make it with these 1969 "sweet streepers" from Mercury

sure footed cat—Cougar 351-4V

Sharpen yourself a set of paws for this wild running Cougar XR-7. (Equipment includes: unique wheel covers, L/H remote racing mirror, tach, elapsed-time clock, 3-spoke rim-blow steering wheel & leather w/vinyl bucket seats). Add 4-V carb, 290 hp/351 cid perf group (comp hand pkg, dual exhausts & striping). Optional: Traction-Lok axle, F70x14 belted traction tires on 6" rims, close ratio 4-speed or Select-Shift transmission & P/B (front disc/rear drum)

Diego Rosenberg

Selling the
AMERICAN
Muscle Car

The Great One by Pontiac.

You know the rest of the story.

Marketing Detroit Iron in the 60s and 70s

CarTech®

CarTech®, Inc.
838 Lake Street South
Forest Lake, MN 55025
Phone: 651-277-1200 or 800-551-4754
Fax: 651-277-1203
www.cartechbooks.com

Edit by Wes Eisenschenk
Layout by Monica Seiberlich

ISBN 978-1-61325-203-1
Item No. CT542

Library of Congress Cataloging-in-Publication Data

Names: Rosenberg, Diego, author.
Title: Selling the American muscle car: marketing Detroit iron the 1960s and 1970s / Diego Rosenberg.
Description: Forest Lake, MN: CarTech, [2016]
Identifiers: LCCN 2015033482 | ISBN 9781613252031
Subjects: LCSH: Muscle cars–United States–Marketing–History–20th century. |
 Muscle cars–United States–History–20th century. |
 –Automobiles–United States–History–20th century. |
 Automobile industry and trade–United States–History–20th century.
Classification: LCC HD9710.U52 R65 2016 | DDC 381/.456292220973–dc23
LC record available at http://lccn.loc.gov/2015033482

Written, edited, and designed in the U.S.A.
Printed in China
10 9 8 7 6 5 4 3 2 1

DISTRIBUTION BY:

Europe
PGUK
63 Hatton Garden
London EC1N 8LE, England
Phone: 020 7061 1980 • Fax: 020 7242 3725
www.pguk.co.uk

Australia
Renniks Publications Ltd.
3/37-39 Green Street
Banksmeadow, NSW 2109, Australia
Phone: 2 9695 7055 • Fax: 2 9695 7355
www.renniks.com

TABLE OF CONTENTS

ACKNOWLEDGMENTS

The author of a project such as this cannot escape recognizing those who played a part: I'd never written a book before, but Wes Eisenschenk and CarTech approached me with an idea for the book that is now in your hands. I offer gratitude to them for thinking I was qualified for such a project.

This book also wouldn't be possible without Mom and Dad, as they fostered my automotive interests at a young age. The support and encouragement of my wife, Tatiana, is duly noted, too.

My automotive education continued into adulthood thanks to Jim Campisano, Don Keefe/*Poncho Perfection* magazine, Tom Shaw, and Terry Boyce. Beyond being afflicted with the automotive gene, they're also fine human beings whom I'm proud to call friends.

Martyn Schorr was more than just a good interviewee; he also handled the role of mentor. For the editor of *Cars* magazine to have my back was simply too good to be true.

Richard Truesdell also was a pillar, and I picked through his stellar image archives for photos for this book. You can view them at http://bit.ly/ATCCphotos.

Over the years, Chuck West, Dan Foley, Kevin Laing, and Jude Hettick have recognized my automotive proclivities despite being a low-compression kid. Their inspiration has been invaluable.

The GM Heritage Center is an unbelievable archive of automotive history; its greatness is matched by Christo Datini and Kathy Adelson.

Linda Skolarus warrants kudos for her guidance with the Benson Ford Research Center. Ditto for Paige Plant and the National Automotive History Collection at the Detroit Public Library.

Up the road in Flint, Jacob Gilbert and Heather Moore gave me the red carpet treatment at the Buick Automotive Gallery and Research Center.

Danielle Szostak at FCA Group was instrumental in making the Mopar and AMC chapters substantive.

Chris Ritter and Hershey's AACA Library & Research Center also deserve thanks.

The Enthusiast Network's Tom Voehringer was perfectly accommodating with the Petersen Photo Archive. Thanks also go to the *Hot Rod* crew (Sean, Kennedy, Brandan, Elana, Thom, Finnegan, Freiburger, and Dave Wallace, Jr.).

I lent my ear to several gentlemen who were only too happy to talk cars: Bob Johnson, Joe Oldham, Jim Wangers, "Mr. Norm" Kraus, Carl Schieffer, and Jim Luikens. Their contributions back in the day (and today) don't go unnoticed.

Mopar collector Steve Juliano is "one of the good guys" in the hobby; he lent this total stranger his valuable literature to study and present to you in this tome. Cougar expert Jim Pinkerton deserves similar praise; he had never met me, but allowed me to visit his abode.

And others: Tony D'Agostino, Ian Webb, John Becker, Larry Daum, Mark Fletcher, Tony Rose, Roberta Vasilow, Doug Jones, Stefano Bimbi, Richard Peters, Lynn Yenko-Zoiopoulos, Steve Frys, Joe Barr, Valerie Harrell and Dale Pulde, Chuck Morris, Dennis Pierachini, Gavin Schlesinger, John Brantmeier, Kevin Marti/Marti Auto Works, Dan Pausch, Nick Taylor, Alan Munro, Mike Jansekok, Andy Cockroft, Doug Hammer, John Skalka, Ken Bowser, Barry Washington, Ola Nilsson, Larry Weiner, David Hakim, Geoff Stunkard, Fred Mandrick, Kurt Shubert, Tweed Voorhes, Casey Marks, Ryan Weaver, Dave Heilala, Jasen Ramsey, Rocky Rotella, Tim Dye/Pontiac-Oakland Museum and Resource Center, Eric White (1955-2016), Keith Seymore, Mike Noun, Chris Phillip, Tim Costello, George Pappas, Wesley Poley, Ken Craig, Bob Dornblaser, Steve Johns, Jim Mattison, Bob Palma, George Krem, Ted Harbit, Richard A. Bennett III, Andrew Beckman/Studebaker National Museum, Dale Dotson/Hurst, Bob McClurg, Roger Grotewold, and the Automotive History Preservation Society.

FOREWORD

by Bob Ashton, Managing Member
Muscle Car and Corvette Nationals

My, how times have changed. Packard may have suggested that you "Ask the man who owns one" way back in 1901, but who could have imagined that in 1969, Dodge would present an ad titled "Mother warned me . . ." showing a lovely young lady named Julia behind what appears to be her suitor's Charger RT/SE. "I'm attracted to you because you have a very intelligent face." Uh-huh!

This is just one example of the outrageous and often controversial ad campaigns that the manufacturers of American muscle presented during the heyday of the muscle car era. In 1963, Ford touted the Cobra's versatility: "The Cobra glides along in 15-mph traffic in fourth gear as effortlessly as it tows a ski boat at 70." In 1964, we witnessed the introduction of the all-new small car/big engine concept with the Pontiac GTO: "For the man who wouldn't mind riding a tiger if someone'd only put wheels on it."

This was only the beginning. As we moved into the 1970s, ad campaigns were wilder and the colors were even more outrageous. Plum Crazy Purple and Hugger Orange, or in the case of the GTO, Carousel Red, may be among the most recognized of the brash, in-your-face colors, but let's not forget about the ones that didn't hit the showroom floor, such as Statutory Grape (really!).

The battle for attention (and the all-important dollar) from young consumers who were beginning to earn a few bucks reached fever pitch during the late 1960s and early 1970s and that is what this book is all about. "Win on Sunday, Sell on Monday" was the mantra, and even the manufacturers known for their conservative cars and marketing jumped onto the bandwagon.

Who would have ever thought that Buick would produce the 455-ci spoiler-clad Saturn Yellow GSX? Even Oldsmobile offered the in-your-face Hurst/Olds, first in subtle silver and black but later in glowing gold and white, featuring some of the wildest bolt-on spoilers and scoops ever offered. And speaking of outrageous, how about the 1969½ 440+6 Road Runner and Super Bees, sans hubcaps and featuring a matte-black pinned-on fiberglass lift-off hood, or the budget-priced, mailbox-scooped red, white, and blue SC/Rambler? Yes, it was a different era.

I first met Diego Rosenberg when he wandered into my Detroit area automobilia store, known as Auto-Know. I had started a business to sell original sales brochures at swap meets, but it quickly grew to include literally thousands of original car ads, all carefully razor-cut from the magazines and wrapped loosely on acid-free backer boards, ready to frame or display with your car. As an avid ad collector myself, the original concept was to "fill the gaps" in our brochure inventory. It was much easier and far more affordable to expand the inventory while offering a neat collectible. We soon found ourselves searching for the elusive ads, much to the delight of our customers, and traveling offering our wares literally coast to coast. We eventually opened a full-fledged retail store.

As the ad inventory grew, so did our selection of car magazines, books, out-of-production model car kits, and promotional models. Diego could spend hours perusing the racks, searching for information on a particular Oldsmobile or Pontiac. Conversations eventually led to our shared interests and before long we forged a friendship that lasted for years. Sharing the passion for what many would consider useless information (yes, we can both whip out production numbers and discuss for hours the pros and cons of cubic inches!), we both knew we shared a certain, well, sickness!

Diego moved on to further his education and career until one day we crossed paths at the Pure Stock Muscle Car Drag Races in Stanton, Michigan. Diego was the track announcer that day and the funny thing is, whenever I heard his voice, I thought, "Gee, that guy sounds familiar!" I couldn't place just who it was until we met later while looking under the hood of one of the participant's cars. "Hey, what have you been up to?" The rest, as they say, is history!

These days I am proud to be at the helm of the Muscle Car and Corvette Nationals show, which is the world's largest all-indoor specialty show devoted to muscle cars, dealer-built supercars, and the rarest Corvettes. The show takes place each November in the Chicago suburb of Rosemont. Earning a living by traveling throughout the country, meeting and inviting enthusiastic car collectors, and often getting to spend quality time behind the wheel of many of the rarest and most sought after examples of American muscle is indeed a dream job. It has also allowed me the opportunity to work directly with the movers and shakers of our hobby, as well as talk to the guy down the street whose eyes light up when they hear about what I do, knowing that I will most likely enjoy hearing the stories of the car he used to own.

There is no doubt in my mind that Diego Rosenberg is the right guy to write this book. With his attention to detail, willingness to go the extra mile to properly research the facts (something that seems to be rare these days), and of course, to share something that quite simply cannot be taught, true *passion*.

Merriam-Webster defines passion as "a strong feeling of enthusiasm or excitement for something or about doing something." This is how Diego approached this project, and I am proud to be able to contribute to what is not only educational, but just good, old-fashioned fun.

CHAPTER 1

SOME HISTORY

War has never been a fortunate by-product of our existence, but when the Allies prevailed against the Axis powers, returning veterans were ready to resume life in the good ol' U.S. of A. A restless faction managed to exploit its wartime penchant for adrenaline and adventure and funnel it into modifying and racing cars at abandoned airports and dry lakes. Many had received technical training courtesy of Uncle Sam that would contribute to the ingenuity used in building hot rods and especially adapting surplus aeronautical equipment. Although hot rodders were considered hoodlums by some, they were far from the outlaws who challenged the gentility of the era.

From the Lakes to the Pavement

With the introduction of Oldsmobile and Cadillac's high-compression V-8s in 1949, the hot rodding paradigm began to change. Soon, those Ford flatheads made way for modern V-8s. And those who didn't have eight-cylinder engines in their rosters? That too would change.

During that time, Robert Petersen began publishing *Hot Rod* magazine with Wally Parks as editor. Parks had been president of the Southern California Timing Association but, in an effort to "discourage illegal racing and to promote safety standards, rules, and classifications," he engaged Los Angeles police officials about creating a national drag racing organization. "There was an awful lot of street racing in outlying communities," Parks told Reuters in 2001. "People were inconvenienced when a road was blocked off, usually at night, and they had tires screeching around the neighborhood. Street racing had a very bad image." This led to the creation of the National Hot Rod Association (NHRA) and, in 1953, it held its first sanctioned event in Pomona.

By 1955, horsepower became a populist phenomenon as both Chevrolet and Plymouth debuted V-8s. Although Plymouth's was a fine effort, it was Chevrolet's that truly transformed the company, becoming the darling of the industry thanks to the skilled efforts of chief engineer Ed Cole and deft leadership of design chief Harley Earl. The Turbo-Fire 265 was quickly embraced by the hot rodding establishment, becoming the *de facto* engine of choice.

Mercury Marine's Carl Kiekhaefer brought professionalism and a competitive spirit in the early days of NASCAR with his team of Mopars. Tim Flock drove this 1956 300-B to 139.37 mph in the two-way flying mile at Daytona. (Photo ©TEN: The Enthusiast Network. All rights reserved.)

Ed Iskenderian was a dry lakes racer when the hot rod scene emerged in the late 1940s. His experience led to the creation of Isky Cams. (Photo ©TEN: The Enthusiast Network. All rights reserved.)

The NHRA hosted the Southern California Championship Drags in April 1953. Two years later, the NHRA had its first national event in Kansas. This race in Pomona was held in August 1953. (Photo ©TEN: The Enthusiast Network. All rights reserved.)

Genesis of "The Hot One"

Two events contributed to the embrace of the small-block. The first came by way of Zora Arkus-Duntov, the Chevrolet engineer who felt the Corvette could show the world it was a viable contender except for being saddled with the Blue Flame Six. In a December 1953 inter-organization memo, "Thoughts Pertaining to Youth, Hot Rodders, and Chevrolet," Duntov observed that many publications catering to the hot-rodding set were full of Fords "from cover to cover," who then "graduate from jalopies, to second-hand Fords, then to new Fords.

"The slide rule potential of our RPO V-8 engine is extremely high, but to let things run their natural course will put us one year behind [Ford's Y-block V-8] and then not too many people will pick up Chevrolet for development.

"It seems that unless by some action the odds and the time factor are not overcome, Ford will continue to dominate the thinking of this group. One factor that can largely overcome the handicap would be the availability of ready engineered parts for high output.

"If the use of the Chevrolet engine would be made easy and the very first attempts would be crowned with success, the appeal of the new RPO V-8 engine will take hold and not have the stigma of expensiveness like the Cadillac or Chrysler, and a swing to Chevrolet may be anticipated. This means the development of a range of special parts (camshafts, valves, springs, manifolds, pistons, and such) should be made available to the public.

"The association of Chevrolet with hot rods, speed, and such is probably inadmissible, but possibly the existence of the Corvette provides the loophole. If the special parts are carried as RPO items for the Corvette, they undoubtedly will be recognized by the hot rodders as the very parts they were looking for to hop up the Chevy.

"If it is desirable or not to associate the Corvette with speed, I am not qualified to say, but I do know that in 1954, sports car enthusiasts will get hold of Corvettes and whether we like it or not, will race them. The most frequent statement from this group is 'we will put a Cadillac in it.' They are going to, and I think this is not good! Most likely they will meet with Allard trouble; that is, breaking sooner or later, mostly sooner; everything between the flywheel and road wheels.

"In 1955, with V-8 engine, if unaided, they will still be outclassed. The market-wise negligible number of cars purchased for competition attracts public attention and publicity out of proportion to their number. Since we cannot prevent the people from racing Corvettes, maybe it's better to help them to do a good job at it."

In September 1955, Duntov entered a 1956 210 in the Pikes Peak International Hill Climb and managed to shatter the sedan class record by more than two minutes.

The other event that helped make enthusiasts "Chevrolet-minded" was the 1955 Speed Weeks at Daytona, where 12 Chevrolets equipped with the 180-horse 265 participated without factory support. A Chrysler C-300 was the fastest, but a Chevy 210 two-door sedan was runner-up at more than 112 mph in the measured mile. This impressive achievement made the newswire, but when potential customers approached dealers, salespeople had no clue about Chevrolet's high-performance offerings. Within months, Chevrolet provided guides to teach salesmen about the brand's success at Daytona and the special options available. The advertising campaign changed from a "low-cost motoring" theme to "The Hot One."

Chevrolet engineer Zora Arkus-Duntov drove this 1956 210 in the Pikes Peak International Hill Climb, destroying the sedan class record. A Chevrolet media blitz commenced. (Photo ©TEN: The Enthusiast Network. All rights reserved.)

The public started taking notice of Chevrolet's impressive transformation from a low-priced brand with no performance history to, two years later, an automaker with a racing program and an engine offering 100 more horsepower via fuel injection.

Racing Subversions, Part I

But the fun didn't last. In June 1957, the board of the Automobile Manufacturers Association (AMA) made a recommendation to its members not to participate in, engage in, or encourage (1.) any public contest, competitive event or test of passenger cars involving or suggesting racing or speed, and (2.) the advertising or publicizing of (a) any race or speed contest, test or competitive event involving or suggesting speed, or (b) the actual or comparative capabilities of passenger cars for speed.

The AMA's directors included top executives from the Big Three and other automakers. "If the decision is adhered to rigidly, the days are

The Chrysler 300 may have been the 1950s performance leader, but the 1958 Mercury Super Marauder 430 with triple Holleys offered 400 horses, a 10-horse edge over the 300-D. (Tom Shaw Photo)

HURST-CAMPBELL

Hurst made a name for itself with quality motor mounts, but George Hurst and Bill Campbell's next product developed the company's reputation: the Hurst shifter. By installing a smooth-shifting shifter on the floor, Hurst gave would-be racers the ability to run faster ETs without spending money on the engine. There were less-expensive shifters in the market, but Hurst developed a reputation for quality and workmanship, eventually leading to OEM status for several manufacturers, notably Pontiac.

Bill Campbell's mechanical prowess gave Hurst shifters their quality reputation, but George Hurst's talent for promotion elevated Hurst-Campbell's success. George stopped by the Petersen Publishing offices in 1961 to peddle his wares. (Photo ©TEN: The Enthusiast Network. All rights reserved.)

The Hurst Performance Clinic, a mobile repair shop complete with configured truck and team of technicians, was launched in 1961 to handle questions, installations, and repairs at events. (Photo ©TEN: The Enthusiast Network. All rights reserved.)

probably gone when Car A will claim it won the Pikes Peak race while Car B says it swept the field at Daytona Beach," read an article in the June 7, 1957, *Santa Cruz Sentinel*. Instead, the industry wanted to emphasize safe and reliable transportation, sharing "the public interest in increasing the safety of highway travel."

Car racing had long been used as a laboratory for the automotive industry. Ban supporters felt it would reduce the number of fatalities yet, several months later, Mercury offered a 400-hp 430, and Chrysler offered 390 hp with fuel injection. Chevrolet had a new big-block 348, and Pontiac continued to offer several 370 "NASCAR" engines. Although not breaking the rules outright, manufacturers resorted to using local dealerships to deliver the goods to racers. With the inaugural Daytona 500 in 1959 and the first nationally televised NASCAR race the following year, it was clear to the automobile industry that horsepower was here to stay and the AMA racing ban hindered their efforts in promotions, sales, and performance.

Harnessing the Horsepower

During this time, several automakers began offering 4-speed manuals. Chevrolet was the first to market, with the 1957 Corvette and then with full-size models in 1958. The advantage wasn't so much the extra gear as much as its position on the floor, perfect for harnessing horsepower in competitive sprints. The clumsy column-mounted linkage was gone, although aftermarket companies such as Hurst-Campbell demonstrated that they had a better idea of how to make a good floor shifter.

Through 1963, an estimated 750,000 American cars featured a 4-speed manual transmission. For 1963 alone, four percent of the market (300,000) were 4-speeds, a 100,000 increase from 1962. Most of those were supplied by BorgWarner, but Chevrolet and Chrysler were confident of the rising demand and developed their own for the 1964 model year.

A Ford engineer told *Automotive News* on September 9, 1963, "Some people said there was a deliberate effort by the industry to shunt people into automatic transmission cars. Then, when people began driving for the fun of it again, many felt compelled to buy the 4-speed box."

So what happened to the AMA ban? "To hell with those guys," quipped Pontiac's general manager, Semon E. "Bunkie" Knudsen. "I've got a division to save and we're going racing." Perhaps manufacturers were officially out of racing, but enthusiasts were racing *for* them, with the NHRA appearing to supersede NASCAR in showcasing Detroit's high-performance offerings. The first NHRA Nationals, hosted by Detroit Dragway in 1959, drew

GM's reaffirmation of the AMA ban in February 1963 put the kibosh on factory race cars such as this 1963 Z11 Impala. (Photo ©TEN: The Enthusiast Network. All rights reserved.)

80,000 spectators. The following year, a Royal Pontiac–prepared Catalina featuring Super Duty components won the Stock Eliminator class with a 14.1 ET at 100 mph. The following year, a Royal Pontiac-prepared Catalina, piloted by Pontiac adman Jim Wangers and featuring Super Duty equipment, won the Stock Eliminator class with a 14.1 ET at 100 mph. Five years after the first "Horsepower Race," the second one was on.

Plymouth and Dodge both offered big-block engines with long-ram induction and a superb automatic transmission. Chevrolets lost the fuel-injected small-blocks, relying instead on the 348 with up to 350 hp. Midway through the 1960 model year, Ford introduced a 360-horse 352, but it was saddled with a column-shifted 3-speed that compromised performance.

In 1961, Pontiac continued to subversively supply Super Duty parts through dealerships, while Ford responded with a solid-lifter 390 offering up to 401 hp. Mopar's ram-inducted 383s carried over from 1960. And Chevrolet finally got serious with the 360-horse 409.

For 1961, Pontiac continued to subversively supply Super Duty parts through dealerships; Ford responded with a solid-lifter 390 offering up to 401 hp. Mopar's ram-inducted 383s were carried over from 1960, and Chevrolet finally became serious with the 360-horse 409. It all came to a head in 1962: All High Performance brands offered purpose-built vehicles with more than 400-hp for the racetrack. Chevrolet, jealous of Pontiac's quasi-disregard of the AMA ban, introduced the Z11 Impala. Pontiac drilled holes in the frames of Super Duty Catalinas to lighten them. And then the hammer fell again: No more racing! And this time it was for real, but only at General Motors.

Racing Subversions, Part II

Legend has it that General Motors was concerned that the Department of Justice would split the company due to its huge market share. To hedge its bets, General Motors felt it wise to stall future incremental growth by removing its investment in motorsports.

As part of Ford's "Total Performance" campaign, Dan Gurney won the 1963 Riverside 500 in this Holman-Moody–prepared Ford Galaxie. (Photo ©TEN: The Enthusiast Network. All rights reserved.)

Yet Ford's Lee Iacocca spoke about how the race among manufacturers was aimed at performance, not speed. "One reason for the continuing strength of the automobile market is the industry's responsiveness to a growing demand for better performance. Today's customer is the principal beneficiary of an all-out competition to give him more value in terms of greater dependability and finer quality," he said in the April 22, 1963, *Automotive News*.

Pontiac Makes Lemonade

Pontiac had banked its well-honed image on performance, so the reaffirmed ban was a major blow. However, the renegade brand had moxie: Pontiac decided to take performance to the street with the GTO. With a name stolen from Ferrari (*Gran Turismo Omologato* meant "Homologated Grand Touring"), the GTO was unique: a mid-sized vehicle packaged as a performance car with its own identity. "We kind of like to let individual customers build their own cars. We probably have the largest variety of engines, ride packages, transmissions, and axle ratios in the industry. This permits the customer to pick almost any kind of a drivetrain to meet his particular driving requirements," said John DeLorean in the March 16, 1964, *Automotive News*.

According to veteran automotive journalist Joe Oldham, "The thing that changed with the GTO was that you didn't have to option out a whole car piece by piece. You could visit a Ford dealer to buy a 1963 Galaxie 500/

There were muscle cars before the GTO, but they were full-size performance vehicles lacking unique identities. In contrast, the "Goat" was solely a high-performance car with, thanks to Jim Wangers, image and marketing behind it.

XL that featured bucket seats, cool emblems, and image, but it came with a 289. You then had to spec out a higher-performance engine. Most people bought a 390 4-barrel, which made for a peppy car with nothing finicky about it. But if you opted for the 406 or 427, you would be talking about a very high-performance street car with all the idiosyncrasies. But you had to option it.

"The difference with the GTO was you got the trim, emblems, buckets, big engine, and image; it was the whole package. That concept was the game-changer. And that's why most people credit the Pontiac GTO with starting the muscle car era. It was the first car that came prepackaged as a hot rod with everything in it already.

"There are some people who will say, 'He's full of it. The Chrysler 300 Letter Series was the first car that came prepackaged like that.' And that's true, but those were full-size cars. The difference was that the GTO was an intermediate, a mid-size car with a big engine."

Marketing Smarts and Marketing Success

The marketing behind the GTO wasn't just ads and magazine press. Suburban Detroit-based Royal Pontiac was hand-picked to become the prototype of what ended up being a stillborn dealer program. Says Jim Wangers, "It was apparent to me that a huge percentage of the folks out in the field (the salesmen and even the dealers themselves) really had no idea of the complexity and sophistication of the revamped 1959 Pontiac. I went to the top folks at the division and put together a traveling performance seminar (which my ad agency backed) that would go out to most of the major zones. Dealers in the zone would be invited to send a sales representative or mechanic to the seminar and learn about sales, service, and parts for Pontiac, which was going through a major image change.

"When I presented this idea, sales manager Frank Bridge was against it; his comment was, 'I'm having enough trouble selling regular Pontiac cars. I don't need to bother with those hot rods.' Yet those hot rods were out building an image that was enabling him to sell his regular cars! Those were things that so many sales-type people never understood.

"Knudsen liked it and suggested we needed proof. 'Why don't you go out and find a dealer that would be willing to be a guinea pig willing to take on this performance personality?' He understood that it was a small but very important image-building effort, not only for the car, but for the dealership. 'You find that dealer and you can be sure we'll support him.'"

Royal Pontiac was enthusiastic about the proposition and became a complete performance-oriented dealership.

Adds Wangers, "They weren't just a dealership with their name on the side of a race car. When you came to Royal interested in a performance car, there were only three salespeople on the entire staff they'd let you talk to. That in itself is the thing that separated Royal from a dealership that simply put its name on the side of a race car for exposure. You could go to the dealership and spend several minutes looking at the racer, but you were really there because you were interested in *your own* performance needs. They used the race car as a traffic-builder, but when you visited the dealership genuinely interested in buying the performance version of their car, you quickly learned that you knew more about *their* car than they did! *That* was the most significant difference between Royal and other performance-oriented dealers."

Changing Demographics and Psychographics

The timing of the GTO may have been serendipitous but, for the Mustang, April 17, 1964, was pure business smarts. In Robert A. Fria's *Mustang Genesis: The Creation of the Pony Car*, Ford public relations specialist Robert Hefty made two observations around 1960: The post-war baby boom created new market opportunities as the kids approached driving age, and two-car families were increasing in popularity.

Iacocca assembled an exploratory team to discuss developing a product that embraced a new market segment based on this evolving demographic and psychographic. The committee determined that 18- to 36-year-olds purchased more than 50 percent of new-car sales through the 1960s. Ford also discovered 36 percent of those under 25 wanted a 4-speed manual, and 35 percent liked bucket seats.

"All the things youngsters want in a car are available on the market today, but not in the right combinations," said Iacocca. "They wanted the

appeal of the Thunderbird, the sporty look of the Ferrari and the economy of the Volkswagen. But you can't buy a T-Bird for $2,500, get exceptional gas mileage in a Ferrari, or get whistled at in a VW. What they wanted, really, was a contradiction in terms." The committee determined there was a group big enough to create demand for a youthful, sporty vehicle.

The group was divided into four audiences: two-car families with money to spend, young drivers with little money to spend, those who wanted a car that was easy to maintain, and sport-minded folks seeking new fun toys.

The resulting Mustang certainly was the right car at the right time, embraced by the Boomers and generations to come.

Even AMC got in on the act. At the 1964 Chicago Auto Show, Rambler introduced the Tarpon, an American with a fastback roof. But AMC squandered a pony-car opportunity by producing the mid-size Marlin for 1965. (Photo Courtesy Mitch Frumkin)

426 Hemi

Chrysler was doing well in racing with its Max Wedge but, in a competitive market, constant development was necessary. Every manufacturer did its darndest to upstage the competition. Chrysler responded in kind, from the 413 Max Wedge to several stages of the 426 before the 1964 hemispherical-head upgrade.

Due to changes in homologation rules, Chrysler brought the Hemi to the street for 1966, giving enthusiasts the opportunity to be king of the street through 1971.

Every Plymouth's a champion

THE CAR WITH THE 5-YEAR-50,000-MILE POWER-TRAIN WARRANTY

CHRYSLER
CANADA LTD.

At Daytona, two 1964 Plymouths qualified at a record-setting 170+ mph with the all-new Hemi; the official race finish was even more amazing. (Dodge, Plymouth and the AMC design are registered trademarks of FCA US LLC)

The 1960s Finally Arrive

The pivotal year for something indirectly related to automobiles was in 1964. The Beatles. Before the Fab Four and the British Invasion, American popular music consisted of leftover 1950s fare, Motown, girl groups, crooners, folk music, and surf tunes. The Beatles began to catch on in America in December 1963, culminating in their February 1964 arrival and appearance on *The Ed Sullivan Show*. America wouldn't be the same: the 1960s had finally arrived, and the kids had taken over.

The role of women also was about to change drastically thanks to Betty Friedan's *The Feminine Mystique*, which investigated women's identity in American society and the patriarchy that led them to say, "I want something more than my husband and my children and my home."

The 1960s were no accident; there was a convergence that changed the status quo. American youths rejected the path of their parents and tossed off the social constructs that had been placed upon them. This was reflected by music, women's rights, civil rights, and automobiles.

The Market Reacts

Oldsmobile was the first with a GTO competitor: the 1964 4-4-2. Its 310-horse 330 and 4-speed made any F-85/Cutlass a fully capable machine, but the 330 was no match for the 389.

Ford's Total Performance program was already in full force. The September 9, 1963, *Automotive News* quoted E. F. Laux, Ford's general marketing manager: "Our Total Performance concept has paid off where it counts, in terms of sales. No one can prove that sales can be attributed to winning a particular performance event, but statistics do spell out very clearly the public acceptance of our new sporty models, which have been leading the way in competitive events."

For 1965, Oldsmobile introduced a new 400 for the 4-4-2. Buick joined the fray with the 401-powered Skylark Gran Sport. Chevrolet relied on the Malibu SS, a buckets-and-console model that lacked a performance image, because any engine was available, including a six.

Plymouth and Dodge featured a 383 and a more competitive 426 Street Wedge for its B-Bodies but, like the Chevelle, there were no true performance models. On the other hand, Mopars were on fire at racetracks across

In September, Studebaker president Sherwood Egbert told Automotive News *that he was "convinced that a new corporate image of speed, performance, and endurance would attract the nation's young buyers into Studebaker showrooms" and proved it by unveiling the 1964s during a series of performance runs at Bonneville. (Photo ©TEN: The Enthusiast Network. All rights reserved.)*

"If we didn't participate [in drag racing], we'd run the risk of Plymouth and Dodge getting a conservative school-teacher image that doesn't appeal to the younger generation," a Chrysler engineer told Automotive News *in 1965, the same year this Coronet with an altered wheelbase was built. (Photo Courtesy Mitch Frumkin)*

NEW MARKET: SOLDIERS IN VIETNAM

American involvement in Vietnam began during the Kennedy administration, but the 1964 Gulf of Tonkin incident resulted in an increased military presence, with the escalation coming to a head in March 1965 when 3,500 Marines were dispatched. By December, 200,000 Marines were deployed.

In response, Hurst Performance conceived the Hurst Armed Forces Club. At its peak, the club distributed the *Hurst Armed Forces Performance Report* to more than 100,000 individuals around the world. When the newsletter began in January 1966, Pontiac had no idea that more than 96,000 GTOs would be built. Soldiers fighting the good fight missed out on an evolving automotive scene, and the automakers and the aftermarket missed out on sales. The newsletter kept enthusiasts abreast of the goings-on in Detroit and in motorsports, but it also offered support for a conflict that sometimes felt as if there was no support at all. Through March 1972, the *Hurst Armed Forces Performance Report* gave veterans hope that an exciting civilian life lay ahead.

The automakers already had distribution channels to bases around the world. "Business is especially brisk in Vietnam, where some sources report that orders placed by GIs for stateside delivery are running about 450 a month and growing," reported the November 21, 1966, *Automotive News*. "The GI in Vietnam is an unusually good prospect. His savings build up rapidly while he's in combat, and he's a good financial risk."

At the time, there were three approaches to taking delivery in the United States: through distributor representatives at post exchanges, independent brokers, or dealers willing to negotiate through the mail. Automakers published targeted brochures featuring photos, descriptions, options, and prices. A down payment of 20 to 30 percent with a $50 deposit was routinely required. A month before a scheduled return home, the order was forwarded by a representative or broker to a dealer near the GI's destination, where the vehicle was prepped and payment was forwarded to the manufacturer or broker.

One man took Detroit action directly to overseas troops. U.S. Lawman Performance Team leader Al Eckstrand told *Automotive News* in September 14, 1970, that his objective was morale building by bringing "a message of speed, skill, and performance to servicemen to fill them in on what U.S.-style driving on civilian highways is all about today."

At first with Dodge, Eckstrand went overseas with eight 1970 Mustangs, including two supercharged Boss 429s running on nitromethane. Each of his shows and seminars included a 90-minute slalom competition, 60 minutes on "practical automotive theory," plus talks on horsepower, the mistake of overbuying horsepower, and engineering innovations.

Wes Poley's gold 1968 GTO convertible (with Hurst wheels, naturally) was prepared by Royal Pontiac. (Wesley D. Poley Photo)

AIR FORCE SGT. POLEY RECEIVES GTO AT NATIONALS

●INDIANAPOLIS -- A proud and happy Sgt. Wesley D. Poley, winner of the Hurst Armed Forces Club "Firecracker 400 - Win the GTO" contest, received his award, a brand-new Pontiac GTO convertible, at the recent NHRA Nationals in Indianapolis. Sgt. Poley, who had come all the way in from Castle AFB, California, was thrilled beyond words with his prize.

As a special surprise, Poley's parents came to Indy from their home town of Ackley, Iowa, to participate in the presentation. Just after the dragster parade on Monday morning, Sept. 2, George Hurst escorted Poley to the starting line at Indianapolis Raceway Park. The Sergeant's GTO convertible was waiting for him at the line, along with his parents and NHRA President Wally Parks.

Mr. Hurst and Mr. Parks both congratulated Poley on his win. Congratulations were sent by telegram from Pontiac Motor Division Vice-president and General Manager John Z. DeLorean, who could not be present due to a last-minute unavoidable change in schedule. Poley was then invited by Wally Parks to take a parade lap down the strip. And so, amid the cheers of some 90,000 drag fans, Poley and his parents drove down the 1/4-mile. Sgt. Poley, however, was a little enthusiastic with the "loud pedal" and Wally Parks sneaked a look over his shoulder to see whether NHRA's Chief Starter Buster Couch had tripped the Christmas Tree for Poley's "hot lap."

As Sgt. Poley stepped from his new car after the parade lap, one of the first of many top-notch racers to congratulate him on his win was none other than Mike Landy, Dick Landy's younger brother, who drives Dick's Super Stock Dodges. Mike is currently serving on active duty with the 81st Armor, 1st Airborne Div. of the U.S. Army at Fort Hood Texas.

The Sergeant and his parents then settled down to watch the fine drag action at the 14th annual NHRA Nationals before their drive home to Ackley, Iowa. But we can be sure that this was a weekend they'll never forget.

★Wally Parks congratulates Sgt. Poley's Dad on his son's tremendous win.

★HAFC Skipper George Hurst (left) and NHRA President Wally Parks congratulate Sgt. Poley on the winning of his brand-new 1968 GTO.

★Sgt. Poley, with Mom and Dad, takes a ride down the drag strip at Indy Raceway Park in his brand-new Ram-Air II GTO convertible.

Iowan Sgt. Wes Poley won a Hurst Armed Forces Club trivia contest and was awarded a GTO at the NHRA U.S. Nationals in 1968. (Photo Courtesy Hurst Inc.)

The U.S. Lawman Performance Team featured half a dozen Cobra Jet Mustang Mach Is that were used in military performance driving seminars, plus two match race cars with supercharged Boss 429s. (Photo Courtesy Hurst Inc.)

America. General manager Phillip Buckminster said in the February 5, 1965, *Automotive News*, "Chrysler-Plymouth Division believes that racing helps sell cars, and is thus in racing to stay."

Three days later, Chrysler chief engineer Robert Roger added, "Probably the most important objective is to build and maintain a youthful, sporty image for the Plymouth and the Dodge among the nation's youth." Each division often had its own cheering section at dragstrips, evidence that racing affected a manufacturer's image.

Ford and Mercury were even more at a loss. Both the Fairlane and Comet Cyclone with the rare High-Performance 289 were rare and easy prey for the GTO. The redesigned 1966 Fairlane and Cyclone GTs were chock full of image and powered by a 390, but these cousins were "stones" compared to the competition. Over at General Motors, Chevrolet introduced the Chevelle SS 396, leaving Chrysler as the only Big Three member lacking image-based performance models.

More Than Muscle: The Specialty Car Market

The year 1967 could be characterized as the year of the specialty car. The October 31, 1966, *Automotive News* listed four characteristics of the specialty car:

- A unique appearance that relied on contemporary styling themes, often featuring a distinct body.
- Tended to be sport coupes.
- Distinguishing features included concealed headlights, full-width taillights, and/or special paint or trim.
- A sporty flavor.

The 12 specialty cars available for 1967 were AMC Marlin, Buick Riviera, Cadillac Eldorado, Chevrolet Camaro, Chevrolet Corvette, Dodge Charger, Ford Mustang, Ford Thunderbird, Mercury Cougar, Oldsmobile Toronado, Plymouth Barracuda, and Pontiac Firebird.

Thanks to the new Eldorado, Camaro, and Cougar, the specialty car market had increased its penetration, and high-performance versions created an overlap with traditional vehicles such as the GTO.

From Horsepower Race to Horsepower War

Horsepower continued to increase across the board. As consumer desire for more accessories increased, power *needed* to rise. This coincided with the rising popularity of V-8s, which was up more than 18 points to 73.71-percent market share between 1962 and 1966.

Tire technology also advanced, with the Goodyear Polyglas bias-belted tire making its first appearance in 1967. Featuring fiberglass belts and a wider tread, the Polyglas (and its Firestone Wide-Oval and Uniroyal Tiger Paw competitors) became *de rigueur* for high-performance cars. The more sophisticated radial-ply tire also began to gain attention (the 1968 Cougar

Pony cars were a subset of the so-called specialty car, but the Dan Gurney–inspired 1968 Cougar XR7-G distinguished itself with a non-functional hood scoop, Marchal or Lucas fog lights, special console with rocker switches, bullet-shaped remote sideview mirror, and other custom touches. Conversion was handled by A.O. Smith, the same facility that converted Shelbys.

NASCAR could be sexy, but some felt that racing, horsepower, and marketing encouraged reckless driving. (Photo Courtesy Paula Mitchell)

GT-E was an early adopter), but mass acceptance did not increase until the following decade.

In turn, aftermarket wheels grew in popularity. The aftermarket industry did its part to convince dealers that there were profits in performance. "Improved new-unit grosses were possible by sales emphasis on performance and 'dress-up' items," said publisher Robert Petersen in the January 30, 1967, *Automotive News*. He pointed out that consumers were jazzing up their new cars with "whitewalls and deluxe trim." Why not sell "performance-improving options" and other profitable accessories normally available through speed shops and mail-order?

However, all the fun and games had a cost: Safety gadflies had been emboldened by Corvair critic Ralph Nader. The January 23, 1967, *Automotive News* reported that a University of Illinois law professor "charged that the auto ads aimed at youngsters in enthusiast magazines are designed to encourage these young people to drive recklessly."

Some began to push back. Daniel Jedlicka, auto editor for the *Chicago Sun-Times*, claimed that industry officials should "defend 'super cars' for the sake of the general public" rather than letting "unknowledgable self-appointed critics" control the narrative. Jedlicka told *Automotive News* in August 25, 1969, that super cars often incorporated safety features such as disc brakes, meatier tires, heavy-duty suspension, and powerful engines for improved passing power. He added that critics "are threatening to rob the American public of the very things they're supposedly lobbying for, safer automobiles, because a super car is far superior, safety wise, to a conventional automobile."

It was only going to become worse.

But for now, things were getting better for American Motors. Rambler finally entered the performance segment with the 1967 343 American as it began to seduce the youth market.

After answering enthusiasts' prayers with the 1968 428 CJ, Ford introduced the Shaker for the 1969 Mustang.

Plymouth Changes the Rules

The year 1968 could be considered "Muscle Car Era 2.0" because of the introduction of the Plymouth Road Runner.

The Road Runner's success was based on the idea that muscle cars had evolved into mature vehicles that had become out of reach for the average kid bagging groceries. This demographic/psychographic was being ignored by the automakers, but Plymouth catered to this group by equipping the Road Runner with the bare essentials: standard big-block and 4-speed, simulated hood scoops, ETs under 15 seconds, and a base price south of $2,900.

"Of all of the GTO's competitors, the 1968 Plymouth Road Runner was by far the most successful," says Wangers. "It not only was a good package, but also the image was of a very stripped-down vehicle with rubber floor mats, bench seat, and hubcaps instead of steel wheels. But after some serious research, we discovered the car they were selling was exactly the opposite: a deluxe-trimmed, big-engined vehicle. Still, the Road Runner was the *only* real *serious* competition that was ever mounted against the GTO."

Ford had been an also-ran at that point. "When Ford came out with the Cobra Jet, it was like their whole scene changed," says Joe Oldham. "Before that, Ford had 390 Mustangs and Fairlanes, which were dogs compared to other cars. You could order

The 1968 Road Runner coupe became so successful that Plymouth introduced a companion hardtop midyear. More than 45,000 were built, showing how smart marketing could affect success. (Photo Courtesy Mitch Frumkin)

a no-compromise solid-lifter 427, but few were willing or able to pay more than $1,000, so Fords were a non-entity on the street scene. Everything changed with the Cobra Jet; Mustangs were immediately competitive with just about anything you could buy from the factory.

Oldham continues, "The street-racing scene may have influenced sales more than what was happening on sanctioned tracks. That's something that Ford never understood until the Cobra Jet. They thought that track success made for bigger sales, and to a certain extent, it probably did. But how many people cared that Ford was 1-2-3 at Le Mans? None! But if you were humiliated at a stoplight on Woodward Avenue, you did care."

Turning On

After San Francisco's 1967 "Summer of Love," psychedelia in popular culture was ingrained in America's consciousness: Peter Max-esque illustrations pervaded graphic design, from the most mundane publications to drug-addled underground 'zines. Even straight-laced pop groups began to inject psychedelia into their repertoire because it was "in." Bright colors and stripes were in vogue. Stripes may have had their foundation in racing, but eventually they were used to make a car look wilder, such as the 1969 GTO Judge with its Fillmore West–like font and signature day-glow paint.

There was no better example than Plymouth and Dodge's roster of 1970 High-Impact colors, which had cutesy names, such as Plum Crazy and Sassy Grass Green. In some cases, they could be paired with trippy fluorescent stripes that would even "turn on" Dr. Timothy Leary. Chrysler

Inspired by popular culture, Chrysler offered several 1970–1971 Hi-Impact colors complete with punny names. The 1970 Challenger R/T in Panther Pink was also available with fluorescent pink stripes. (Ken Bowser Photo)

continued the madness into 1971 even when the rest of the market was leaving psychedelia (and high performance) behind.

Performance cars dolled up with the latest and greatest accessories also gained prominence. Cars such as the GTO Judge, Hurst/Olds (H/O), Cyclone Spoiler, and GSX were striped and spoilered vehicles that were somewhat the antithesis of the Road Runner. By 1970, plenty of manufacturers offered options to equip a car with bling, but the above models were packaged with almost everything already.

Trends from the Street

Chrysler continued to demonstrate marketing savvy in 1969 with the A12 Road Runner and Super Bee. Noting that kids on the street personalized their cars, Chrysler created a package with the good stuff already done. The *pièce de résistance* was an outrageous fiberglass hood.

According to Oldham, "Some people at Chrysler looked around and saw what was happening and said, 'Let's get on this and sell some cars!' Their answer was a package that included a new tri-carb 440. There were no hubcaps, a blacked-out fiberglass hood with a big scoop; what guys were doing to their street cars. One of the first things street racers did was take the hubcaps off so they didn't lose them while racing. You had to take them off if you raced your car on a dragstrip anyway, so the A12 cars came with no hubcaps right from the factory. They were very smart about it." For years, manufacturers had encouraged dealers to prepare for the high-performance customer because it would lead to greater profits. "The market is wide open. The people involved seem to have an endless supply of money. It can be very profitable, but it has to be handled correctly. The business requires personnel who know what's going on in the field," said one Chevrolet dealer.

A survey in the May 19, 1969, *Automotive News* on high-performance profit opportunities for dealers, however, showed that most dealers were not interested in catering to enthusiasts. For all the hype about horsepower, the youth market, and profits, only 21.3 percent said they pushed high-performance sales, and 63.1 percent said they did not sell parts or accessories used in modifying the looks or engine to increase performance.

Another Chevy dealer admitted, "We do not sell the super-hot cars or the kill-the-driver type. We tell these sons of silly fathers to check their insurance costs. And then if they still want these cars, we tell them to buy them elsewhere." Many dealerships were not interested in dealing with a kid who was going to cause warranty issues, or a long-hair who didn't look like he had the scratch to purchase a new high-performance car.

The End Is Near

In 1970, General Motors finally lifted its cubic-inch ban, meaning that more than 7.4 liters was the norm. The irony is that GM's edict may not have hurt the company at all.

"It forced the engineers to look at other components," says Joe Oldham. "I didn't realize it at the time, but the Ram Air IV GTO was one of the quickest and fastest cars I drove back then. To make up for the engine-size deficit, GM engineers spent time on cylinder head flow with the accompanying intake manifold design and camshaft profile."

Emissions Requirements

Ironically, high-performance sales were half of what they were two years before. An economic recession didn't help, but the writing was already on the wall due to impending emissions requirements. General Motors announced that all of its 1971 engines would have lowered compression and could run on low-lead or unleaded fuel, a full year ahead of the government mandate.

Air quality had become an issue over the years: "The state department must establish new standards which may be used as criteria for subsequent evaluation of control devices," said S. Smith Griswold in the February 3, 1964, *Automotive News*. The auto industry was accused of dragging its feet in efforts to develop effective exhaust-control devices.

Auto Insurance Rates

Insurance had impacted sales for several years but didn't become dramatic until the new decade. The insurance industry clamped down on cars that had any semblance of high performance. "When a car has an engine that can attain speeds of 120 or more miles an hour, and can accelerate from a standing start to 60 mph in less than 8 seconds, it contains elements of danger not possessed by ordinary cars," said Insurance Exchange general manager Ed Daniels in the February 9, 1970, *Automotive News*.

"Combine this car with racing stripes, 'four on the floor' gear shifts, big, bulging racing tires, air scoops, and spoilers to hold down the back end and you have more than transportation. You have an invitation to race, to use the street for a dragstrip, to forget about safety. And you have a car that is much more attractive to young auto thieves."

Jim Wangers adds, "Insurance, even more than the drive for safety or economy, had more to do with putting a lid on the 'performance era.' Insurance really became an unrealistic monster; it was slow getting started, but when it came on, it came on as a 'killer,' and it was aimed at young people."

According to *Car Craft*, "The increase in rates is based upon a statistical survey of past accidents and thefts of 'performance type' cars, as the insurance companies involved in the rate raising maintain that the past record on these cars, from a claims standpoint, is considerably worse than that of 'normal' cars" regardless of driving record.

There were several attempts to come to terms with these new values while bringing exciting vehicles to the tire-squealing public. "Market demand has been moving sharply toward performance cars with smaller engines to avoid the excessive insurance rates that many insurance firms have placed into effect or scheduled for cars having a low weight to horsepower ratio," said Don Yenko in the February 27, 1970, *Automotive News* while touting his Yenko Nova Deuce. "The insurance companies are putting the squeeze on large engines and I don't think there will be any letup."

Some manufacturers tried to beat the insurance industry by introducing budget supercars with standard low-performance engines, such as the 1970–1971 Pontiac GT-37 and 1971–1972 Chevrolet Heavy Chevy. There also were "cosmetic supercars," including the 1971 Plymouth Duster Twister, which looked like a Duster 340 but was powered by a Slant Six or 318.

A New Market

With emissions, safety, cost of ownership pressures, and even a 1970 fuel shortage scare that may have been manufactured hype, the performance market was brought to its knees.

"The 1960s was a glorious era for Pontiac. It was because management found a niche and ran it all the way 'up the tree,' so to speak," says Wangers. "I don't think that anybody had any idea that that big-engined intermediate was going to develop into a segment. To Pontiac's credit, the idea and development of the GTO was one thing, but the way in which it was handled was effective."

So effective, in fact, that a new market segment was created. The way Brand X responded is what makes the era so interesting.

The 1973 Trans Am, especially the SD 455, represented everything that was glorious about the era when it seemed as if horsepower was dead. (Rocky Rotella Photo)

CHAPTER 2

PONTIAC SETS THE PACE

When Bunkie Knudsen became general manager of Pontiac in 1956, he had his hands full. Although a stalwart GM brand, Pontiac didn't have much distinction compared to the rest of the stable: Chevrolet enjoyed entry-level popularity and had just become the "Hot One." Oldsmobile was the "Rocket Division" that benefited from experimental status. Buick was the "banker's hot rod," an upper-middle class brand known for its brawn. But Pontiac? Cars for librarians. Sure, Pontiac introduced a new V-8 in 1955, but it was just the beginning, and the perfect opportunity for Knudsen. He began by removing the trademark Silver Streak bands that had appeared on every Pontiac exterior since 1935. He also removed all Chief identification. Pontiac began moving from "conservative, reliable, and dependable" into something a bit more exciting. Unfortunately, the marketing didn't keep pace with this supposedly exciting new vehicle. "Built to last 100,000 miles" said one ad. Assisted by Knudsen's vision, Pontiac began to offer Tri-Power carburetion in 1957 and even fuel injection for the special-edition Bonneville, which made its debut at Daytona Beach Speed Weeks.

Knudsen had assembled a crack team to assist in Pontiac's metamorphosis. Oldsmobile's Pete Estes became chief engineer; John DeLorean was recruited from Studebaker-Packard and named his assistant. When the 1959s (the first completely under Knudsen's control) were ready, Pontiac's transformation was complete: a sharply styled cruiser with Wide-Trac" stance and a new 389 with Tri-Power performance to support the Division's new image as America's sportiest brand.

Performance and Racing

Although 1959 was Pontiac's watershed year, 1960 was pivotal for performance enthusiasts. Despite the Big Three's gentleman's agreement with the 1957 AMA to back out of its support of organized racing, Knudsen subversively continued Pontiac's racing effort because the brand's reinvention depended on performance. He formed the Super Duty Group to create high-performance parts. When Super Duty equipment began to trickle down to NASCAR racers, Pontiac became the car to beat. And as the 1960 NHRA Nationals was to take place in Detroit, Pontiac had the perfect platform to put on a show in sanctioned drag racing.

This was "Win on Sunday, Sell on Monday" in action. For the street, Pontiac offered a slew of performance engines topped off by the 389 425A, but the Super Duty association was never far from the minds of enthusiasts. This was the brilliance of Jim Wangers, who understood the difference between *racing* and *performance*. As Pontiac's account manager at the MacManus, John & Adams agency, Wangers used marketing smarts and his familiarity with high performance to educate consumers: The cars they read about in the buff books used parts that they could purchase from any Pontiac dealership.

Pontiac's stock with enthusiasts increased with the 1961 introduction of the 421, which was initially

Pontiac introduced the Firebird several months after the Camaro. Five models were available, all catering to different segments of the market. (Photo ©TEN: The Enthusiast Network. All rights reserved.)

The Tri-Power 3x2 induction system first appeared in 1957. For 1958, the 347 grew to 370 ci; Tri-Power offered 300 and 330 hp.

At the 1960 U.S. Nationals in Detroit, Jim Wangers (second from right with both hands on the fender) won NHRA's Top Stock Eliminator driving a Royal Pontiac–prepared Catalina. (Photo ©TEN: The Enthusiast Network. All rights reserved.)

The 1959 Wide Track Pontiac was cleaned up for 1960. The 389 425A produced up to 348 hp. Over-the-counter Super Duty parts boosted output to an arbitrary 363 horses. (Chris Phillip Photo)

The NHRA put racing shenanigans to rest by requiring manufacturers to build their Super Stockers at the factory. Pontiac responded with 179 421 Super Duty vehicles, some with aluminum body parts. (Rocky Rotella Photo)

available as a 373-hp Super Duty engine. The 421 was further developed for 1962 as a mild 4-barrel 320-horse torquer and a 405-horse dual-quad Super Duty Super Stocker. Otherwise, the 425A was Pontiac's top street engine, available with up to 348 horses with Tri-Power. Although a Catalina two-door sedan may have been a racer's choice, the most stylish way to go fast was with the new, personal-luxury Grand Prix. The redesigned 1963 Pontiac featured vertical headlights, but only the Grand Prix had a recessed grille with parking lights and voluptuous "Coke-bottle" side flanks notable for their lack of trim. Out back, a unique concave backlight was complemented by full-width trim hiding the taillights.

Although still not a performance car in essence, the Grand Prix was the perfect showcase for the expanded 421 lineup, which now included two 421 HOs with up to 370 hp with Tri-Power. Pontiac's trusty 389 continued, but the 425A was gone; the top Tri-Power now featured 313 horses. Transistorized ignition was a new performance option, with DeLorean declaring it "greatly superior in performance, maintenance, and economy," as it combined increased output and voltage with greater ignition stability. For racers, the Super Duty 421 with up to 410 horses continued its winning ways. Facing pressure from the Federal government, General Motors decided to reaffirm the 1957 AMA racing ban early in 1963, putting an end to the Super Duty fun and games. At the time, General Motors had almost 60 percent of the American auto market (with Pontiac number three in sales). Fearing an mule was a hoot, but General Motors dictated that the A-Body could not have an engine larger than 330 ci. In a clever move, Pontiac made the 389 part of the GTO package instead of a model, which meant it could be pushed through the approval process under the radar because the company's Engineering Policy Committee did not involve itself with options.

To protect themselves, the key players convinced Pontiac's sales manager to send a memo to district managers to garner support of the GTO package from dealers. Within a few days, 5,000 orders had been placed for the GTO, giving engineers the equity to push the package through to GM management. When management saw so many orders, how could they say no?

According to Wangers, "The GTO brought to life everything Pontiac had been trying to say about the entire product line." In a public relations coup, *Car and Driver* compared the Pontiac with its namesake, the Ferrari GTO. Two Pontiacs were used for the comparison; the red one was a Royal Pontiac–prepared ringer capable of running 0–60 in 4.6 seconds and 0–100 in 11.8. After the March 1964 issue hit newsstands, the American automotive landscape was forever changed. So the racing ban was not the end of the world after all. And if anyone was serious about performance, he or she would have a Hurst shifter resting by his/her knee. Wangers was instrumental in convincing Pontiac management that a Hurst shifter should be standard equipment on every floor-shifted manual Pontiac thanks to its precision and street reputation. This was a beneficial relationship because every time Hurst debuted a new product, you could count on a Pontiac to appear in its ads and promotions.

To lighten the 1963 Super Duty Catalina, Pontiac drilled more than 100 holes into the frame rails. Only 14 "Swiss Cheese" Catalinas were built before the AMA ban. (Photo ©TEN: The Enthusiast Network. All rights reserved.)

anti-trust suit, the corporation felt exiting all sponsored motorsports would be one way to push against market penetration while promoting safety.

This put Pontiac in an awkward position because Bunkie Knudsen had built its image on performance and exploited it in sanctioned racing. Now there would be no more Super Dutys, no more racing victories, and no more performance image. Without racing, Pontiac's performance image could only rely on the Wide-Track chassis, some great street engines, and a robust parts catalog.

GTO Changes Everything

Pontiac's saving grace was the GTO. A group of Pontiac engineers were playing around with the idea of dropping a 389 in the redesigned, larger 1964 Tempest, as the engine shared external dimensions with the 326. Their test

If the *Car and Driver* test was considered a PR victory, Pontiac still had a lesson to learn from the media. *Hot Rod* magazine wanted to test a GTO but the press pool had none available. An eager zone manager offered his wife's loaded convertible for the test, resulting in a lukewarm article thanks to the base 389/325, two-speed automatic, and 3.08 open rear.

After this episode, Wangers asked DeLorean for two cars to promote Pontiac's image to the press. All these GTOs would have the "proper" gearing and options and be tuned by Royal Pontiac so they could perform at their peak. Over the model year, Wangers had changes made to tuning,

The concept was mundane, the effort subversive. The 1964 GTO came to fruition thanks to a loophole in GM's rules. By the time executives objected, more than 5,000 dealer orders had been placed. (Rocky Rotella Photo)

Sound the trumpets or something, Hurst is out with the safest custom wheel ever made! The only forged wheel in the industry!

Pontiacs figured prominently in Hurst advertising (1965 GTO) and promotions (1966 Bonneville). Hurst's forged aluminum wheel was over-engineered and expensive, but it came with a lifetime warranty against defects or failures, just like Hurst's shifter. (Photo Courtesy Hurst Inc. & ©TEN: The Enthusiast Network. All rights reserved.)

gearing, suspension, and brakes, then invited an editor to sample an exclusive take on this GTO. This kept the GTO's image visible and positive in the media, and all Royal tweaks were divulged, yet they were simple tricks that could be done by anyone.

Full-size Pontiacs weren't ignored, however. The facelifted 1964 models featured a return of high-performance 389s, with the top Tri-Power having 330 hp. Because there were no more Super Dutys, the 421 HO with 370 hp was as good as it got. A sporty 2+2 package for the Catalina included buckets, console, and a tepid 389, so it wasn't a complete performance package as was the GTO.

GTO's Big Brother

Pontiac redesigned its 1965 full-size line with coupes that showed off a sweeping semi-fastback roofline. The 2+2 package featured a standard

421 plus the new availability of GM's Turbo-Hydramatic three-speed automatic. As a follow-up to the GTO versus GTO article, *Car and Driver* ran a 2+2 vs. 2+2 comparison in March 1965 with race driver Walter Hansgen piloting both the Pontiac and Ferrari around Bridgehampton.

Officially a performance package for 1965, the 2+2 came standard with a 338-hp 421. A 421/356 or a 421 HO with 376 horses, both with Tri-Power, were optional. (Photo ©TEN: The Enthusiast Network. All rights reserved.)

In another nod to Ferrari, the 1964 2+2 package gave the Catalina a sportier flavor thanks to bucket seats and a console, among other features. The standard engine was a 2-barrel 389, but order the 421 HO and you practically had the GTO's big brother. (Donald J. Keefe Photo)

Restyle and Ram Air

The restyled 1965 GTO featured vertical headlamps, taillights that wrapped around the fenders, and a new hood design with single scoop that could be made functional with a midyear dealer accessory. The base 389 was upped to 335 hp while Tri-Power put out 360 horses. This truly was Pontiac's moment. More than 75,000 GTOs were built and competitors scrambled to capture the GTO's essence. *Motor Trend* awarded the whole Pontiac Division "Car of the Year."

And it only got better. The GTO was heavily restyled for 1966 and now enjoyed full model status. Engines were basically carry-overs, but the first of Pontiac's Ram Air engines became available on February 28. Known today as the XS (its stamped engine code), this was a Tri-Power 389 with beefier components, including "744" camshaft, heavy-duty springs, and mandatory

Midyear 1965, a factory ram-air induction accessory became available for the GTO via dealer installation.

With less slab and more curves, the 1966 GTO was as handsome as any performance car in the market. Production reached a rousing 96,946 units. (Chris Phillip Photo)

4-speed with 4.33 gears. The XS was rated at 360 horses, as was the conventional Tri-Power, but it was clearly a breed above. The 2+2 returned for 1966 as its own model, cleaner thanks to a facelift that also featured simulated vents on the rear flanks. The GTO's popularity, however, was making full-size performance cars less attractive, as only 6,383 2+2s were built.

Ram Air also continued as a dealer-installed accessory for the regular Tri-Power.

1967: Year of Transition

This was the first year of a new performance trademark: the hood tachometer. Having a tach in the driver's line of vision was practical because many factory versions were often difficult to read. A Pontiac with a hood tach made an impact on the street scene, told the rest of the world that this car meant business.

The 1967 GTO debuted with a new grille, trim, and a squared-off rump with new taillights. Pontiac bored the 389 to 400 ci, but standard horsepower remained at 335; the 360-horse 400 HO was the first step up. The top engine was the 400 Ram Air, which also was rated at 360 horses but at a higher RPM; the Ram Air accessory package continued to be available for lesser 4-barrel engines. (For the first time, a 2-barrel 400/255 combined economy with the GTO's image.)

Thanks to government regulations, all U.S. automobiles were required to use a dual-master cylinder, which helped make the 1967 GTO a more refined driver.

All big Pontiacs were redesigned for 1967, still with trademark vertical headlights but now with more sculpted "longer/lower/wider" styling. The 2+2, having reverted to option status, featured front fender louvers and a

THE MAGNIFICENT FIVE

Released several months after the Chevrolet Camaro, the Firebird wasn't just a me-too version of the Chevy; it had several improvements underneath (especially the suspension). The Firebird was available in five models with entirely different personalities: Firebird (Starter), Firebird 326 (Family Sports Car), Firebird Sprint (European), Firebird HO (Light Heavyweight), and Firebird 400 (Thriller).

The Sprint was a high-output OHC-6 with a 4-barrel carburetor that could blow away many V-8s, but it wasn't high-performance in the muscle car vein. The striped Firebird HO with its 285-hp 326 HO was capable of surprising some challengers. The Firebird 400 was the *de facto* high-performance F-Body, rated at 325 horses. Later, the 400 Ram Air became available, also rated at 325 horses.

ENDING A PERFORMANCE TRADITION

For 1967, General Motors enacted yet another edict: no multiple carburetion for anything other than the Corvette. That was the biggest blow to Pontiac's image since the 1963 racing ban as Tri-Power was a huge part of its image. Because Pontiac relied on Tri-Power as a performance trademark, the division needed to demonstrate that performance wouldn't be compromised by the new Rochester Quadrajet.

Wangers commissioned Royal Pontiac to prepare two 1967 GTO press cars (one a 4-speed, the other with the new TH400 3-speed automatic) and *Motor Trend* was invited to test the new cars. Not only did they perform as well as the 1966 Tri-Power, they also demonstrated that the TH400 could launch better than the stick. Only a "hot shoe" driving a stick could outsmart the new automatic.

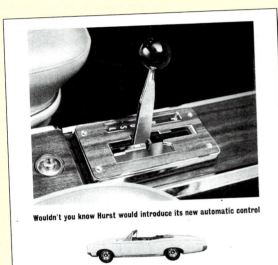

Wouldn't you know Hurst would introduce its new automatic control

wrapped in a '67 GTO?

It's only proper. Hurst has been in GTOs since the first GTO was born. Now that they've kicked loose the Great One for '67, with a new engine, drive train components and a 3-speed Turbo-Hydramatic, Hurst is in there with something new of its own. A console-mounted Dual Gate control that's going to switch a lot of manual-shift levers over to automatic.

The reason is simple. Because the manual side of the Hurst automatic control is for *real*. This is no merchandising gimmick that promises you manual shift control, but in reality makes you guess your way through the automatic gears. The new Turbo-Hydro is a gutsy, performance-prone transmission that's as home on a race track as it is on the highway. And controlling it can

be as precise as handling a fully synchronized manual transmission. The Dual Gate gives you that control with its positive latching mechanism that takes the guesswork out of gear-changing, going up or down. It eliminates any possibility of missing a gear, or accidentally hitting neutral and blowing an engine.

You're in complete control. You've got the automatic side when you feel shiftless and all the advantages of the manual side when you want to let it happen.

Soon you'll be able to buy Hurst automatic controls (along with all the other Hurst products) at your speed shop. Right now, though, you'll have to buy a Pontiac to get one. Write for details: Hurst Performance Products, Dept. 61B, Warminster, Pa. 18974.

HURST

Dual-transmission control became a reality when Hurst introduced the "His and Hers" shifter at a 1962 trade show. Pontiac offered the rebranded "Dual/Gate" as a factory option for 1967 GTOs. (Photo Courtesy Hurst Inc.)

Motor Trend tested two 1967 GTOs: One with the new Turbo-Hydramatic automatic, and the other a 4-speed, and both with the new Rochester Quadrajet. Pontiac wanted to show that the Quadrajet was as good as the banned Tri-Power. (Photo ©TEN: The Enthusiast Network. All rights reserved.)

new 428 engine offering 360 hp, with the 376-horse 428 HO optional. By then it had become obvious that enthusiasts preferred the GTO and its brand-new little brother, the Firebird, so 2+2 production ended after 1,768 were built.

1968 and 1969

"The Great One" was brought to the forefront once again for 1968. Even with tough competition from Dodge's redesigned Charger and others chipping away at the GTO's success, the Goat continued to sell a ton and

even garner "Car of the Year" status from *Motor Trend*. The curvaceous new body was on a smaller 112-inch wheelbase. The pillared coupe was missing for the first time.

Most noteworthy was the GTO's front bumper made from plastic Endura, which could return to its natural shape after low-speed impact. If the Endura bumper wasn't your style, you could opt for the "Endura-delete," which substituted the Tempest/LeMans chrome bumper. Pontiac's signature vertical headlights were now a thing of the past, and the new GTO could be ordered with optional retractable headlamp covers.

After GM issued its cubic-inch edict, Pontiac engineers improved power output in other ways. The Ram Air II, introduced in April 1968, featured round-port heads and an upgraded cam and exhaust manifolds. (Rocky Rotella Photo)

A May 8, 1969, memo read, "The Judge was conceived to stimulate Pontiac's youthful, sporty, good performance image among the young car enthusiasts. According to market surveys, these images have been decreasing over the past year. The Judge was to be a strong image car with excellent performance, yet it was not to hurt GTO sales." (Richard Truesdell Photo)

The base 400 was now rated at 350 hp, likely due to the GTO's increased weight (remember the 10 pounds per horsepower edict?). The dealer-installed Ram Air accessory was available for the last time, and the D-port 360-horse Ram Air engine was superseded in May 1968 by the 366-horse Ram Air II featuring round-port heads, improved exhaust manifolds, high-lift 041 camshaft, forged aluminum pistons, and other improvements.

A new 350 HO replaced the 326 HO for the Tempest/LeMans. Featuring 320 hp, it bore no markings to suggest what was within, but it made for a good Junior Supercar. Alas, fewer than 6,000 350 HOs were built.

The 350 HO also became the new engine for the 1968 Firebird HO. The Firebird 400's standard engine was upgraded to 330 hp; the new 400

HO was rated at 335 horses. The 400 Ram Air was rated the same, but the midyear Ram Air II replacement had 340 horses. Firebird styling was mildly tweaked, the most noticeable change was the wrap-around parking lights.

Only detail styling changes marked the 1969 GTO, notably the grille, parking lights, taillights, and badging. The standard 400/350 continued; the 400 HO now featured standard air induction to become the 400 Ram Air ("Ram Air III") with 366 hp. Despite being available for only a few months in 1968, the round-port Ram Air II was upgraded with revised heads and an aluminum intake and called Ram Air IV. Ram Air cars now featured identifying decals on the scoops, plus the system now was cable-operated from the driver's seat.

Thanks to the success of the Plymouth Road Runner, Pontiac was keen to develop a competitor. What started out as a day-glow orange Tempest-based ET (elapsed time) with a 350 HO evolved into a GTO-based package called The Judge. The name came from a popular Flip Wilson (later, Sammy Davis, Jr.) quip from a recurring segment on TV's *Laugh-In*.

The Trans Am package for the 1969 Firebird 400 aroused consternation among purists because the engine wasn't legal for Trans-Am racing. All 697 built (including 8 convertibles) were white and blue. (Wade Ogle Photo)

The package included a spoiler, stripes, Rally II wheels sans trim rings, and Ram Air III with 3-speed manual, among other items. Production began in January 1969 with an initial run of 1,000 "pattern" Judges in Carousel Red with specific equipment. Then the option list expanded, with the GTO's full-color palette becoming available in mid-February.

In addition to representing new blood in the Pontiac line, the Judge also functioned as bait to bring people into showrooms.

So perhaps the ET was stillborn, but anyone could pick a Tempest pillared coupe (even with special-order Carousel Red) and spec out the 330-hp 350 HO, but only 85 did. The 1969 Firebird received its first major facelift. It displayed a smaller chrome "beak" surrounded by the GTO's Endura plastic. Rectangular parking lights were shared with the GTO. The Firebird HO continued as the entry-level performance F-Body, now rated at 325 hp and lacking the HO stripes of the past.

The Firebird 400 featured 330 horses standard. Unlike the GTO, the 335-horse 400 HO did not include air induction. Pontiac issued a bulletin to remind dealers that the "Ram Air inlet" was not included and had to be ordered separately. The top engine was the 345-horse Ram Air IV.

Pontiac introduced a special midyear Firebird package called the Trans Am. Only available in Cameo White with Tyrol Blue stripes, this be-spoilered Firebird was created as an "American GT," highlighting Pontiac's effort in the Trans-Am racing series.

The 400 Ram Air III with a special Ram Air hood was standard. A 3-speed manual transmission, functional fiberglass front fender air extractors, front and rear spoilers, and heavy-duty shocks and springs were among its features.

The Grand Prix went on a crash diet for 1969 by moving to a stretched 118-inch A-Body platform. With Model J and SJ trim levels (note the Duesenberg references), the Grand Prix came standard with a 400/350, but performance fans appreciated the 428/370 and 390-hp 428 HO.

Growing Pains

The year 1970 was to be a big one for the performance segment, but for Pontiac it didn't quite happen. General Motors lifted its cubic-inch limit, so Pontiac offered a new 455 HO with 360 hp, less powerful than the carryover Ram Air III and RAIV 400s. In addition to the 455 (which featured air induction as an option), the restyled GTO appeared sleeker and featured a redesigned Endura nose with no provision for concealed headlights. A new rear stabilizer also was a long-overdue feature. As before, the 400/350 was standard.

VOE System

Perhaps you've seen the commercial on YouTube with a 1970 GTO stopping by a drive-in restaurant looking for someone to race. While scoping the scene, the driver tugs on a cable under the dashboard, resulting in a throatier rumble. That lever was the vacuum-operated exhaust (VOE).

The original idea for this "Tiger Button" supposedly came from John DeLorean, who wanted a system that opened the mufflers, advanced the timing, and opened the Ram Air scoops all at once. The system that made it to production was nowhere near as complicated: vacuum-operated baffles in the muffler reduced back pressure and deepened the exhaust note with a simple tug.

Sounds neat, but the VOE system met with opposition. A December 1969 *Car Distribution Bulletin* stated that the system was "illegal for vehicles operated and registered in the State of Pennsylvania. Effective immediately, we will remove the optional Vacuum Controlled Exhaust System from all orders for dealers in the State of Pennsylvania."

By February 1970, the VOE system was canceled after 233 VOE-equipped GTOs had been built.

The 1969 Judge's intent was to kick-start GTO sales, enhance its image in the face of more aggressive competition, and draw folks to showrooms. The 1970 Judge featured much of the same equipment although it was redesigned. (Tim Dye Photo)

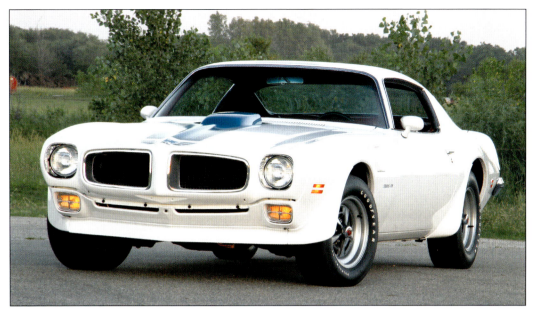

After a tepid launch in 1969, the redesigned 1970 Trans Am earned some praise thanks to the latest in handling and racing accoutrements. (Rocky Rotella Photo)

ahead of the static boundary layer that rendered most air-induction systems inefficient.

The Trans Am also became a more fully realized package, equipped with functional doo-dads and a well-thought-out suspension to give stellar stability and handling. Standard full instrumentation sat directly in front of the driver. The Ram Air III was standard, but 88 consumers bought the 370-horse Ram Air IV.

The Grand Prix continued into 1970 after a very successful revamp, so changes were few. The 400/350 remained standard, with the 455/370 replacing the 428. However, the Hurst SSJ, an $1147.25 conversion package that included a landau-type half-top, Fire Frost Gold accents, and a host of other custom touches sparked sales. SSJs generally were Polar White or Starlight Black, but other colors could be special-ordered. The SSJ package continued through 1972.

1971 and 1972: The Lean Years

Although eschewing wild graphics in standard form, the GTO could be ordered with the 1969 Judge stripe. The 1970 Judge featured new tri-color "eyebrow" stripes over each wheel arch. Also new was a flying spoiler and black Ram Air inserts. The signature Carousel Red was replaced by Orbit Orange, complemented with blue/pink/orange stripes. Standard power continued to be the Ram Air III, with the Ram Air 455 HO and Ram Air IV as options. GTO production fell to 40,149, including 3,797 Judges.

The 350 HO was gone for 1970, but, for the first time, pedestrian A-bodies were available with the 400. The 4-barrel was rated at 330 hp but was identical to the GTO's 400/350 when equipped with a manual tranny (automatics featured small-valve heads from the Catalina). It was perfect for the mid-year GT-37, which was a performance option for a new Tempest sub-series called the T-37. Somewhat a combination of a "junior supercar" (think the stillborn 1969 ET) and a "cosmetic supercar," the GT-37 came standard with a 2-barrel 350 with dual exhausts, hood pins, 1969 Judge stripes, and meaty tires with Rally II wheels less trim rings. Only 1,419 GT-37s were built.

The second-generation Firebird was delayed until February 1970 because of a United Auto Workers (UAW) strike. Reeking of European influences, the Firebird was now available only as a hardtop coupe. The refreshed lineup included Firebird, Firebird Esprit, Firebird Formula 400, and Firebird Trans Am.

The Formula 400 became the standard Firebird performance model, which included a 330-hp 400; the 345-horse Ram Air III was optional. The new fiberglass hood featured scoops that reached out front to grab air

The facelifted 1971 GTO featured a less graceful Endura nose that appeared tacked-on rather than integrated, with new forward-jutting hood scoops inspired by the Formula Firebird. Optional "eyebrow" stripes were similar to the Judge's but featured two colors instead of three. Also new was the polycast Honeycomb wheel option.

Although the 1970 455 HO was a disappointment to some, that all changed for 1971, which was ironic, considering that Pontiac lowered the compression on its engines. The GTO's 10.25:1 400/350 fell to 8.2:1 and 300 hp. The 455 fell from 360 to 325 hp.

Pontiac's new, round-port 455 HO was included in the 1971 Judge package, a throwback to the excesses that had been curtailed by emissions rules and insurance. Pontiac apparently agreed, canceling the Judge midyear after 357 hardtops and 17 convertibles were built. (Rocky Rotella Photo)

The 1971 GT-37 offered the same basic equipment as before but now included a choice of two 455s. Eyebrow stripes in white and red or black and red were replaced in March with longitudinal sword stripes.

Marginal styling changes, such as front fender vents and an inset grille, marked the 1972 GTO. However, the GTO also became a performance package offered only for the LeMans hardtop or pillared coupe. (Richard Truesdell Photo)

The new top engine also used the 455 HO designation but was a completely different animal thanks to round-port heads similar to the Ram Air II/IVs. With 8.4:1 compression, the 455 HO produced 335 hp, yet it was faster than the 1970 455 HO. Ram Air was optional, but included when the Judge package was specified.

The Tempest line for 1971 fully absorbed the budget-minded T-37. Although not a performance car, the T-37 could be ordered with any GTO engine including the 455 HO. But if you just *had* to have something that looked the part, the GT-37 was back, advertised as "From the people who brought you Wide-Track, Ram-Air, standard Hurst shifters, the protective Endura bumper, variable-ratio power steering, GTO, Grand Prix, and the Firebird Trans Am." Performance enthusiasts could move up from the 2-barrel 350 to the 400/300, 455/325, or 455 HO.

In another sign of the times, Pontiac compromised the GTO's image by making the T41 Endura nose optional for certain LeMans models. Order a LeMans Sport with T41 and 455 HO and you could pretend you were driving a GTO. Your insurance company may not have caught on, but it diluted the GTO brand.

Thanks to an abbreviated 1970 model year, the 1971 Firebird had few changes. The basic performance model continued to be the Formula, but for 1971 it was expanded to Formula 350, Formula 400, and Formula 455. The Formula 400 featured 300 hp; the Formula 455 could have either 455, with the HO available with Ram Air. The Trans Am also changed little but came standard with the 455 HO.

Although changes for 1972 were minimal, new horsepower formulas made things appear worse. For example, the 455 HO fell from 335 gross to 300 net horsepower. These engines were marginally different from 1971. The HO featured new heads with slightly reshaped ports to enhance low-lift

flow, and a leaned-out carburetor without a booster venturi on the primary side allowed for more flow.

The biggest shock was the demotion of the GTO to an option package for the LeMans, which included the standard 400 4-barrel and just about everything else familiar to GTO fans. The convertible was gone, but the GTO (pillared) coupe returned for the first time since 1967. Engine choices remained the same, but the 455 HO now featured standard Ram Air and unitized ignition. A new WW5 package included the HO and a handling package.

The 1972 Formula Firebird continued to offer a 350, 400, or 455. Choose the 455 HO (with standard Ram Air for 1972) plus the Y99 Ride and Handling package and you'd have all the Trans Am's power and handling but with less weight. (Michael Sparks Photo)

Styling upgrades featured an inset grille and new front-fender air extractors designed to "keep the engine compartment cooler and reduce air-pressure build-up." GTO identification migrated to the rear fenders and full-width "sperm whale" side stripes were a new option. A unique ducktail spoiler was featured in early marketing material but canceled at the beginning of the model year.

The LeMans moved down to replace the T-37, but the GT package lived on in the 1972 LeMans hardtop or convertible with standard equipment similar to the 1971 GT-37. When the 455 HO was ordered, the T41 Endura nose and Ram Air were required for any LeMans.

The 1972 Firebird received minimal changes, the most noticeable was a new honeycomb grille. Engine choices for the Formula remained the same except the D-port 455 was discontinued, leaving the HO as the only 455. The Trans Am continued to feature the HO engine as standard equipment.

The Best of Times, the Worst of Times

A new A-Body was introduced in 1973 after being delayed a year. However, due to new safety standards mandated after the design started taking shape, a clumsy 5-mph front bumper was implemented. The LeMans looked awkward and lost the sleek lines that were part of the original sketches.

This affected the GTO's traditional good looks, not to mention that the new Grand Am stole the GTO's trademark Endura look. Nevertheless, the GTO package included a 230-hp 400, G60x15 blackwalls, NACA hood scoops, blacked-out grille, and firm shocks with heavy-duty front and rear stabilizer bars. Because performance was a bad word, horsepower was not even mentioned in the brochure.

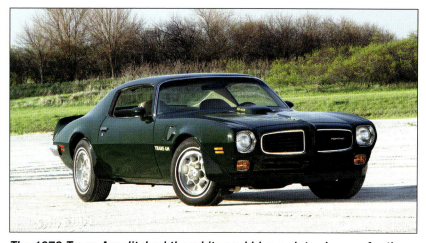

The 1973 Trans Am ditched the white and blue paint schemes for three new colors. Also new was a "Screaming Chicken" decal for the hood. (Rocky Rotella Photo)

Engine options started with a 250-hp 455, but Pontiac had something special up its sleeve: the Super Duty 455. As the successor to the 455 HO, the 8.4:1-compression SD455 featured a four-bolt main block, improved round-port heads with revised intake and exhaust ports, a slightly more radical cam, forged pistons and heat-treated forged-steel connecting rods, a specially machined cast-iron crankshaft, and dry-sump oil system, among other items. It was initially rated at 310 hp but, due to a more emissions-friendly cam change and the EPA requiring retesting (for several manufacturers) for exhaust gas ratio and spark timing issues, the Super Duty was re-rated on paper at 290 hp. Regardless, the SD 455 performed in ways that people had forgotten about, which is why the 1973 Super Duty GTO won *Cars* magazine's Top Performance Car of the Year.

Something interesting happened along the way, however: No Super Duty GTOs were ever factory-produced. In March 1973, Pontiac sent a bulletin to dealers announcing the cancellation of the Super Duty for all A-Body vehicles. Only 4,806 1973 GTOs were built.

After several years of ups and downs in sales, the second-generation Firebird began to gain traction in 1973. Amber parking lights and a coarse egg-crate grille were new, but the engine lineup was shuffled. As before, Firebird Formula engines began with a 350 2-barrel, with the 230-hp 400 the first choice for enthusiasts. The D-port 455 made a return, and the new Super Duty replaced the 455 HO.

The all-new 1973 GTO was based on the LeMans Colonnade coupe. The Super Duty 455 was offered but, thanks to emissions issues and parts shortages, Pontiac eventually restricted SD 455 production for the Firebird, making this 1973 a fine "what-if." (Donald J. Keefe Photo)

The Trans Am ditched the white and blue color combinations from 1970–1972 and was now available in Buccaneer Red, Cameo White, or Brewster Green, all of which could be complemented by the "Screaming Chicken" decal for the hood.

The Trans Am ditched the white and blue color combinations from 1970–1972 and was now available in Buccaneer Red, Cameo White, or Brewster Green, all of which could be complemented by an optional "Screaming Chicken" decal for the hood. Newly standard was the D-port 455 with the Super Duty optional, but the latter's availability was delayed thanks to the EPA testing debacle plus a parts shortage, limiting installations to 252 Trans Ams and 43 Formula 455s.

The 1974 Trans Am was restyled to comply with new federal bumper regulations. The Super Duty 455 became more widely available, but it did not return for 1975. (Rocky Rotella Photo)

1974: End of an Era

The sun was setting on an era in Detroit as the GTO made its final appearance in 1974. Pontiac felt that the GTO's essence could be revived by installing a 200-hp 350 4-barrel in the compact Ventura. "You can't inherit a name like GTO. You have to earn it. And we built our compact 1974 GTO to do just that," proclaimed the brochure.

Pontiac added parking lights in a blacked-out grille (shades of 1966), body-colored sport mirrors, shaker hood scoop, Rally II mags, "beefy" suspension, and "contemporary" GTO identification. Available as a coupe or hatchback coupe, both in Ventura and Ventura Custom trim levels, the GTO was a minor success with 7,058 built, but Pontiac felt it was time to bury the name and finish the era that it helped foster.

That wasn't Pontiac's only nail in the coffin. The 1974 Firebird received its first facelift since 1970, featuring a sloped nose and conventional bumper design (also made of Endura); out back, a urethane bumper with elongated and segmented taillights were also new. The Formula featured a familiar engine lineup, while the Trans Am's standard engine was downgraded to a 225-hp 400, with the 455 4-barrel and 290-horse Super Duty optional.

Thanks to pent-up demand due to its late introduction in 1973, SD 455 production increased to 943 Trans Ams and 58 Formulas. After that, Pontiac put an end to high-compression performance in a low-compression world and marked the end of an era, performed by the same company that arguably started it a decade earlier.

The Ventura-based 1974 GTO may have seemed like a fall from grace, but it was a logical evolution for the times. This one is still in the hands of its original owner. (Denis "Diz" Dean Photo)

Royal Pontiac: Dealer Extraordinaire

Many Pontiac dealerships experienced performance-car success, such as Knaffel Pontiac in Akron, Myrtle Motors in Queens, Gay Pontiac in Dickinson, Texas, and Packer Pontiac in Detroit. However, none made an impact like Royal.

Thanks to Royal Pontiac's increased visibility from campaigning a car at the dragstrip, customers began to visit Royal *en masse*. By Labor Day weekend 1960, Royal's Super Duty Catalina was victorious in NHRA's Top Stock Eliminator. In just four years, Pontiac went from being a "stick in the mud" to the hottest car in America.

Pontiac winning a racing title in 1960 was great for the brand's image, but what about for the average performance enthusiast? It's easy to pretend to be Arnie Beswick while dodging cars on the highway entrance ramp, but it's another thing to want to know what made Arnie's car tick. Enthusiasts often discovered that, although Pontiac promoted special high-performance parts, only a handful of parts managers knew how to sell performance. Hence, dealerships needed to be educated on how to cater to those enthusiasts.

"Any effort we could make to help our dealers better understand this new generation of Wide-Track performance would make a huge difference," said Jim Wangers in his book *Glory Days*. This was important because a knowledgeable dealership staff could help elevate Pontiac's image. Wangers put together a traveling seminar that included a "performance service expert" and a "performance parts expert" who held training sessions at the zone offices. Wangers used metro Detroit–based Royal Pontiac for this pilot program.

First on the agenda was to ensure the dealership stocked the right performance equipment. Next, the salesmen were schooled on understanding the product so that they knew how to assist the customer in ordering a car with the proper equipment. Mechanics who knew how to service high-performance vehicles were retained. Royal had demonstrators with the

Royal Pontiac came up with the Bobcat name by borrowing letters from Catalina and Bonneville. (Dennis Koss Photo)

latest performance options so customers could get an idea what they could expect from the option list. Unsurprisingly, Royal Pontiac's sales shot up. Sometimes other dealerships called Royal when they needed a part.

Street Bobcat

Royal's win led to the opportunity to offer super-tunes. By placing ads in newspapers, the dealership developed another way to promote the Pontiac brand. Magazines were attracted to what Royal was doing on the track and at the dealership, but what about on the street? In 1961, Royal decided to brand vehicles that received a super-tune and created the Royal Bobcat.

Bobcats were usually Catalinas powered by Pontiac's top street engines with a 4-speed. Heavy-duty suspension, performance axle ratio, tachometer, and even Pontiac's eight-lug aluminum wheels were common equipment on Royal Bobcats. They also included the tune-up package that turned any Pontiac into a Bobcat: thin head gaskets, progressive carburetor linkage (for Tri-Power), special distributor advance curve, blocked intake heat riser gaskets, richer carburetor jets, and special locknuts for more positive valve adjustment.

Open House Success

The dealership held a Royal Pontiac Performance Open House where a host of Royal Bobcats were on display, complemented by an array of components that made up the Bobcat package. The service department also showed films of the 1960-1961 Daytona 500. Some customers were

also invited to display their own vehicles, and even Pontiac's 1962 Super Duty Catalina factory racer was on site for enthusiasts to pore over. For many, this was the first time they were able to see one up close. Sponsors such as Hurst displayed their products, too. More than 15,000 folks visited Royal Pontiac that weekend.

Business Expansion

By the start of the 1963 season, Royal Pontiac started a mail-order business. This could have only been possible thanks to its active racing presence, knowledgeable sales staff, service managers who knew how to build a performer, and parts managers who knew what to keep in stock.

Pontiac's ad agency also exploited the marque's accomplishments at the 1962 Daytona 500 and the NHRA Winternationals, both of which had a Pontiac in the winner's circle. Ads were placed in magazines that featured race coverage to show readers that the very same parts that made those cars winners were available to every Pontiac owner.

In October 1963, the dealership hired a mechanic named Milt Schornack, who became the face of Royal Pontiac to millions of magazine readers. Milt improved the Bobcat package, raced for the Royal Racing Team, and found himself involved with Pontiac's skunkworks.

Royal Pontiac became the premier Pontiac dealership in the United States, thanks to an integrated effort that included knowledgeable sales talent, astute mechanics, and well-versed parts managers. A robust national catalog business was a logical extension. (Photo Courtesy Keith Seymore Collection)

Royal Pontiac continued with the Bobcat package through 1969 but, in 1970, the Royal Racing Team was sold to George DeLorean (John's brother), who ran Leader Automotive; Royal Pontiac was sold in 1974.

Marketing Strategy

The GTO's success was buoyed by co-branding efforts. Not only did the GTO start a performance movement, but it also was a marketing success that demonstrated how proper support could make a positive impact on sales.

Goats on 45

Promoting the GTO in song was a stroke of luck that fell into the lap of Jim Wangers. John Wilkin, a teenager whose mother owned a Nashville-based publishing company, gave Wangers a call about a song he'd written about the GTO. Wangers thought the song was "close" but needed several specific references to the GTO, such as "three deuces and a 389." Wilkin was paired with several session musicians and then recorded "G.T.O." as Ronny and the Daytonas for Mala Records. The surf-inspired 45 reached number four on the Billboard Pop Singles chart in 1964.

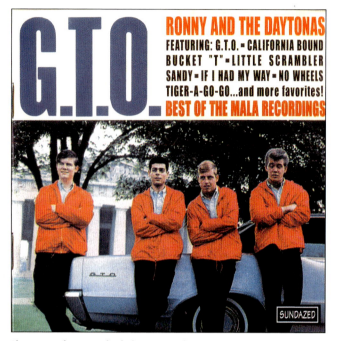

The Beatles may have ruled the roost in 1964, but Ronny and the Daytonas came out of nowhere and had a number four hit with "G.T.O." Pontiac had a hit car, and now it had a hit song to help promote it!

The GTO returned to the studio for 1965 with a promotional 45 produced in conjunction with Hurst. "GeeTO Tiger" backed by "Big Sounds of the GeeTO Tiger (at the GM proving grounds)" was part of a contest for listeners to submit how many times the word "tiger" was mentioned and, in 50 words or less, write why they'd like to own a GeeTO Tiger. The lucky winner won a 1965 GTO painted Hurst Gold with several custom touches.

GeeTO as a nickname may not have caught on the way Goat did, but the promotion was successful for Pontiac.

Thom McAn

Using sharp research skills and creativity, Wangers discovered that shoes resonated with young people. Thom McAn was one of the largest shoe stores at the time. It also was among the biggest advertisers on Top 40 radio, a market that catered to youths. With Wangers' lead, MacManus, John & Adams approached the shoe company in 1966 with the idea of "taking the image of our GTO and applying it to one of their shoes."

Thom McAn subsequently created a "mod" shoe called The GTO and referred to it as "America's first high-performance shoe," complete with a sole that resembled tire tread. All 1,500 Thom McAn shops featured point-of-sale window displays with GTOs racing toward the finish line on a miniature dragstrip.

Recognizing a good thing, Pontiac agreed to provide 50 GTOs in a contest whose only requirement was filling out an entry form. Every entrant

Count the tigers!

Listen to the Colpix recording "GeeTO Tiger" by the Tigers (a great new group of swingers), and count the number of times the word *tiger* is sung in the record. (Complete rules are listed below.)

And win one in the HURST-GeeTO Tiger Contest!

Win the original GeeTO Tiger—a wild '65 GTO with special Hurst-gold paint and unique tiger-appointed interior. It's set up to go. Features Pontiac's big-gun 360-hp mill with 3 deuce carbs, transistorized ignition and 4-speed close ratio box with a gold-plated Hurst shifter. All riding on a full set of gold anodized Hurst custom wheels. Wild!

(To see a "live one" stop by your local Pontiac dealer's. He's got his own version of this one-of-a-kind Hurst hustler.)

6 more prizes from Hurst!
To runner-up winners Hurst is giving away: two sets of Hurst custom wheels. Two Competition Plus 4-speed shifters. And two Synchro/Loc 3-speed shifters.

100! Prizes! 100!
Still more. Like auto-stereos. Record albums from Colpix Recordings. And subscriptions to *Hot Rod, Motor Trend, Car Craft, Rod & Custom,* and *Teen.* The editors of these magazines are honorary judges and will assist George Hurst in selecting the winners. Their decision is final.

One more time!
All you have to do is: 1) Listen to the record "GeeTO Tiger" by the Tigers. 2) Put down on a sheet of paper the number of times the word *tiger* is sung in the record. 3) On the same sheet write, in 25 words or less, "Why I would like to own the original GeeTO Tiger"—the car that inspired the song. 4) Send

your entries to:
Hurst Performance Products
P. O. Box X509, Dept. "CD"
Glenside, Pa.

That's all you have to do. But do it quick. Entries must be postmarked no later than July 31, 1965 and become the property of Hurst Performance Products. Contest not valid where prohibited by state or local law.

Out of more than 100,000 contest entries, one person was chosen to win the Hurst GeeTO Tiger, which was painted in special Hurst Gold paint and equipped with a gold-plated Hurst shifter and gold-anodized Hurst wheels. (Les Kletke Photo, Courtesy Hurst Inc.)

received a set of decals featuring GTO emblems. All told, more than 500,000 entries were received.

Another Pontiac/Thom McAn tie-in involved Hurst and Promotions, Inc., the company that ran the Detroit Autorama and similar events around the country. The purpose, according to Wangers, was to attract "a new generation of high-performance car enthusiasts." MacManus, John & Adams designed a display where kids and adults could sit in the cockpit of two GTOs (with Hurst shifters) to race MPC GeeTO Tiger slot cars down a 1/25-scale quarter-mile strip. The Mystery Tiger was always on hand to arouse excitement and distribute tiger tails and GTO decals. Through 1966, this scale-model dragstrip visited 32 cities with 150,000 participating enthusiasts.

The Monkees

A new TV show about a pop group and their hilarious hi-jinks was planned for 1966. The sponsor for this new show (*The Monkees*) was Kellogg's. When Wangers met with Kellogg's marketing department he proposed a sweepstakes that included a GTO convertible plus a trip

Pontiac teamed with Thom McAn to produce the GTO shoe, then promoted a give-away for 50 1966 GTOs. It was so successful, another 22 1967 GTOs were given away. (Brian Stumbaugh Photo, ©TEN: The Enthusiast Network. All rights reserved.)

to Hollywood for a starring role in a *Monkees* episode; fifteen runners-up would win GTO hardtops. Kellogg's planned to promote the contest on 42 million cereal boxes, and research showed that the average cereal box was viewed six times before disposal.

Dean Jeffries was commissioned to build a custom Monkeemobile and, of course, it was based on the GTO. The popularity of *The Monkees* and the car was such that MPC produced more than 7 million scale-model plastic kits of the Monkeemobile.

Was it any surprise that Dean Jeffries used a GTO for the Monkeemobile? In conjunction with Kellogg's, one GTO convertible and 15 GTO hardtops were given away as part of a TV Screen-Stakes. (Photo Courtesy Leisa Hurley-Richardson, ©TEN: The Enthusiast Network. All rights reserved.)

CANADIAN PONTIAC MARKET

If you lived near Burlington, Bangor, Buffalo, Detroit, or Seattle in the 1950s and 1960s, you may have caught glimpses of vehicles that looked familiar but couldn't put your finger on it. Much of that was due to a combination of Canadian tariff and Canadian pride.

The Cars

Canada's population density is much less than the United States', so large-scale manufacturing tends to have higher costs. Starting in 1936, the government's way of protecting its automotive industry was through tariffs. A 17.5-percent duty was imposed on all vehicles imported into the Great White North. Using economies of scale while providing consumers something unique at marginal cost, Pontiac started using Chevrolet bodies with Pontiac grilles in the 1930s, eventually evolving into Chevrolet chassis with Pontiac styling. By the 1960s, it became even more diverse.

Big Ponchos

During the dawn of the muscle car era, Oshawa-built Strato-Chiefs, Laurentians, and Parisiennes could be found at Canadian dealerships. Enthusiasts could opt for a Super-Flame 409 with up to 425 hp in 1963. In 1965, the Astro-Jet 396 replaced the 409. In 1966, the Jet-Flame 427 was added to Pontiac's engine line-up.

For 1967, the Parisienne 2+2 debuted, but it was a sporty buckets-and-console model instead of a performance entry like the American version. Similar to the Impala SS, the Parisienne 2+2 was available with everything from a straight-6 to the 385-horse 427, lasting through 1970 with the LS5 454/390 as the top engine.

Acadian

When it comes to the Canadian version of the Chevy II, things get a bit more interesting. The compact Acadian featured a Pontiac-like split grille plus other unique trim not found on its American cousin. For 1966, the L79 327/350 became available but was dropped for 1967, leaving the 327/275 as the top engine.

Along with the redesign of the 1968 Chevy II, the 1968 Acadian featured a new 295-hp Astro-Flash 350 that was standard with the new Super Sport package; unlike the Nova SS, a big-block Acadian was never available.

The Pontiac-inspired split grille was gone, but minor trim variations set the Acadian apart. SS horsepower was bumped to 300 for 1969–1970 but, in a familiar story, compression was lowered for 1971, resulting in a 30-horse loss. The Acadian was replaced by the Ventura II in 1972.

Chevrolet's L79 327 was available for the 1966 Acadian, including the utilitarian Invader to the top-line Canso Sport Deluxe. Only 63 of the 350-hp small-blocks were built. (Joe Calla Photo)

The 1965 Beaumont Sport Deluxe featured standard buckets and console plus rear fender louvers and other distinctive trim. Only 23 L79 Beaumonts were built among the Deluxe, Custom, and SD. (Tim Costello Photo)

Beaumont

In 1962, when the Acadian was introduced, the top trim level was called Beaumont. When the 1964 Chevelle was introduced in the United States, Canada followed suit with the Acadian Beaumont. With unique trim, taillights, and split grille, the Acadian Beaumont appeared to be a Chevelle pretending to look like a 1963 Buick Wildcat. The top-line Acadian Beaumont Sport Deluxe (similar to the Chevelle Super Sport) came standard with buckets and a console (the latter was included with the optional automatic or 4-speed). But performance enthusiasts had to wait until 1965 when the L79 327 became available.

For 1966, the redesigned Beaumont split from its Acadian roots and simply became "Beaumont." The Sports Option for the Beaumont Custom replaced the Sport Deluxe model and gave you bucket seats, a console, front fender louvers, Sport Deluxe identification, and the availability of a 360-hp Econo-Jet 396. Of course, the grille, trim, and taillights gave the Beaumont a very unique look.

A 1967 facelift mimicked the Chevelle, yet looked uniquely Beaumont. The Sports Option now featured fender louvers on the rear quarter panels, and the optional 396 was available in 325- and 350-horse variants. Wide SD 396 stripes running along the lower body were also available for the 396-equipped Sport Deluxe. In December 1966, the Sport Deluxe reverted to its own Beaumont model and featured a standard 396, louvered hood (from the Chevelle SS 396), and bench seat.

The Beaumont was completely redesigned for 1968, still resembling a Chevelle with a Pontiac-inspired split grill. A new louvered hood, again borrowed from the Chevelle SS396's American cousin, hid a 396 available

in two states of tune as before. The SD 396 came standard with unique full-length lower-body stripes proclaiming "SD-396." Production was 702 SD 396 hardtops and 65 convertibles. The Beaumont's final year was 1969. Except for a slight facelift, the biggest change was symbolic: the SD 396 reverted to an option package, now based on the low-line Beaumont Deluxe hardtop or, for the first time, a (pillared) coupe. Although it donned redesigned lower-body stripes, engines remained the same. Only 91 Beaumont SD 396s were built, all featuring one of two Econo-Jet 396s as before.

A 1965 meeting between Prime Minister Pearson and President Johnson led to the creation of the Auto Pact. This agreement allowed automotive parts and

Midyear, the 1967 Beaumont Sport Deluxe transformed from sporty package to full-fledged performance model with standard 396. This SD 396 features optional stripes. (Richard Truesdell Photo)

completed automobiles to cross the border duty-free (and, for Pearson, the hope for the creation of more Canadian jobs). Hence, there was no reason to produce the Beaumont after 1969, and full-size Pontiacs began to feature Pontiac engines after 1970, although the latter retained their Canada-specific names.

Canadian Dealer Specials

Thanks to a sparse population density and less disposable income than its southern neighbor, Canada's high-performance market in the 1960s was rather small. Yet judging by the old-car hobby today, Canadians have a certain fervor that is unique (befriend a Beaumont enthusiast and see).

It should not be a surprise that Canada did not lack in home-grown dealer specials. Grant Hamilton Pontiac-Buick and Conroy Pontiac-Buick are two noteworthy examples.

Comanche

Grant Hamilton, president of Grant Hamilton Pontiac-Buick in Montreal, Quebec, was an ardent racer. He had taken notice of Carroll Shelby's efforts with the Mustang and wanted to do something similar with the Pontiac Firebird.

Starting with a 1968 Firebird 400, Hamilton loaded it with options, among them Koni adjustable shocks, Custom saddle leather interior, and dark green paint (survivors have been found in either Verdoro Green or a special-order green). He then added high-speed driving lights and Comanche badges on the hood scoops and trunk lid.

The 1969 Comanche was built in the same spirit and, thanks to a Firebird restyle, it was even more distinctive. Hamilton ordered Expresso Brown

Grant Hamilton fancied the estimated 13 Comanches he built in 1968 were Canada's first true GT. In 1969, he built approximately 30 more, once again based on the Firebird 400. (Photo Courtesy Chris Phillip)

Firebird 400s with heavy-duty air cleaner and radiator, Positraction with 3.36 gears, Koni adjustable shocks, and Rally gauges plus Sun SuperTach, Custom gold leather interior, and other items.

A customer could add factory options such as the 400 Ram Air, but what truly made the Comanche unique were the following modifications:

- Off-white tail panel paint
- Off-white front fender louver striping
- Marchal fog lamps
- High-speed quartz driving lights
- Chrome hood-scoop inserts
- Hood pins
- Pirelli Cinturato radials (205 x 14 front/225 x 14 rear)
- Special Comanche emblems

Ever the enterprising individual, Hamilton created a small syndicate to sell the Comanche, including Ontario dealerships City Buick-Pontiac in Toronto and Surgenor Motors Limited in Ottawa.

According to an article in the March 1969 issue of *Track & Traffic* magazine, "We feel that [the Comanche] could make converts of a lot of sporting enthusiasts who might not otherwise buy an American car. Grant Hamilton has created a GT car in the true sense."

Cheetah

Conroy Pontiac-Buick in West Vancouver, British Columbia, was the location of one of western Canada's most popular high-performance dealerships. With a portfolio that included GTOs, Gran Sports, and Chevy-powered Beaumonts, Conroy covered much of GM's performance portfolio.

Michael Carmichael, Conroy's general manager, had noticed an uptick in high-performance automobile sales, which was complemented by the opening of Mission Raceway in 1965. Carmichael decided to offer his own branded performance car and call it "Cheetah."

Conroy built a handful of Beaumont Sport Deluxe Cheetahs in 1965 with various engines and equipment that included Buick mags, racing mirrors, and special badging. Thanks to the availability of the big-block the following year, the 1966 Cheetah started life as a Beaumont Sport Deluxe hardtop with the 396, 4-speed, and other options that enthusiasts tended to gravitate to, such as limited-slip differential, tachometer, heavy-duty suspension, and upgraded brakes.

Cheetah-exclusive items were Buick mags, racing mirrors, stripes, and several "Cheetah by Conroy Pontiac" badges both inside and out. Conroy campaigned a 1966 Cheetah, driven by the Ambassadors Car Club, on the opening day of Mission Raceway.

For 1967–1968, Cheetahs were based on the Beaumont SD 396 model. Although the 375-hp L78 was not available for Beaumonts, Conroy could build one for you. A handful of 427 Cheetahs were built in 1966–1968. All Cheetahs featured similar equipment as before, although stripes were now available from the factory.

The 1969 Cheetah was based on the Beaumont Deluxe thin-pillar coupe. All three that are believed to have been built featured the 300-hp 350, including one automatic campaigned for Conroy by the Ambassadors.

It is estimated that close to 50 Cheetahs were built from 1965 to 1969.

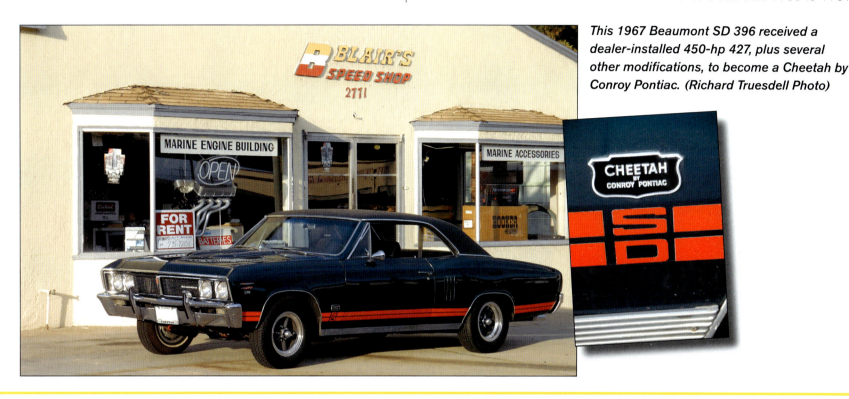

This 1967 Beaumont SD 396 received a dealer-installed 450-hp 427, plus several other modifications, to become a Cheetah by Conroy Pontiac. (Richard Truesdell Photo)

Advertising Program

When Pontiac's transformation was completed for 1959, the cars were advertised as Wide-Track Pontiacs. Originally conceived to promote the relatively wide spacing of the chassis' wheels, this theme lasted through 1971. Other campaigns were used throughout the 1960s, especially to promote performance or appeal to youths, but Wide-Track defined Pontiac.

Pontiac also published a specialized brochure with performance models beginning in 1965, something unique that became common several years later.

The Tiger

The tiger theme was popular in the early to mid-1960s: Esso had the "Put a tiger in your tank" campaign and U.S. Royal had the Tiger Paw tire. Pontiac jumped on the bandwagon through its association with Tiger Paw and used the tiger theme for the 1965 GTO: "For the man who wouldn't mind riding a Tiger if someone'd only put wheels on it—Pontiac GTO." Pontiac even named its studio group The Tigers to record the GeeTO promotion with Hurst.

The Tiger theme continued into 1966 with an attempt to improve the GTO's image at the dragstrip. With sanctioned drag racing forbidden by General Motors, the Goat generally wasn't the top car at the track. In response, Pontiac's ad agency came up with the idea of sending a pair of Royal-prepared GeeTOs for exhibition around the country. One GeeTO was driven by a "Mystery Tiger" in a tiger suit; the other was piloted by a guest driver/spectator through a lottery.

Meanwhile, the racing digest (and co-sponsor) *Drag Week* featured a weekly column reporting the previous week's Tiger races. *Drag Week* also featured a contest for readers to guess the identity of the Mystery Tiger, with the grand prize being a free trip to the 1966 NHRA Nationals in Indy where the secret was revealed.

By the end of 1966, Pontiac had moved on from the Tiger theme.

The Rest of the Story

General Motors' no-racing policy didn't mean that Pontiac couldn't demonstrate performance in advertising. But in 1966, General Motors initiated another policy that forbade any evidence of performance

Feline imagery was everywhere, including a Tom Jones hit, "What's New, Pussycat?" Pontiac was part of that brigade, even using a live tiger for its commercials

Car Craft had the opportunity to test the 1966 GeeTO Tiger. The Goat, er, Tiger also received Royal's Bobcat package.

demonstrations or aggressive driving. Although Ford touted "Total Performance" and Chrysler exploited the Hemi's success, Pontiac had to make do with image and attitude. It worked well for Pontiac but, in 1968, the division's cleverness got the best of it and aroused the consternation of a suburban Detroit municipality and, hence, General Motors.

Everyone knew that Woodward Avenue was *the* cruising spot in America. Stretching from the center of downtown Detroit through the suburbs until it reached the city of Pontiac 26 miles later, Woodward Avenue was a regular pike by day. According to the September 1969 issue of *Esquire*, at night it became a place where "a large part of the future of the American automobile is being determined. If a car is respected on Woodward, it will be a best seller in the youth market anywhere. The auto makers know this."

Pontiac's advertising agency created an ad that took advantage of Woodward's equity while eschewing tire-smoking, power-shifting GTOs. A 1968 GTO in signature Verdoro Green was pictured making a U-turn with a sign in the foreground pointing toward Woodward Avenue North: "The Great One by Pontiac. You know the rest of the story." Of course, the rest of the story was that the driver was reversing direction to find a challenger. A complementary billboard appeared along Woodward with the headline, "To Woodward Avenue with love from Pontiac."

The latter was the campaign's undoing. A local city council person complained to General Motors about promoting irresponsible street racing as a way to sell cars. GM bosses ordered Pontiac to remove the billboard and put the kibosh on any future Woodward advertisements.

The Great One by Pontiac.　　　You know the rest of the story.

Enthusiasts knew that Woodward Avenue was America's premier place to cruise and street race. General Motors prohibited racing imagery, but Pontiac's ad agency created this clever ad that implicitly suggested this GTO was trolling for a victim. The ad was axed after a companion billboard appeared and the local establishment complained to General Motors. (Photo Courtesy General Motors)

THE GTO CLUB

Pontiac published *How to Start a GTO Club* in 1964 to encourage dealerships to support car-oriented and social activities. In August 1967, the GTO Club of Elkhart County (Indiana) was formed, which published a newsletter called *The Great Wide-Tracker*. In addition to their shared enthusiasm for the Great One, the club also organized a field trip to the 1968 Indianapolis 500, took part in a Memorial Day parade, held parties, discussed topical issues such as insurance rates, and more.

The GTO Club of Elkhart County caravanned to the Pontiac, Michigan, plant in 1968. After being treated to dinner, Club members were given a tour of the plant before heading to Royal Pontiac. Pontiac documented the trip in its **Chieftain** *magazine and asked, "An idea for your dealership, too?" (Photos Courtesy Pontiac-Oakland Museum and Resource Center)*

The GTO Club of Elkhart County in 1968. Notice the youthfulness of its members. (Photos Courtesy Pontiac-Oakland Museum and Resource Center)

CHAPTER 3

CHEVY OUT IN FRONT

When it comes to Detroit automakers, it's basically Chevrolet versus the world. *USA-1* has demonstrated that it can handle all comers and come out on top, whether it's sales or performance. Chevrolet's market power was so great that legend says the federal government wanted to break up General Motors for anti-competitive practices. The new-for-1955 small-block quickly became the hot rodder's choice, and the 409 was the first performance engine enshrined in song during the muscle car era.

But let's back up a bit. The 348 was the first of the Chevrolet big-blocks. Introduced in 1958, the 348 often had detractors who falsely called it a "truck engine." What truck engine had up to 315 hp with 3x2 carburetors, solid lifters, and an available 4-speed? Horsepower options grew to 335 horses in 1959, all wrapped up in the low and sleek "bat-wing" body. The fuel-injected 283 with up to 290 horses made its final appearance that year.

The 1960 model year had similar big-block options, but Chevrolet was beginning to be outclassed by other manufacturers. According to a confidential internal letter from April 27, 1960, Zora Arkus-Duntov articulated, "We are facing the prospect of losing our position of a top high performance automobile," especially with strong multi-carbureted competitors from Ford, Pontiac, and "sundry Chrysler products."

1961's Real Fine

Chevrolet's turning point was 1961. The 348 (with up to 350 hp) endured through 1961, but it was the midyear introduction of the 360-horse 409 that changed the pecking order of the high-performance market.

The 409 was most at home in an Impala with the midyear Super Sport package, which Chevrolet touted as "For discriminating customers who like sports car flair and go, teamed with big car elegance." The package included performance items, such as an electric tachometer, sintered-metallic brake linings, and heavy-duty suspension, among others, and required the 348/305 or better. Don Nicholson ran a 409 victory with a 13.19 ET at the 1961 NHRA Winternationals.

Thanks to bigger valves and larger ports for 1962, the 409 was upgraded to 380 hp, and a new dual-quad version put out 409 horses. This was the 409 enshrined in song by the Beach Boys.

The Super Sport package returned for 1962 as a fully realized trim level with buckets and console. Impala two-door hardtops featured a new convertible-like roofline, but the sleek style of 1961's "bubbletop" roofline was available in the Bel Air hardtop. A handful of NHRA Impalas also were sold with aluminum front-end components.

Chevrolet's Last Stand

The 1963 model year brought an expanded 409 lineup, starting with a more streetable 340-hp version that also was available with Powerglide. The two

Dana Chevrolet's Hi-Performance Center served as home for new and used Corvettes, Chevy-powered Lolas and McLarens, and 427 Camaro conversions. (Geoff Stunkard photo)

Trim styling and a selection of performance options made the 1961 Chevrolet attractive, but it was the midyear introduction of the 360-hp 409 that upped the ante. Only 142 were built in 1961. (Photo ©TEN: The Enthusiast Network. All rights reserved.)

Enthusiasts often had to choose between looking stylish or going faster. Chevrolet offered a compromise with the 1962 Bel Air "bubbletop," which was lighter yet sleeker than the Impala SS. (Richard Truesdell Photo)

Dick Harrell's 1963 Impala Z11, sponsored by Morran's Gateway Motor Company in Carlsbad, New Mexico, was one of a handful of factory race cars built with the W-block 427. Harrell won Stock Eliminator at the 1963 AHRA Winternationals with this car. (Photo Courtesy Dick Harrell® Estate Records, dickharrell.com)

The 425-hp 409 was dropped for 1965, leaving only 340- and 400-horse variants. They were replaced midyear by the Turbo-Jet 396 with up to 425 horses. (Richard Truesdell Photo)

carryover 409s were upgraded to 400 and 425 horses. The bubbletop Bel Air was gone, but a new Z11 drag package for the Impala hardtop was introduced after a handful of similar parts were scattered to some racers in 1962:

- 430-hp 427 W-block engine
- Special heads and intake manifold
- 2x4 Carter carburetors
- Cowl plenum
- Aluminum hood, front fenders, front and rear bumpers, grille filler panel and brackets, hood catch, and two-piece fan shroud

- Sintered metallic brakes with special venting screens and air scoops in the backing plates
- T-10 4-speed manual transmission
- Heavy-duty Positraction rear axle with 4.11 gears
- 327 V-8 badges

Records show that 50 Impala hardtops were built with this package, but GM's renewed interest in the 1957 AMA ban took hold early in 1963, spelling an end to Chevrolet's specialized drag efforts.

The top 1965 Chevelle engine was the 350-hp L79 327, but Chevrolet had no purpose-built model like the GTO. Except for the quasi-promotional Z16, Chevy fans had to wait until 1966 for a regular-production big-block Chevelle with its own identity. (Richard Truesdell Photo)

The 1966 Chevy II featured an L79, giving Chevrolet a small-block screamer that was capable of beating much more substantial machinery, as demonstrated by Grumpy Jenkins. (Photo ©TEN: The Enthusiast Network. All rights reserved.)

After their 1965 debut, Chevrolet expanded both the Caprice series and the Mark IV big-block for 1966. Few ordered both together. (Mark Clawson Photo, Courtesy Leigh Scott)

The 409 was a carry-over for 1964, but the big news was the new mid-size Chevelle. It was available in trim levels from the 300 to the Malibu Super Sport, the latter with buckets, console, and fancy trim reflecting its place at the top. There were no performance options when the Chevelle was introduced, but eventually the 327/300 became available, with a rumored 327/365 from the Corvette never materializing.

From Mystery Motor to Mark IV

Full-size Chevys were all-new for 1965, with styling that showed General Motors at the top of its game. The Super Sport remained the sportiest model, but the 409 was pared down to 340 or 400 hp, unacceptable in a world where the GTO was killing it and the Pontiac 2+2 offered the GTO's recipe in a full-size bruiser.

Of special note was the new Turbo Hydra-Matic 400 three-speed automatic. At midyear, enthusiasts were presented with a replacement for the 409: the 396 Turbo-Jet V-8, an all-new, modern design that featured canted valves, free-flow exhaust manifolds, and tons of potential.

The 325-horse L35 was the base 396, but the L78 (also available for the Corvette) had 425 horses thanks to mechanical lifters.

The Chevelle continued into 1965 with marginal changes, but the engine roster improved considerably with the advent of the L79 350-hp 327. That was 15 horses more than the base GTO engine, but Tri-Power made things a bit tougher against the small-block. Luckily for Chevrolet enthusiasts, the Z16 Chevelle SS 396 made an appearance to whet their appetites. A veritable custom-built car, the Z16, included an L37 375-horse 396, reinforced convertible frame, 3.31 gears *without* Positraction (Chevrolet felt the rear stabilizer would assist), M20 4-speed, special 14x6 wheels with mag-style wheel covers, and plenty of other sporty and heavy-duty equipment.

Other than the hydraulic camshaft, the L37 and the L78 were the same engine. All 201 Z11s built (including a rumored convertible) were strategically distributed for promotional purposes.

A Compact Comes On Board

The compact Chevy II started to show signs of muscle in 1965 with the 327/300. For 1966, the L79 became available for any body style, from the lowly Chevy II 100 to the snazzy Nova Super Sport. In a market where cubes and horsepower reigned supreme, the L79 Chevy II was perhaps the first "giant-killer" released from a manufacturer; just ask Grumpy Jenkins.

Full-size Chevrolets received a handsome facelift for 1966, but the big news was a big-block upgrade. The L35 396 remained, but the L78 was replaced by the L72, a 425-hp 427 in the same state of tune. Despite its size,

Chevrolet introduced the SS 396 as a full-fledged model for 1966. The top 375-hp L78 was the same engine rated at 425 horses in the 1965 full-size models and Corvette. (Richard Truesdell Photo)

If the SS 396 formula worked well for the Chevelle, why not the Impala? The SS 427 package for the Impala SS included a 427/385. Only 200 ordered the SS 427-exclusive D96 "eyebrow" stripes. (Richard Truesdell Photo)

a L72 Chevy was a formidable competitor on the street and strip. For those who wanted 427 power but desired an automatic, a hydraulic-cammed L36 offered 390 easy horses.

The Masses Finally Get Their Big-Block Chevelle

The Chevelle was redesigned for 1966, which was perfect timing for the regular-production SS 396 to debut. Simulated hood intakes gave a hint as to what was underneath: 325 hp to start, with a 360-horse L34 and 375-horse L78 as options. Thanks to a horsepower rating that defied GM's

"10 pounds per horsepower" rule, the L78 was not often advertised and relied on word-of-mouth and magazine press. Even more obscure was the introduction of the heavy-duty M22 Rock Crusher 4-speed manual.

The El Camino also featured the 396 as an option but without Super Sport equipment.

Lots of News for 1967

Chevrolet had a huge year in 1967. The full-size models were redesigned. Impala coupes highlighted dramatic fastback styling that was both

After a year-long absence, the L79 327 reappeared for any non-SS 1967 Chevelle, but it was a big-block world and only 4,048 were built. (Richard Truesdell Photo)

graceful and sporty. "Heavy. The way most people want an Impala, nearly two tons," said one ad.

The model lineup was similar to before, but a new Z24 SS 427 package for the Impala SS gave it the Chevelle SS 396 treatment with the standard L36 427, heavy-duty suspension, special hood with simulated intakes, and other trim.

Strangely, the L72 427 took a year off from the order form but the L36 (now rated at 385 hp) continued to be available for any full-size Chevy.

The Chevelle received a mild facelift for 1967; the SS 396 received new simulated hood intakes. Engine choices remained the same except the L34 was re-rated at 350 hp.

Also re-rated was the L79 327 for pedestrian Chevelles, now with 325 horses. This engine was mysteriously missing from the option list of the compact until late in the model year.

Camaro

The biggest news for 1967 was the Camaro. Order the Rally Sport package and you received hidden headlights and other trim. The Super Sport package, which included simulated hood intakes and a "bumblebee" stripe around the nose, was initially available only as an SS 350, showcasing the new 295-hp small-block. In November, the SS 396 was introduced with the L35, joined several months later by the L78.

A Camaro SS/RS convertible was chosen to be the pace car at the 1967 Indianapolis 500.

The 1967 Camaro Z-28 Special Performance Package didn't receive much recognition from enthusiasts until magazines began to hype its greatness. A 302-ci small-block and "Band-Aid" stripes were two unique features. This one includes the RS package. (Photo ©TEN: The Enthusiast Network. All rights reserved.)

A complete redesign for 1968 brought new semi-fastback styling, but the SS 396's engines remained unchanged. Car Craft pulled a 14.02 ET with an L78. (Photo ©TEN: The Enthusiast Network. All rights reserved.)

In addition to the SS, another performance option was available: the Z28 Special Performance Package. Created to homologate Chevrolet's bid for the fledgling Trans-Am series launched by the Sports Car Club of America (SCCA), the Z28 featured a 283 crank in a 327 block to create 302 ci, which was just under the 5-liter limit per Trans-Am rules.

An aluminum intake, Holley carburetor, and "30-30 Duntov" solid-lifter cam produced 290 hp. The rest of the package included Rally wheels with front disc brakes, 4-speed manual, and two wide racing stripes over the hood and trunk lid. The press brought this special package to the attention of the masses, but only 602 Camaro Z28s were built for 1967.

Carryovers and Redesigns

The facelifted 1968 full-size Chevrolets saw the return of the L72 427. The Z24 SS 427 package returned for its second year, with louvered front fenders and a unique "power bulge" hood hiding the standard 427/385. In addition to the Impala fastback and convertible, the SS 427 package was available on the Caprice-inspired Impala Custom Coupe with formal roofline. Big muscle wasn't in demand, so only 1,778 enthusiasts ordered the Z24 package.

The Chevelle Grows Some Curves

The El Camino SS 396 was new. Super Sport engines were carry-overs, although the 375-hp 396 continued to be omitted from most Chevrolet marketing material.

The 1968 Chevelle SS 396 was redesigned on a new 112-inch wheelbase, which helped emphasize a new long-hood/short-deck look.

Despite the lack of publicity, awareness was strong enough that 4,751 L78 Super Sport hardtops/convertibles/El Caminos were built.

The L79 327 also made its final appearance, available in all Chevelles and El Caminos except the SS396.

The Camaro's 350 and 396 found their way to the all-new 1968 Nova SS, which now was a full-fledged performance package. Only 901 of 5,571 Nova SSs had the big-block. (Photo ©TEN: The Enthusiast Network. All rights reserved.)

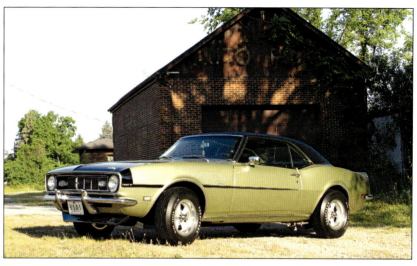

The 1968 Camaro SS and Z/28 continued to carry the performance banner, but regular Camaros could still be ordered with the 327/275, a nice balance between pedestrian and performance. (Steve Frys Photo)

The Fastest Chevy?

The Chevelle wasn't the only Chevy that was all-new for 1968. The Chevy II was redesigned with semi-fastback styling and a heftier presence. Although the L79 327 lingered for the last time, the Nova SS featured the Camaro SS 350's engine and borrowed its simulated hood intakes. Eventually, the L34 and L78 396s were introduced, making the Nova SS one of the great performance surprises of 1968.

The L78 was only available with a manual transmission but, thanks to Fred Gibb Chevrolet and racer/builder Dick Harrell, Chevrolet was cajoled into building the L78 Nova with a beefed-up TH400 via Central Office Production Order (COPO), a channel normally reserved for fleet vehicles. To be legal for NHRA racing, 50 COPO 9,738 Nova SSs were built. A handful of the COPOs also received 427 transplants from Dick Harrell Performance Center.

The Camaro received enough styling tweaks for 1968 to keep things including fresh, oval parking lights, an inset V-shaped grille, and taillights with a center lens divider.

The Rally Sport featured a new grille pattern and body sill trim. The Super Sport's bumblebee stripe returned but was replaced in January by a "sport stripe" that extended from the nose to the front fenders. With the addition of the L34 396/350, the Super Sport buyer now had three big-blocks to choose from, plus a new L89 aluminum head option for the L78.

The press continued to rave about the Z28 Special Performance Package, giving it enough visibility that Chevrolet replaced the front-fender 302 identification with "Z/28" badges in March 1968.

1969 Redesign

The big Chevys were completely redesigned for 1969. The sporty fastback was replaced by a more typical hardtop roofline. Strangely, although the Super Sport was discontinued, the SS 427 package remained. The standard L36 was bumped up to 390 hp again, with the L72 available for those who understood its magic. Also included were 15-inch wheels, heavy-duty suspension, black accented grille, and SS identification.

SS427 sales actually were up, but 1969 was the swan song for full-size performance Chevrolets.

After a slow start in 1968, the Nova SS increased in popularity in 1969. Only detail trim changes were made, but engine choices remained the same. The SS 350 received a 5-hp bump. For the serious enthusiest, the SS 396 with the L78 may have been Chevrolet's best weapon.

Chevrolet didn't bother to give the 1969 SS 427 distinguishing features such as a special hood or louvers, but 2,455 buyers felt 390 hp (425 optional) was distinguished enough. (Rick Pawlenty Photo)

The SS 396 became a performance package in 1969, so an enthusiast could spec out a SS 396 pillared coupe that was on equal footing in price and performance with the Plymouth Road Runner.

The Cowl Induction hood was new for the 1969 Camaro and was available with any performance engine. This SS 396 is one of 4,889 L78s.

The 1969 Camaro Z/28 featured four-wheel disc brakes as an option. A dealer-installed cross-ram dual-quad unit was available for those serious about getting their inner Penske on.

Chevrolet Responds to the Road Runner

The Chevelle received a mild facelift for 1969, but the SS 396 moved from being a model to being an optional performance package for any Chevelle two-door, including the Chevelle 300 Deluxe pillared coupe. This wasn't so much a demotion as much as a way for Chevrolet to compete with the super-successful Plymouth Road Runner. Engine options were the same as in 1968 besides the addition of L89 aluminum heads for the L78.

The most notable 1969 Chevelle was the Malibu sport coupe with the COPO 9562 package. General Motors still limited A-Bodies to 400 ci, but the high-performance market was ultra-competitive in 1969.

Chevrolet dealer/racer Don Yenko convinced Chevrolet Engineering manager Vince Piggins to create a 427 Chevelle through the fleet channel. Yenko received 99 of the estimated 323 COPO Malibus built, then added Yenko Super Car stripes and badges, monogrammed "sYc" logos on the headrests, and performed a super-tune. These COPOs were otherwise trimmed like basic Chevelle SS 396s but without SS markings.

Other equipment included a unique heavy-duty rear axle with heat-treated 4.10 gears, Positraction, and 4-speed or TH400 automatic. Yenko Chevelles also featured power front disc brakes and the COPO 9737 Sports Car Conversion, which included F70 x 15–inch Goodyear Wide Tread GT tires on 15x7–inch Rally wheels.

Although the 1969 Camaro carried over much of the same equipment, a restyle gave it new personality. The Super Sport continued to feature simulated hood intakes, but a new Cowl Induction hood gave the Camaro SS its first factory air induction system.

The SS 350 received a 10-hp bump to 300. The SS 396 continued in three states of tune plus the L89 aluminum heads. Thanks to Chevrolet's continued Trans-Am success (and even more enthusiasm from the media), sales of the Camaro Z/28 topped 20,000.

Power, Economy, Luxury

The Chevelle was restyled for 1970, looking stockier thanks to bulges in the right places. The SS 396 package reverted to Malibu hardtop and convertible body styles. A new "power bulge" hood could be made functional with cowl induction (which also included stripes on the hood and trunk lid, although stripes were otherwise optional). Out back, a large black rubber strip on the bumper set the Super Sport apart from lesser Chevelles. The standard SS 396 engine was upgraded to the L34, but the big-block was also bored slightly and actually measured 402 ci.

The L78 and L89 aluminum heads continued to top the range, but they were soon joined by the SS 454 package, which included a 360-horse LS5 (rated 390 for the Corvette and full-size models). Before the end of 1969, Chevrolet introduced a companion LS6 454 with 450 hp, which replaced

In addition to the COPO Chevelle, Don Yenko was involved with the creation of the COPO 9561 Camaro. This COPO started with a base (non-SS) 1969 Camaro with the L72 engine and the following equipment:

- Cowl Induction hood
- Heavy-duty cooling
- Close-ratio 4-speed or TH400 automatic
- Positraction rear with 4.10 gears
- Heavy-duty suspension
- Power front disc brakes
- 14 x 7–inch wheels

When Yenko received the estimated 200 1969 COPO Camaros, he added Yenko Super Car stripes and badges, monogrammed "sYc" logos on the headrests, a rear spoiler, 140-mph speedometer, and a super-tune. Another 800 or so "regular" COPO Camaros were also sold by other dealerships.

But there was another 427 Camaro: COPO 9560. Its 430-hp ZL1 427 was basically an aluminum version of the Corvette's L88 that originated with Jim Hall's Chaparral Can-Am racing team in 1967 before Chevrolet thought to offer it for the 1969 Corvette.

Racer/tuner Dick Harrell and Fred Gibb Chevrolet convinced Chevrolet General Manager Pete Estes to build a Camaro ZL1 for drag racing, but to be legal for NHRA racing, a minimum of 50 needed to be produced. Gibb was told the engine would cost $2,000, but the High Performance Unit package ended up costing more than $4,160. This meant that a typical ZL1 Camaro retailed for more than $7,300 (a hot 396 Camaro SS hovered around $4,000).

In addition to the sticker shock, Gibb was under the impression that he had exclusive rights to this COPO, but 19 ZL1 Camaros were ordered by other dealerships. That made it even more difficult for Gibb to sell 50 very expensive Camaros. Chevrolet eventually agreed to buy back more than 30 ZL1s to sell to other dealerships.

both the L78 and L79. The Chevelle SS 454 (and its companion El Camino SS454) was the only Chevy built with the LS6.

For those pining for something more akin to "econo-muscle," Chevrolet offered the LS3 Turbo-Jet 400 for non-SS Chevelles. Although advertised as a 400, it was really a big-block 402 with 330 hp.

A handsome 1970 restyle brought a domed hood for both the SS 396 and the all-new SS 454. Stripes were optional, but a buyer could order the optional Cowl Induction and stripes were included. (Wesley Allison Photo)

The brand-new 1970 Monte Carlo was Chevrolet's new bid in the personal-luxury market. For performance fans, the SS 454 package included the LS5 454 and TH400 automatic. Little SS 454 badges on the rocker panels were the only way to identify this special Monte.

Yenko Strikes Again

A redesigned Camaro was scheduled for 1970, but a UAW strike delayed its introduction. Instead of waiting, Don Yenko commissioned Chevrolet to install the Corvette's LT1 350 in the Nova. The 370-hp small-block was the perfect foil for insurance companies because the VIN indicated the car was a basic V-8 Nova. With the COPO 9737 Sports Car Conversion Package and COPO 9010 LT1 engine conversion, these Novas received a close-ratio 4-speed or TH400, a three-piece anti-sway bar, 4.10 gears, and other heavy-duty items.

Yenko Chevrolet added unique stripes and a hood tachometer, substituted 14 x 7–inch Magnum 500 or 14 x 6–inch Atlas mags (or whatever a customer wanted), and replaced the column shifter with a Hurst Dual-Gate. Named "Yenko Deuce" (a nod to the Nova's Chevy II origins), Chevrolet delivered 175 of these COPOs to Yenko Chevrolet for conversion (plus two more sent to Canada sans conversion).

Sensing a trend toward smaller performance engines, Don Yenko commissioned Chevrolet to build the Nova with the Corvette's LT1 via COPO order. He called it the Deuce. (Bob McClurg Photo)

For the regular-production Nova SS, the engine lineup was unchanged. Although Nova SS production picked up for 1970, only 5,567 of the 19,558 were 396s.

A Camaro for the Ages

When the all-new Camaro finally hit the streets on February 26, 1970, Chevrolet called it "a 'Super Hugger' from the ground up." The convertible was gone, leaving only a coupe with a semi-fastback roofline. The models and packages were familiar: base, Rally Sport, Super Sport, and Z/28. The RS trim package included a quasi-bumper-less look thanks to an Endura grille surround; as before, it could be combined with SS or Z/28 performance packages.

The Super Sport began with the familiar 350/300, but (like the Chevelle) the base 396 was upgraded to 350 horses with the L78 as an option. However, the Z/28 package was completely revised for 1970, including a 360-hp LT1 350 that gave the Z more flexibility throughout the RPM range. Additionally, an automatic transmission was available for the first time. Other equipment included F60 x 15–inch white-letter tires, heavy-duty suspension including rear stabilizer bar, quick-ratio steering, spoiler, and trademark stripes.

Different Times, Drastic Measures

The hammer fell for 1971 as General Motors lowered the compression on all its engines to comply with impending regulations for 1972. The Chevelle was facelifted with Camaro-esque single headlights and round taillights. Thanks to a dwindling performance market, however, the SS package was watered down to include a standard two-barrel 350, with 350/270, 402/300, and LS5 454 as options (the latter was the only one to receive engine badging).

Interestingly, the LS5 was rated at 365 horses (5 more than for 1970) while the 425-horse LS6 was advertised but never installed. The El Camino, whose Super Sport updates mimicked the Chevelle's updates, was joined by a new cross-town cousin, the GMC Sprint. An SP performance package was much like the SS.

Chevrolet also introduced the Heavy Chevy package for the 1971 Chevelle (the SS was based on the upscale Malibu) as a way to cater to the budget performance enthusiast. Chevrolet touted it as "heavy on looks and light on price" with "low initial cost, low operating cost, low insurance rates, [and] high resale." Included in the package were full-length body stripes, Heavy Chevy identification on all four sides, SS hood with hood

Hurst developed the 1970½ Z/28 Sunshine Special, complete with sliding sunroof and additional Hurst-branded performance modifications, and presented it to General Motors for consideration. General Motors declined. (Richard Truesdell Photo)

The 1971–1972 Heavy Chevy package was a low-cost alternative to the SS. Although more of a "cosmetic supercar" than the SS, the 1971 Heavy Chevy could be optioned with the 402/300, making it a nice competitor to the Plymouth Road Runner. (Photo Courtesy Terry Boyce Collection)

pins, black-painted grille and headlight bezels, and Rally wheels without trim rings. Available engines ranged from a 307 to the LS3 402.

The Monte Carlo reappeared for 1971 with a revised grille, parking lights, and reconfigured trim. The SS 454 package returned one more time; its LS5 delivered 365 hp. Monte Carlo sales were more than 100,000, but only 1,919 were built with the SS 454s package.

The 1971 Nova SS was available only with a 270-hp 350 (no more big-blocks), but the usual goodies were still there, such as a hood with simulated intakes and special suspension components.

After an abbreviated 1970 model year, the second-generation Camaro experienced few visual changes for 1971. Of course, all engines were designed to run on low- and no-lead gasoline, so the Super Sport's standard 350 was down to 270 hp, with the 402/300 the only option. The Z/28's LT1 350 fell to 330 hp, and sales had fallen drastically compared to a few years before, 8,377 Camaro Super Sports and 4,862 Z/28s were built.

An industry-wide switch in 1972 from gross to net horsepower ratings made the state of Chevrolet high performance appear even more dismal. The Chevelle SS was a mild, standard small-block; the 240-hp 402 and 270-horse LS5 454 were the only performers worth their salt. The Heavy Chevy package made a repeat showing, but the LS3 402 was likely the only worthy choice for a performance enthusiast.

The Camaro SS made its final appearance in 1972, with the standard 350 now rated at 200 net horsepower. The big-block was also in its last year; the 240-horse SS 396 was less powerful than the 255-horse LT1 Z/28. Pontiac offered as much as 300 hp in the Trans Am, while the Camaro was a shell of its former self.

The Chevelle was completely redesigned for 1973, but it looked ponderous and lacked the verve of earlier cars. A 245-hp 454 was the top engine for the SS package, which was not competitive in its segment. The Z/28

This 1963 Corvette, a General Motors demonstration vehicle, was at the opening of Grotewold Chevrolet Oldsmobile in Le Mars, Iowa. (Photo Courtesy Craig Hover)

Camaro was the only performance variant left, but the LT1 350 was replaced by a 245-horse 350.

Things became so bleak for Chevrolet performance that even the Z/28 disappeared for 1975–1976. For the company that produced the highest-horsepower engine of the era, it was a sad way to say goodbye.

Dealerships

Before the second round of the AMA racing ban in 1963, Chevrolet dealerships made a name for themselves sponsoring drag racing, culminating with the Z11 Impala. A lot of names came to prominence during the early days, such as "Dyno Don" Nicholson and Bill Thomas, but the dealerships that caught on (several were brands unto themselves) started carrying the Chevrolet performance banner once the division was officially out of racing. All around the United States, Chevy dealerships participated and promoted high-performance activities in ways that Chevrolet was not permitted to do.

Nickey Chevrolet

Nickey was the Midwest's largest high-performance Chevrolet dealer. Its extensive mail-order catalog business, ads in buff books,

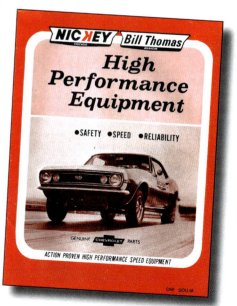

Nickey's mail-order business was backed by a technical department prepared to answer any question. Note the Bill Thomas association on this 1967 Nickey catalog. (Nickey Performance, Inc. Photo)

The standard engine for the 1972 Chevelle SS was downgraded to a 307, but the 402 and LS5 454 were still available. (Photo ©TEN: The Enthusiast Network. All rights reserved.)

If the Nickey Super Camaro was not up to your standards, Nickey had 200,000 parts in inventory for you to build your own. (Nickey Performance, Inc. Photo)

Jim Luikens helped build Berger Chevrolet into America's #1 Chevy high-performance parts dealer, no doubt assisted by a clever ad campaign through the mid-1970s. (Photo Courtesy Berger Chevrolet)

and association with Californian Bill Thomas helped give Nickey exposure from coast to coast. If you desired a 427 Camaro when Chevrolet wouldn't build one, Nickey would build it (or anything else) to your specifications. Nickey also was one of the few dealerships that encouraged enthusiasts to fly to the dealership and drive away in a high-performance Chevrolet.

Berger Chevrolet

This Chevrolet dealership was *the* high-performance Bow-Tie dealership in Michigan during the muscle car era, even outshining Chevy dealerships in Detroit. Beginning in 1968, Berger formed a high performance parts department and took on a young and clever racer named Jim Luikens as department manager. When high-performance manager Bob Delamar left in June 1970, Luikens replaced him. He soon became the face of Berger Chevrolet to millions of high-performance fans. After the agency Johnson & Dean had observed Luikens taking calls nonstop and giving advice, they built a campaign around his personality and knowledge. Luikens inadvertently became a national company spokesman.

Luikens' talent came from his racing experience and understanding how to decipher Chevrolet parts books, which were full of racing items hiding in plain sight (remember, Chevrolet was still officially out of racing). Through 1975, Luikens played the role with aplomb: "The phone never stopped ringing and I had my hands full doing what we were doing." True, the "by Berger" script on the trunk lid of a high-performance Chevrolet was a badge of pride for those in the know, but it was Luikens' knowledge

and work ethic that made Berger America's biggest seller of Chevrolet high-performance parts.

Yenko Chevrolet

Perhaps the best known of the high-performance Chevrolet dealerships, this Canonsburg, Pennsylvania, dealership is most famous for creating several branded performance cars. Race enthusiast Don Yenko began to convert Corvairs into race-going Yenko Stingers from 1966 to 1969. (He even used the COPO system for several non-RPO components.)

In 1967, with the introduction of the Camaro, Yenko sold a handful of Dick Harrell–engineered 427 Yenko Super Camaros through a nationwide dealer network. Through 1968, Yenko Super Camaros were 427 engine transplants but, from 1966 to 1969, Yenko managed to convince Chevrolet to build 427 Camaros via the COPO channel. Yenko also persuaded Chevrolet to create the 1969 427 COPO Chevelle.

In contrast, the few 1969 Yenko Novas built were engine transplants. For 1970, Yenko created the LT1-powered Duce via COPO order, but the death knell was upon the industry and Don Yenko created the Yenko Stinger II Vega for 1971–1973.

After a year of building Yenko Stingers, Don Yenko built the 427-powered Yenko Super Camaro in 1967. In 1969, he convinced Chevrolet to install the 427 at the factory. (Photo Courtesy Lynn Yenko-Zoiopoulos)

Clearly Don Yenko's racing experience, company connections, and familiarity with the fleet ordering system clearly helped Chevrolet get around some of the handicaps imposed by GM edicts.

Dana Chevrolet

Dana's existence as a SoCal performance hub was bright but brief. Ford Special Vehicle Operations' Peyton Cramer made his way to California to help Carroll Shelby run Shelby American through 1965. His experience interfacing with dealerships prompted a desire to run one of his own. Ford wasn't interested, but a chance meeting with dealership owner Paul Dombroski led to the two securing a loan to buy a failed Chevrolet facility in South Gate. They soon purchased another facility down the street and converted it into the 7,000-square foot Dana Hi-Performance Center.

Along with racer Dick Guldstrand as the Center's general manager, Dana's racing exploits included prepping and racing a Corvette at Le Mans, supported via high-performance sales and service. The showroom sold new and used Corvettes and Dana's own 427 Camaros, which they began to build even before Chevrolet announced the availability of the big-block 396.

Dana Chevrolet was among the first high-performance Chevy dealerships to garner national attention. With stellar facilities and plenty of magazine ink, Dana could build anything to suit your style. (Photo ©TEN: The Enthusiast Network. All rights reserved.)

Dana's ads bragged, "Complete preparation for street, strip, slalom, and road racing." After 18 months, Cramer sold his interest to Dombroski due to a disagreement.

Scuncio Chevrolet

Located near Providence, Rhode Island, Scuncio (pronounced "skoon-see-oh") was New England's premier high-performance Chevy

As the high performance manager of Rhode Island's Scuncio Chevrolet and owner of Bob Johnson Racing Enterprises, Bob Johnson was the go-to guy for high-performance Chevrolets in New England and beyond. (Photo Courtesy Edward Scuncio, Sr.)

Chevelle SS

Scuncio Chevrolet's catalog showed different ways you could build a factory Chevy, with Scuncio Super Options for those who demanded more than the factory could provide. (Photo Courtesy Edward Scuncio, Sr.)

The Motion Performance 1967 SS-427 Camaro set itself apart thanks to Joel Rosen's cooperation with Baldwin Chevrolet, factory warranty, GMAC financing, and the (eventually) Motion Supercar Club. The Club's newsletter gave professional tuning, engine, and suspension tips tested in Motion's dyno room, at the dragstrip, and on the Sunrise Highway. (Photo Courtesy Martyn L. Schorr, Co-Founder Baldwin-Motion)

In 1968, Motion Performance marketed the "Fantastic Five" lineup of SS-427 supercars, and added an assortment of dyno-performance Phase I/II/III packages. If anyone ever was King of the Road, it likely was someone driving a Baldwin-Motion Chevrolet. (Photo Courtesy Martyn L. Schorr, Co-Founder Baldwin-Motion)

dealership, with enough of a reputation to pull enthusiasts from the Mid-Atlantic States. Scuncio always had top-shelf Chevrolet performance models on the premises to give discerning customers something to test and drive away, unlike dealerships that sometimes shied away from high-performance cars due to pesky kids or potential warranty issues.

According to High Performance Manager Bob Johnson, "Most of the ones I sold were the highest-performance versions. The average buyer didn't know what was available from Chevrolet. For example, the 375-horse wasn't advertised.

"Enthusiasts often found us through Connecticut Dragway because we put 50 to 60 flyers in cars in the parking lot. I sold a lot of cars that way and, of course, a lot of people saw our cars racing. Spectators talked to the owners [of dealer-sponsored cars] and they would see my name on my race car and then chat with me about ordering a car. They subsequently visited Scuncio and looked at Chevelles or other models and then we made a deal; just like that.

"Knowledge and cars in inventory was key in running a good high-performance dealership. We had the biggest selection around."

Baldwin-Motion Chevrolet

Marty Schorr, editor of *Cars* magazine, knows Baldwin-Motion Chevrolets well. His magazine featured many of the creations that came out of racer Joel Rosen's facility and he also was the advertising manager for the Baldwin-Motion enterprise. All three companies are pertinent to the Baldwin-Motion story.

"The Baldwin-Motion program was very unique because it involved a Long Island-based 'Mom and Pop' dealership [Baldwin Chevrolet] that didn't sell performance cars, and a speed shop [Motion Performance] that only built performance cars," says Schorr.

The two businesses joined forces after Rosen approached Baldwin in the fall of 1966 about racing a Camaro under a Baldwin/Motion/*Cars* banner. It was a tough sell, but Baldwin's parts manager convinced his bosses that a successful race car would bring people into the showroom. Rosen was given a Camaro. He tore it apart and rebuilt it with an L88 for Modified Production. That car set AHRA and NHRA records, the latter with shop manager Bill Mitchell behind the wheel.

The experience led Rosen and Schorr to imagine building a "super-street" 427 Camaro. They approached Baldwin about their idea, which was to be "the ultimate in one-stop performance car shopping," including national marketing exposure through *Cars* and drag racing.

"Winning NHRA national meets got us into the big leagues of promoting our products," adds Schorr. "The Motion name became well known at tracks all over the country, which trickled down to the street cars. A Motion car could be made from anything from Chevrolet's portfolio. You could order anything you wanted if you were willing to pay for it, and you would pick it up at Baldwin Chevrolet like any other car; and the car could be financed by GMAC!" To boot, base SS-427 B-M models were covered by factory warranties honored by Baldwin Chevrolet.

At the time, *Cars* was developing a reputation for a New York City style of "telling it like it is" journalism, but the magazine didn't have the staff, money, or cars to compete with the West Coast magazines. Says Schorr, "We had to fight harder to get Detroit's attention because we weren't their first choice; *Hot Rod* was."

This also was true when it came to advertising because Baldwin-Motion couldn't afford to advertise in *Popular Hot Rodding* or *Car Craft*. Rosen focused on buying ad space with publications with smaller circulations while Schorr wrote the ads. The small budget ended up being to their benefit as it allowed the ads to be brazen without scrutiny from General Motors.

The partnership's quick success led to the creation of the Motion Supercar Club in 1967 to capitalize on enthusiasts who requested a Motion Performance catalog. It also served as a branding opportunity. Club membership included trinkets such as decals and patches; a subscription to the *Motion News* publication, which showcased Baldwin-Motion race cars and products; discounted speed equipment; and performance tips.

"That was the way Joel brought people in the shop to modify their cars, and that's how Baldwin Chevrolet brought customers into their business. It was a very successful concept. And it helped sell magazines, too," says Schorr.

In 1968, Rosen and Schorr created the Fantastic Five, a team of vehicles touching on all segments of the high-performance market: Nova, Camaro, Chevelle, Corvette, and the $2,998 Street Racer Special 427 Biscayne. All could be ordered as a Motion SS-427 or the much more radical Phase III models. The latter helped inspire Motion's famous money-back guarantee: "We guarantee that our Phase III Camaro will turn at least

120 mph in 11.50 seconds or better, with an M/P-approved driver on an AHRA- or NHRA-sanctioned dragstrip. The Phase III Camaro is a completely street-able, reliable machine that will run these times off the street."

Fred Gibb Chevrolet

A strong participant in sanctioned drag racing, the LaHarpe, Illinois-based Gibb (along with Dick Harrell) initiated the production of 50 1968 Nova SS 396s with the L78/TH400 combination. The combination initially was not available from the factory, but Chevrolet was asked to beef up the TH400 via a COPO order. The production run met the requirements for homologation in NHRA SS/CA.

Gibb was also instrumental in instigating the production of the Camaro ZL1 the following year.

Dick Harrell Performance Center

Several of the above-mentioned players may not have become known for their high-performance operations if it weren't for the talents of drag racer and engine builder Dick Harrell. Raised in New Mexico, Harrell picked up the racing bug as a teenager, both as tuner and driver. After a stint in Korea, Harrell began drag racing in his spare time, ultimately racing as an amateur in 1961 with a factory-sponsored Chevrolet before becoming a professional the following year. Then, with his 1963 Impala Z11, Harrell won Top Eliminator at the NHRA Winternationals. Unfortunately, his sponsorship dried up due to GM's AMA racing ban.

Nevertheless, Harrell stayed loyal to the Bow-Tie brand. Over the next several years, he worked with California's Bill Thomas Race Cars. In the fall of 1966, they fabricated components to assist in the installation of a big-block 427 in the brand-new 1967 Camaro. Nickey Chevrolet, the Chicago dealer known for its high-performance parts business and successful

This 1962 Bel Air bubbletop featured a 409 built by Dick Harrell, tuned by Charlie Therwhanger, and driven by Bryan Teal. (Photo Courtesy Dick Harrell Estate Records, Valerie Harrell, dickharrell.com)

The Dick Harrell Performance Center offered 427 Camaros, Chevelles, and Novas with strip-proven Turbo-Hydros and Super-Duty 4-Speeds. Harrell also had a syndicate of dealerships that allowed Chevy enthusiasts to "see Dick Harrell, he's got what you need." (Photo Courtesy Dick Harrell Estate Records, Valerie Harrell, dickharrell.com)

It's ironic that Chevrolet was the last of General Motors' performance divisions to properly respond to the GTO. With a new big-block introduced early in the 1965 calendar year, Chevrolet should have been poised to introduce the 396 for the Chevelle, but the Division chose a different route with the Z16.

1965 Z16 Chevelle

There was a lot more to the Z16 package than just a limited-edition preview of what was to come for the 1966 Chevelle. It was a semi-custom vehicle used to promote the Chevrolet brand and its all-new Turbo-Jet 396. Or, in Chevrolet's words, the purpose was "to draw attention to the new 396 cu.in. engine, as well as to create interest in a powerful, smooth, high performance cruising coupe in the medium size car, for future market exploration."

The 200 Chevelles slated to receive Z16 equipment resulted in "a street machine that may be the *most potent and 'fun' car in the country*. Since it is not advertised, etc. (making it an 'unlisted' car), it could with good exposure become the *most wanted* car in the country, especially in view of the fact that only 200 (all coupes) are to be built.

"The 'Malibu SS 396' is a smooth, very powerful, easy-handling luxury touring machine that is a real bear-cat. A name plate carries the name 'Malibu SS 396,' and a fender insignia will show the '396' designation too.

"The car will get special distribution, in that it will be offered directly to the people who:

The Z16 SS 396 wasn't just a preview of what was to come for 1966; it was a veritable custom-built vehicle used to showcase Chevrolet's brand-new big-block. Z16s were sold only to enthusiasts who could give the car maximum exposure. (Photo ©TEN: The Enthusiast Network. All rights reserved.)

racing program, was chosen to sell one of the first 427 Camaro conversions. Nickey chose Harrell to run its High Performance division.

This led to meeting Chevrolet dealer and road racer Don Yenko, who commissioned Harrell to engineer the 1967 Yenko Camaro. By this time, Harrell had set up his Dick Harrell Performance Center in East St. Louis, Illinois, followed in 1968 by a move to Kansas City, Missouri.

A chance encounter with Herb Fox, a drag racer from Fred Gibb Chevrolet, proved to be fortuitous as it led to a business relationship between Harrell and Gibb. It was pure serendipity because Harrell and Yenko were already on the outs, and it allowed Harrell to continue building his own branded 427 conversions with cars supplied by Gibb and Bill Allen Chevrolet. This led to a coast-to-coast network of 12 dealerships selling Harrell's conversions.

Along with the 1968 COPO Nova SS 396 (and several 427 transplants), the association with Gibb took on a new meaning when Chevrolet used Harrell's expertise in developing the aluminum ZL1 427 for 1969. Although the ZL1 was initially developed for Can-Am racing, Harrell saw Pro Stock potential and, with Gibb, convinced Chevrolet to build at least 50 for homologation.

But the dragstrip was never far from Harrell's mind. In fact, he was named 1969 AHRA Driver of the Year. Passionate about his fans as much as the finish line, Harrell's life was cut short when his Camaro funny car crashed during an event in Toronto in September 1971.

- Have demonstrated their enthusiasm for 'special' performance products of Chevrolet
- Have the means and potential for getting maximum exposure of the car

"'Maximum exposure' may mean:

- In newspaper auto columns, in magazines, on TV
- At events where crowds of spectators may see the car, and/or see it perform
- In the hands of 'prestige' people at prestige places

"We [Public Relations] will campaign for nationally known magazine and newspaper auto editors to drive and write about the cars. Dealers who have them should do likewise in their towns, and lend them to very important people, put them in parades, on special TV programs, etc. Certain owners that we know will modify these cars and run them on dragstrips and perhaps in other events. (No support from us, however.) The general policy of placing the cars should be to get a wide spread in high-visibility areas.

"To summarize: Since the objective is to create *talk* and *print* about the new engine, and this interesting car, we would like to have reports, news clippings, etc. on results obtained in your area."

The statistics gathered include: 200 cars produced, 175 sold to customers in all sales regions, 25 assigned by Public Relations for press driving in 12 cities, and 88 top magazine and newspaper auto editors received Detroit-mailed special invitations for test drives (hundreds more were invited locally).

Chevrolet's preliminary report showed that one magazine article and 11 newspaper articles had been published from Washington, D.C., Charlotte, Chicago, New York, Denver, Indianapolis, Dallas, San Francisco, Van Nuys (Los Angeles), Oakland, and Cincinnati.

"Consensus is that this is a very exciting and well-engineered car, and a forerunner of a new model for 1966. *Motor Trend* calls it 'King of the Road.'"

Chevrolet Sports Department

Yep, it's good to be the King. Want a sports car in your showroom? Sorry, Pontiac. The men upstairs at General Motors won't let that happen. Corvette sales can't be cannibalized.

Legend says that really did happen, but when you're the 500-pound gorilla, you get to do what you want. Starting in April 1968, all of Chevrolet's performance models were grouped under the Chevrolet Sports Department banner. Dealers were encouraged to align themselves with the concept based on three ideas:

1. Chevrolet had better products than any competitive brand, with sports models in every line.

Milton Bradley's *Chevyland Sweepstakes* was a "game for the entire family" that simulated the experience of managing the day-to-day opportunities and challenges of a Chevrolet dealership. (Nik Kolenich Photo)

2. There was a growing pool of affluent, youthful, sports-minded prospects that accounted for more than 20 percent of the total Chevrolet sales.
3. National advertising support across different media urged tens of millions of readers, listeners, and viewers to visit their nearest Chevrolet Sports Department.

By creating a "genuine, physical Sports Department complete with display cars and special point-of-purchase materials" and "staffed with experts who can answer the most discerning questions [to] help people buy exactly what they want or need," Chevrolet was prepared to help cooperative dealerships build the Sports Department into the "strongest dealer-oriented selling concept in [the] market."

The Chevrolet Sports Department continued for 1969, proclaiming that "Chevy goes big on Super Sports" A new twist was added: the Sports Shop engine department. "Now that the Sports Department has focused the public's attention on the sportier Chevrolet convertibles, hardtops, and even recreational vehicles on your floor, the Sports Shop goes a step further, directing their attention to the 'Engine Room' of your Sports Department. The Sports Department is where prospects can learn all the details of the 1969 Super Sports team: Camaro SS, Camaro Z/28, Chevelle SS 396, Nova SS, Impala SS 427, and the Corvette Stingray."

Chevrolet backed up its marketing push with Super Sport in major markets consisting of radio and TV spots (the latter with emphasis on NCAA football, *Bonanza*, and *Bewitched*), and outdoor billboards. Four-color Super Sport print ads also appeared in 16 magazines.

In the January 1970 issue of *Central* magazine, the division reflected on the previous 10 years of the automotive market and how "the average young driver was more appearance-conscious than performance-conscious." But drag racing's popularity had changed the tastes of American youths, as it was noted that flashy trim alone didn't win races.

With sales for Bow Tie performance cars increasing for 1968 and 1969, Chevrolet stated the obvious: "You don't need to be a marketing expert to read the performance car trend. Performance sells. The performance car future looks

SETUP ASSISTANCE

Chevrolet made recommendations to help dealerships determine the best place for the Chevrolet Sports Department:

- Find a spot to create a "smart and appealing" Chevrolet Sports Department, even in the Service Department or outside in the used-car lot. Arrows or rally striping could direct customers to the display.
- A two-car Sports Department for a four- or five-car showroom was suggested to be optimum for most dealerships.

To promote high-performance Chevys, the division created the Chevrolet Sports Department in the spring of 1968. In 1969, athletes such as Olympic skier Jean-Claude Killy and NFL star O. J. Simpson tied their athleticism to Chevrolet's more athletic offerings. (Photo Courtesy General Motors)

- For a five-car Sports Department, the full line of Super Sports (four) was encouraged, plus a Corvette or a Corvair Monza.
- For two-car dealerships, a one-car Sports Department still fit the bill; just put it in the center of the showroom for maximum traffic exposure, and alternate sports models frequently.
- Emphasize product.
- Use local printers or silk screeners to create banners to identify a dealership as Sports Department headquarters. Car-top displays and other collateral were supplied by Chevrolet.
- Make sure your most capable salesmen share duties on the Sports Department floor.
- A traveling Sports Department works "anywhere and everywhere that traffic congregates," such as shopping centers, sports events, college campuses, county fairs, transportation terminals, and hotel lobbies.

Chevrolet also made suggestions for mapping out advertising and promotional plans. It offered three approaches for success:

Distinct Approach
Set up a separate advertising budget to help give the Sports Department a look and identity with a personality all its own.

Integrated Approach
Inject the Sports Department flavor wherever possible, including existing ads and commercials. Chevrolet suggested a moderate budget increase to create awareness of the Sports Department.

Initial Accelerated Push
With enough funds, a three- to six-month advertising and merchandising push in print, radio, TV, direct mail, showroom promotions, and publicity was recommended to give the Chevrolet Sports Department heavy exposure. The largest share of the budget was in newspapers (including college papers to capture the youth market). Sponsoring a Little League team or donating vehicles to a college's homecoming (with Sports Department logo on doors) were secondary suggestions.

The January 1970 issue of *Central* magazine.

Communication came in the form of a monthly kit promoting product knowledge and new sales strategies. Included were flyers, quizzes, filmstrips (with accompanying records), and Central magazine, "a management publication for Chevrolet retail executives." The January 1970 kit showed how performance cars could open the door to future sales. (Photo Courtesy General Motors)

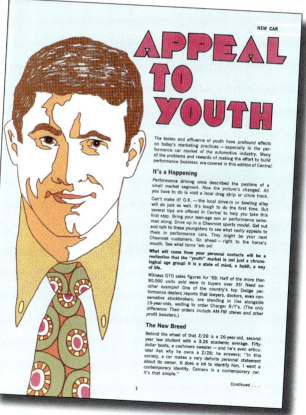

The youth market was more than just a demographic; it was a "state of mind, a habit, a way of life." (Photo Courtesy General Motors)

Thanks to GM's anti-racing edict, Chevrolet didn't promote performance clinics. Instead, Dave Strickler hosted his own clinic with support from Ammon R. Smith Chevrolet and Grumpy Jenkins. (Photo Courtesy Steven Frys)

as bright as a dragstrip 'Christmas Tree.'

"Selling performance may take more effort, but it's worth your investment in time, money, and that extra effort. Know what the customer wants and the typical young performance buyer will often pay sticker price or close to it for the car he wants."

And what happens when that performance buyer marries and raises a family? "Their thoughts about performance today will give way to thoughts of buying a home or furniture. And more practical transportation."

Chevrolet High-Performance Clinic

Chevrolet was noticeably absent when it came to corporate performance clinics, but there were opportunities at the dealership level.

During the summer of 1968, Super/Stock driver Dave Strickler announced that he would run a clinic sponsored by Ammon R. Smith Chevrolet of York, Pennsylvania. Technical assistance was courtesy of Grumpy Jenkins plus some of its sponsors, including Hooker, Hurst, Champion, and Penzoil.

The team coordinated 11 dealers in New York, New Jersey, and Pennsylvania to play host to their own clinics. Unfortunately, the effort wasn't able to expand beyond the region due to a declining high-performance market.

Advertising Program

Chevrolet was rather coy with its promotions in the 1960s due to a General Motors rule that required 10 pounds per horsepower or more for anything other than the full-size Chevy or Corvette. The solid-lifter L78 396 in 1965 was rated at 425 hp, but when the 396 became a regular production engine for the 1966 Chevelle, the L78 was rated at 375 hp, a 50-horse difference for the same state of tune. However, the L78 did not show up in most brochures or ads. Considering that the Chevelle weighed less than 3,750 pounds, the reason was clear.

In 1968–1969, a series of ads paired the Corvette and Camaro, hinting that there was a little bit of Corvette in the pony car. During this time, Chevrolet started marketing the Chevrolet Sports Department, an umbrella campaign touting all sporty Chevrolets. A year later, Chevrolet also began hiring famous athletes, including skier Jean-Claude Killy and football star O. J. Simpson, to support Sports Department marketing.

Following are some of Chevrolet's suggestions to appeal to the youth market.

"It's A Happening"

- Visit a local dragstrip or circle track.
- Can't go to a race? Drive a Chevrolet sports model to a drive-in or bowling alley. Talk with the kids and see what appeals to them in performance cars. They just might be your next Chevrolet customers.
- Youth is a state of mind, a habit, a way of life. The youth market is not just a chronological age group.

"The New Breed"

Performance buyers weren't just youths wanting to go fast, they were a 26 year-old law student who wants his car to make "a very definite personal statement about its owner. It does a lot to identify him. I want a contemporary identity. Camaro is a contemporary car." It's that simple; a 23-year-old graduate with "over $6,000 and a lot of time" tied up in his car; a 25-year-old gas station owner "who is now on his fifth supercar;" a 30-year-old assistant vice president for a local bank who sheds his status quo trappings when driving his Monte Carlo SS 454.

"They Have the Money to Go!"

- There's a performance car market ready to spend money on dealers who want to get involved, but "building a performance reputation requires substantial dealer investment."
- 700,000 supercars were sold in 1968, which was 10 percent of the U.S. new-car market.

"Try These to Sell Performance Image"

- Dealers interested in catering to enthusiasts were encouraged to "go where the action is" with a brightly painted Z/28 or SS and the dealership's name scrawled across the side, and to let interested buyers sit in it, open the hood, and examine the engine. Performance specialists who spoke the language of enthusiasts were encouraged to represent the dealer.
- Donate performance trophies.
- Offer a dealer-represented tow truck to someone who needs help getting to and from the dragstrip.
- Contact the media and loan them supercars for special events or while their own vehicles are being serviced.
- Have a performance representative show high-performance parts along with the cars.

"Project a Strong Performance Image"

- Display local race results and maintain a library of magazines at a designated "dealership performance information center."
- Make performance cars the main attraction in the showroom.

"Go Racing"

- Offer discounted performance parts to "hot shoes" at the track. In return, they can letter their Chevys with your dealership's name.
- Sponsor a car club directly, which can pay off by generating enthusiasm for the brand, keeping the dealership's name in front of the public, and giving enthusiasts the knowledge to win races via a performance clinic.

Chevrolet continued to promote the Sports Department for 1971 but, with the market's paradigm shift, Chevrolet began to redefine "performance" with a focus on "the ever-growing sports-recreation market that demands vehicles like wagons, campers, and Blazers."

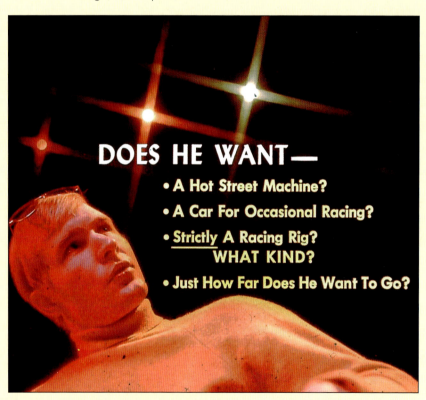

The Sound of Money *filmstrip from the January 1970 Chevrolet Communication kit gave salesmen strategies for catering to the high-performance enthusiast. (Photo Courtesy General Motors)*

CHAPTER 4

BUICK ENTERS THE FIELD

The Buick from the brand's heyday is quite different from the Buick of today, which is now chasing a younger clientele while continuing to offer the understated elegance that has long been a Buick hallmark. And who would have guessed more Buicks are sold in China than in North America? But when General Motors was on top of the world, Buick was known for powerful sedans for the well-heeled. With the advent of the muscle car era, Buick's Gran Sport continued that tradition.

Banker's Hot Rod

Buick's reputation for speed started in 1936 when it introduced the Series 60 Century, which was like the Special behind the cowl but used Roadmaster's larger straight-8. This combination made the Century a bona fide 100-mph automobile; impressive for the era.

The midyear 1970 Buick GSX made just about everything standard, both mechanically and physically. Perhaps the only item that enthusiasts were left wanting was the optional Stage 1 engine. (Photo Courtesy General Motors)

This "Banker's Hot Rod" lasted through 1942 when automobile production was curtailed for the war effort, but the Century didn't return to the Buick lineup until 1954, when Buick combined the Special's smaller wheelbase with the Roadmaster's 322-ci nailhead V-8, which had been introduced the year before.

The Century continued through 1958 when Buick rebranded its 1959 lineup. The new Invicta carried the torch for the small body/big engine formula. By then, Buick's previous NASCAR efforts were already a few years old, and the marque's high-speed reputation had been supplanted by Chevrolet, Pontiac, and Oldsmobile.

Although hardly a performance car, the mid-1962 Invicta Wildcat coupe offered a bit of sportiness with its standard buckets and special side trim. An expanded Wildcat line-up superseded the Invicta in 1963 as Buick's mid-line trim level. Although it (along with the LeSabre) was available with a 4-speed manual, its 401/325 didn't make it a performance car. More muscle came in 1964, as Buick offered a 425 with up to 360 hp with dual-quads.

Enter the Gran Sport

For 1965, the company from Flint introduced a performance package to compete with the Pontiac GTO: the Gran Sport. Based on the upscale Skylark, the Gran Sport package included a 325-hp nailhead 401 and typical heavy-duty upgrades. The Skylark Gran Sport was a fine performer, but the nailhead didn't instill fear in Tri-Power GTOs.

The Riviera also received the Gran Sport treatment, which included a 360-hp 425 with dual-quads. The Riviera Gran Sport was the Banker's Hot Rod incarnate, but it wasn't something that you'd see at the local drags or racing on Woodward Avenue (unless you borrowed Dad's car).

The Skylark Gran Sport became its own model for 1966. Despite a restyle that included a new hood with simulated vents, the Gran Sport was mainly a rerun from 1965. However, in March 1966, Buick announced a special engine option called the L76 Wildcat GS V-8. This special 401 consisted of a new Quadrajet carburetor plus a camshaft and distributor borrowed from the 425.

Buick introduced the Gran Sport package for the 1965 Riviera and Skylark, with the latter receiving the Wildcat 445 401 (although marketed as a 400 to avoid the wrath of GM bosses). Cars magazine named the Gran Sport series "Top Performance Car of the Year." (Andrew V. Kent Photo)

The restyled 1966 Gran Sport contained most of the same equipment: 401 Wildcat V-8, floor-shifted 3-speed manual, notchback seats, heavy-duty suspension and stabilizer bar, reinforced box frame, 7.75 x 14–inch tires, and special trim throughout. (Photo ©TEN: The Enthusiast Network. All rights reserved.)

Another, even more enigmatic Gran Sport engine was also introduced in the spring of 1966. Buick Powertrain Engineer Dennis Manner told *Hemmings*, "There was still some demand from the dealerships that sponsored drag racers to develop the 401 for their cars," so his department created this "skunkworks" engine for those in-the-know. According to the NHRA

Both the GS 400 and its new little brother, the GS 340, featured twin simulated hood scoops and a special grille. (Richard Truesdell Photo)

With tongue in cheek, Buick felt the need to remind the younger generation that it had something to offer that had nothing in common with their Old Man's Electra. (Photo Courtesy General Motors)

specification documents Buick filed, this 11.0:1-compression 401 featured an underrated 332 hp.

Buick Extends the Gran Sport

The Riviera continued to offer a Gran Sport package, although the standard engine was the 340-hp 425, with the dual-quad 425/360 optional. The full-size Wildcat was a new recipient of the Gran Sport package for the only time. A 4-barrel 425 was standard; the 360-horse 425 was optional.

A New Engine, a New Promise

The Gran Sport really found its mojo for 1967. The new "GS 400" featured a brand-new engine design measuring 400 ci with a modest 340 hp. A new 3-speed Super Turbine automatic transmission replaced the previous two-speed.

The engine's true test, however, was on the street, where the 400 ran rings around the old nailhead, thanks to better-breathing heads and other improvements. A handsome facelift gave the GS 400 a more aggressive stance and a pair of simulated hood scoops added to the sporty flavor.

The First Junior Supercar?

The GS 400 was joined by a new companion called the GS 340. Although the 340 was not a new engine, it had never been available in the Gran Sport series. Rated at 260 hp, the GS 340 hardtop distinguished itself from its big brother thanks to Arctic White or Platinum Mist paint. It featured broad red stripes along the sides, red hood scoops, and lower rear deck molding. Buick touted the GS 340 as the one "for people who look for a large measure of sporting flavor at a low price."

A similar car developed exclusively for California was called the California GS. It was a regional promotion based on the low-line Special pillared coupe that used the GS 340's engine and hood (sans red highlights). Buick touted it as "The *in* car for Golden Staters on the GO. High performance and Buick quality at an 'economy car' price."

The 1967 GS 400 featured a unique low-restriction dual-snorkel air cleaner made out of red plastic. (Photo ©TEN: The Enthusiast Network. All rights reserved.)

Dark Horses

The GS series was completely redesigned for 1968. Wheelbases shrank 3 inches, and a sweeping spear ran along the length of the sides as on full-size Buicks. Available only as a hardtop or convertible, the GS 400 featured the 400/340, cowl-mounted simulated hood scoop, and a simulated vent behind each front wheel. Racing stripes above the rockers were a new option.

The 1967 GS 340 hardtop was upgraded to the 1968 GS 350. The result of a .25-inch bore increase, the small-block now developed 280 hp. Looking identical to the GS 400 (no color restrictions or unique trim this time), the GS 350 was also joined by the national debut of the California GS, which continued to be based on the Special Deluxe pillared coupe.

Buick Begins to Set the Stage

It should come as no surprise that Buicks were not the favored brand for performance enthusiasts. The engine offerings were limited and sales were slow. Certainly the 400 was no slouch, but Chevrolet offered a solid-lifter 396, Pontiac offered a Ram Air 400 with 4.33 gears, and Oldsmobile's W30 had a cam so radical that power brakes were not permitted.

In 1968, Buick's parts department began to offer two stages of tuning so Buick enthusiasts could be more competitive in drag racing. Stage 1 and Stage 2 weren't necessarily packages because their parts could be bought separately, but they were designed to work together. The Stage 1 boosted horsepower by 5, to 345, thanks to a high-lift camshaft, heavy-duty valvesprings, upgraded carburetor and distributor, and high-capacity fuel pump, among other things.

The Stage 2 was created as an off-road package not suitable for the street. The special equipment included forged aluminum 11.0:1 pistons fitted with chrome pin assemblies, a valvetrain package including camshaft, intake manifold gasket that provided blocked heat holes for cooler air/fuel mixtures, connecting rod bearings with .001 oversize available, full-groove main bearings, special secondary metering rods, and low tension/friction piston rings.

Buick also introduced a dealer-installed cold-air package for GS models that consisted of an air cleaner inlet hose and two support springs.

The usual yearly styling tweaks were included in 1969; these included a new grille and the elimination of the simulated front fender vents. Standard air induction was a first for Buick (and an unusual feature). A new hood design featured a power bulge with two louvered scoops that sucked the

Buick's A-Body was redesigned for 1968, appearing a bit more luxurious like its bigger siblings. However, compared to its contemporaries, the GS 400 and GS 350 looked quite conservative. The 400/340 continued from 1967, but dealer-installed Stage 1 parts brought a new level of performance. (Photo ©TEN: The Enthusiast Network. All rights reserved.)

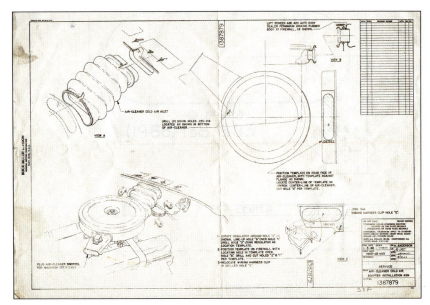

The redesigned 1968 Gran Sport series featured a forward-facing scoop at the cowl, but it wasn't a functional air induction unit. Eventually, Buick offered this over-the-counter system. (Photo Courtesy Roberta Vasilow)

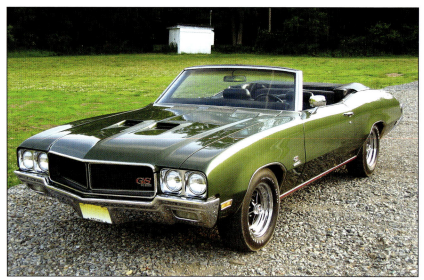

Although 1970 is often touted as the high-water mark for high performance cars, Buick may have had the best year. A nice combination of low-end horsepower and torque, the 455 Stage 1 became one of the fastest showroom-stock cars available. The GS restyle was also easy on the eyes. (Marco Conigliari Photo)

Flint Lights a Fire

Everything came together for the Gran Sport in 1970, especially when General Motors reversed its cubic-inch limit. Buick had just bored the 430 to 455 ci, so the new GS 455 featured 350 hp and 510 ft-lbs of torque. All this was wrapped in a redesign that was as handsome as any performance car in the market.

Ordering the Stage 1 engine bumped horsepower up by 10. Road testers were surprised to be running ETs deep into the 13s; the cat was now out of the bag. *Motor Trend* said in January 1970, "A real performance Buick, stock from the showroom. It's been a long time arriving, but it looks like it's here. The old man's car inbred with a going street bomb."

According to Dennis Manner, "The objective, as we developed the Buick Stage 1 400/455-ci engines, was simply to provide maximum street performance in a vehicle sold from the showroom floor. We allowed no compromise of Buick features. If you wanted air conditioning, power steering, power brakes, power windows or seats, etc., they were available. This was no trick lightweight or stripped-down model, nor were any tinkering changes necessary once you bought it. There were no ifs, ands, or buts about it.

"We optimized the Stage 1 package to move on the street. Furthermore, we did not compromise the car's street performance so that it would be quicker at the dragstrip.

"For example, a wilder camshaft would have provided more power when running without mufflers at the strip, but it would have reduced torque on the street with an exhaust system.

A mild facelift arguably improved the looks of the 1969 GS 400 and GS 350, and standard air induction was a nice touch. The Stage 1 became an official factory option and was competitive with Ram Air GTOs. (Photo ©TEN: The Enthusiast Network. All rights reserved.)

atmosphere into the carburetor. Buick claimed that they delivered cool clean air to the air cleaner "to provide more efficient and powerful engine operation in higher speed ranges."

The GS 350 and California GS remained mostly unchanged, as did the standard GS 400 engine. However, the Stage 1 was now an official factory option. Featuring a high-lift camshaft, stiffer valvesprings, and other heavy-duty upgrades, the Stage 1 was rated at 345 hp.

"The Buick 455-ci engine was designed to produce high-torque durability and power in relatively heavy cars, including the Gran Sports, which weigh in excess of 3,600 pounds in typical street trim. The Stage 1 was an extension of that philosophy, to enhance the high-torque characteristics of the engine, and focus on the automatic transmission for the majority of sales.

"We redesigned the GS cold-air induction air cleaner and developed a low-restriction dual exhaust to improve power and provide a pleasant sound while conforming to legal noise restrictions. The power development engine on the dynamometer was equipped with an exhaust system and air cleaner to ensure that our camshaft, carburetor, spark timing, compression ratio, and valve sizes were focused toward developing real power on the street.

"Significant work was done to the camshaft, including the fitment of special valvesprings and pushrods to ensure clean valvetrain behavior at 6,000 rpm. A higher-pressure oil pressure spring was used to ensure adequate flow to the rod bearings at higher RPM.

"We selected a 3.42 rear axle ratio for air conditioning (3.64 for non-air cars) to maximize performance and driving enjoyment with the high-torque engine and G60 tires. To further enhance street performance, the automatic transmission option was calibrated to allow downshift on demand, all the way back to first gear at speeds below 35 mph. This feature provided exciting acceleration in a rolling situation.

"All of this special engineering was targeted toward the basic goal of maximizing total street performance. The axle ratios, camshaft timing, transmission calibration, valve size, exhaust system, fuel, and spark all played their part."

The Stage 2 remained a set of components available from the parts department, but it now included high-flow heads and forged TRW 11.0:1-compression flat-top pistons for the new 455. An 850-cfm Holley (PN 4781) sat atop an Edelbrock B4B intake, plus prototype Kustom Equipment headers.

The intention was to produce at least 50 10-second Stage 2 cars but, with a low-compression world around the corner, Manner sent an inter-departmental memo in April 1970: "Per the request of the Sales Department, the proposed Stage II engine will not be offered as a production option for 1971 and will continue to be a dealer-installed super high-performance engine package."

Enter the GSX

In February 1970, Buick introduced a performance and appearance package for the GS 455 to make it, what some consider, the ultimate supercar: the GSX. Inspired by the GTO Judge and other be-spoilered performance cars, the GSX package included Saturn Yellow or Apollo White paint, front and rear spoiler, black and red striping, body-colored headlamp bezels, and several heavy-duty upgrades, among others.

The Stage 1 engine cost an additional $113 on top of the $1,196 GSX package. That value proposition was the likely reason that 400 of the 678 GSXs built had the Stage 1.

The 1970 GS 350 was simply called "GS" (the California GS was gone). It received a 35-hp bump to 315 with an impressive 410 ft-lbs of torque.

Buick created the GSX package for the GS 455 as an attention-getter to bring people into the showroom, but it also gave you everything you'd ever want in a well-rounded performer. Front and rear spoilers, fat tires and mags, hood tachometer, rear-sway bar, and prominent stripes were all part of the package, which was available in Saturn Yellow or Apollo White.

Buick rearranged the Gran Sport series for 1971, so the 350 became the base engine (with a small-block GS convertible appearing for the first time). The 455 and Stage 1 were options. The GSX package was back, now available in six colors with a choice of three engines.

Cars magazine named the GS 455 (especially in Stage 1 tune) Top Performance Car of the Year: "The GS 455 offers the best combination of handling, ride, braking, quality control, engine performance and tasteful styling of all the '72 intermediate models offering optional or standard high performance packages." (Photo ©TEN: The Enthusiast Network. All rights reserved.)

The new 1973 Colonnade Century (which replaced the Skylark) was attractive, but the government-mandated front bumpers ruined the look that Buick sought. Nevertheless, the Gran Sport was available as a performance package that could be optioned with the 455 Stage 1. The 270 net horsepower may have paled compared to 360 gross horses from 1970, but the Stage 1 was still one of the fastest cars available at the time. (Photo Courtesy Phillip Roitman)

"Dull transportation, you've just been scorched," Buick said in a GS ad.

Consolidation and Compression

For 1971, Buick merged the GS and GS 455 into one series. Thanks to GM's corporate-wide compression cut, the 350 was relegated to 260 hp, while the 455 and Stage 1 put out 315 and 345 horses, respectively. A new option was the N25 "through-bumper exhaust extensions" where the exhaust system was routed to two rectangular exhaust pipes poking through the bumper.

The GSX package also returned for 1971, but because the GS series now encompassed three engines, it was possible to order a GSX hardtop with a 350. An expanded color palette was new, and the front spoiler, sport mirrors, and hood tachometer were optional. Only 124 GSXs were built.

The 1972 GS added black headlight and taillight trim but otherwise looked identical. Changes under the hood were marginal as well, but engines were now measured in net horsepower instead of gross. That meant the GS featured a standard 350/195, with 455/250 and 270-hp Stage 1 as options. Even more disappointing, Buick's brochure didn't feature pictures of the GS, but Buick continued to offer the GSX. It was available in any GS color, but only 44 were built.

Although many manufacturers were downgrading their performance models, Buick pressed on with the Stage 1 for 1973. Horsepower remained the same, but the car itself changed. The new Gran Sport package was based on the redesigned Century Colonnade hardtop. The package included a standard 4-barrel 350, special blacked-out grille and headlight trim, rear deck striping, and "Gran Sport" fender decals and grille badge. The 455 and 270-hp Stage 1 remained as options. Buick produced 728 Stage 1s, including 92 with a 4-speed.

The Century Gran Sport received a mild facelift in 1974. The Stage 1 remained on the option list, although horsepower was down to 255 and available with only an automatic transmission. The Century GS Ride and Handing Package was offered for the last time in 1975; a standard 231 V-6 with two 350s were the only upgrades.

Although a shell of its former self, the 1975 Gran Sport was the link to the division's future as Buick added a turbo to the V-6 in 1978. It reached new heights with the 1986–1987 Grand National and 1987 GNX.

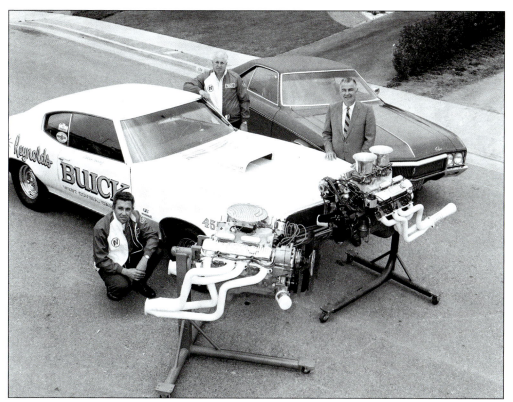

Jim Bell, "Pop" Kennedy, and Pete Reynolds Jr., pose with the 1970 Reynolds Buick Stage 2 GS and a Riviera, plus racing engines built by Kennedy-Bell. (Photo Courtesy Don Reynolds/Reynolds Buick)

Since Buick seemingly was cut from a different cloth than other high-performance GM brands, it may not come as a surprise that the division did not have a strong high-performance marketing component behind the Gran Sport. Add GM's racing ban to the equation and it's no wonder Buick was conservative.

However, there still was a contingency of Buick faithful who demanded more. Reynolds Buick in West Covina, California, stands out as a dealership that helped advance Buick performance for enthusiasts.

The story begins with a Buick racer named Lennie "Pop" Kennedy whose tuning expertise, coupled with quick reflexes that belied his age, made him an unusual sight in the winner's circle. Starting with a 1955 Century, then a 1956, Pop beat plenty of heavy artillery in Southern California.

Bill Trevor, a Buick technical instructor at General Motors Training Center in Burbank, remarked to Reynolds Buick owner Pete Reynolds that if he ever wanted to sponsor a car, he knew of the right driver.

Pop and Reynolds' association began with a 1959 Invicta that ran 14.70 ETs thanks to milled heads and a 4.44 rear end. When Pop switched to a 1961 Invicta, Reynolds sponsored two trips to Indy that resulted in two NHRA

Jim Bell estimated the new 400 put out 75 more horsepower than the old nailhead 401. With his expert preparation, this 1967 Reynolds Buick GS 400 ran 12.10 at 111 mph. The mechanically similar 1968 was eventually used as a skunkworks test mule for 455 and Stage 2 components. Pictured are Pete Reynolds Jr. and Pop Kennedy. (Photo Courtesy Don Reynolds/Reynolds Buick)

Upon delivery, this white 1970 GS Stage 1 was immediately sent to Jim Bell's shop and had Stage 2 parts installed. Pop ran 10.70 ETs, but General Motors made a decision for a low-compression future, killing the chances of a factory Stage 2 car. (Photo Courtesy Don Reynolds/Reynolds Buick)

This Apollo White GSX was built by Buick Engineering and sent to Bill Trevor in Burbank to be used as a test mule for Stage 2 equipment, including the prototype Stage 2 hood scoop. When it was clear that the Stage 2 had no future as a production item because General Motors decided to get a head start in emissions mandates, the GSX went back to Flint and was dismantled. (Photo Courtesy Dennis Manner)

class wins in 1961 and 1962 (despite the fact that he *drove* the Buick to and from Indy). The Invicta's best time was 14.21 at 97.70 mph.

Next came a 1964 Skylark with the 300 V-8 but, when the 1965 Skylark Gran Sport was introduced, Pop switched cars and ran 12.30 ETs. Part of the success with this car can be credited to Jim Bell, who often competed with Pop, but eventually joined forces with him to handle tuning.

Buick sent a letter to dealerships celebrating first-place victories in every class entered at San Fernando Raceway in February 1965. "I am sure you and your salesmen can use this information when you start talking about Buick's performance."

The introduction of the 400 engine in 1967 led Bell to build a Reynolds-sponsored GS 400. This NHRA Super Stock stormer ran .2 second quicker than the nailhead 1965. It was replaced by a 1968 GS 400 that changed roles for 1969: with assistance from Dennis Manner, Bill Trevor supplied Pop and Bell prototype parts for the 455 and Stage 2 (including new heads for the latter) for them to evaluate on the flow bench and at the dragstrip. (During this time, them formed Kennedy-Bell to develop high-performance Buick parts.)

Trevor ordered a white GS Stage 1 automatic through Reynolds Buick and received Stage 2 parts at the Burbank Training Center. A new item was a Stage 2–specific air induction system featuring a large hood scoop and special air cleaner with a foam and rubber baffle. There were two more skunkworks vehicles: the Doug Jones and David Benisek team (acolytes

of Trevor) ordered a bare-bones, red Stage 1, 4-speed through Trevor and received Stage 2 upgrades from Clark Brothers Buick in Torrance; and a GSX Stage 2 4-speed prototype (with Stage 2 hood) built by Buick Engineering that was sent to Trevor for evaluation and promotion.

Jones' and Benisek's red Stage 1 ran 13.30 out of the box, but when it and the white Reynolds car were upgraded with Stage 2 parts, both ran 10.70s at 127 mph. In comparison, the GSX was a bit more "streetable" (it even featured air conditioning), running 11.70 ETs at 118 mph at Lions Drag Strip before it was sent back to Flint and dismantled. The Stage 2 hood was subsequently donated to Jones and Benisek.

The Stage 2 was out of favor because of impending EPA requirements and a changing market. The project was quietly discontinued, but many Stage 2 components became available from Buick's parts catalog.

Already a survivor of several heart attacks and strokes, Pop retired from racing in 1972. Soon after, he sold his interest in Kennedy-Bell to his racing partner, and Bell changed the name to Kenne-Bell. The company became *the* go-to place for Buick performance and turbo 3.8L V-6s before evolving into its current position as a leading producer of superchargers.

Marketing Strategy

Unlike other marques, Buick didn't spend a lot of money on marketing to the high-performance crowd. When the Gran Sport was introduced in 1965, all the magazines were enthusiastic, and even Buick's ad agency was a bit aggressive with the suggestion that the GS was "A howitzer with windshield wipers." But Buick did not have a strong drag racing presence, had no major tie-ins (as Pontiac did), and didn't produce any nifty ad campaigns as did Dr. Oldsmobile.

But the Gran Sport was among the first GTO competitors to apply the same performance formula to several of its car lines. The GS 340 was among the first of the Junior Supercars. It was also was among the first to make prominent use of racing stripes.

GSX: Image Changer

If Buick was not working hard to tempt America's enthusiasts with high-performance machinery, how did the GSX come about? Toward the end of 1969, Buick Engineering's Product Information Department prepared a case to produce an "in" car: "Buick has proven to be equal to competition in terms of those things that appeal to the conservative buyer, such as comfort, durability, and quality of construction. But, until recently, we could not appeal to the all-important ego of the younger buyer by offering him a car that is accepted and desired by others in his social group."

FRONT AND REAR SPOILERS

NEW STRIPING ON DECK LID, HOOD, QUARTERS AND FRONT FENDERS

HOOD MOUNTED TACHOMETER

SPECIAL ORNAMENTATION

4

During the conception of the GSX package in the summer of 1969, it went from a rather understated design (even lacking front and rear spoilers) to this wild production iteration several months later. (Photo Courtesy General Motors)

BASE PRICE OF ALL ENTRIES RANGES FROM $4,171.00 FOR GSX TO $3,073.00 FOR FORD TORINO COBRA. THE DIFFERENCE BASICALLY IS STANDARD EQUIPMENT. THE PRICE RANGE NARROWS CONSIDERABLY WHEN THE VARIOUS CARS ARE COMPARED SIMILARLY EQUIPPED.

	BUICK GSX	PONTIAC JUDGE	OLDS W-30	CHARGER R/T	FORD COBRA
BASE LIST PRICE	$4171.00	$3376.00	$3757.00	$3484.00	$3073.00
EQUIPMENT					
POWER DISC BRAKES	STD	61.00	39.50	66.05	61.70
4-SPEED TRANS.	STD	175.00	STD	N.C.	STD
POSITIVE TRACTION	STD	40.00	STD	40.10	40.80
STYLED WHEELS	STD	STD	70.00	81.60	147.20
SPECIAL TIRES	STD	29.00	STD	STD	STD
BUCKET SEATS	STD	STD	STD	STD	126.30
CONSOLE	STD	53.00	58.00	51.55	51.30
INSTRUMENT GAUGES	STD	48.00	80.00	STD	N.A.
CLOCK	STD	INCL.	INCL.	64.85	15.20
TACHOMETER	STD	60.00	INCL.	INCL.	46.50
SPORT STRG. WHEEL	STD	40.00	15.00	25.30	37.00
DUAL SPORT MIRROR	STD	N.A.	STD	N.A.	24.70
TOTAL COMPARATIVE PRICE	$4171.00	$3882.00	$4019.00	$3813.45	$3623.70

THE CAR NEAREST GSX IN PRICE IS OLDS W-30. THIS CAR, HOWEVER, DOES NOT OFFER APPEARANCE MODIFICATIONS OF THE QUALITY OR SCOPE FOUND ON GSX.

Although Buick considered the GTO Judge, 4-4-2 W-30, Charger R/T, and Torino Cobra as prime competitors for the proposed GSX, some were positioned differently in the market. The one thing they all shared was that they were their respective brand's "image" car. (Photo Courtesy of General Motors)

The first step in changing this image was the introduction of the Opel GT in the spring of 1969, "the original 'light your fire' special-interest car" (a reference to an theme that became Buick's ad campaign for 1970).

The increase in showroom floor traffic (up to 5,000 people one weekend) made Buick realize it needed to maintain the fire that the Opel GT had started. For the approaching spring, Buick hoped to stoke the flames once again, this time with the "high-potential 1970 Buick A car line."

Skylark sales had lagged behind the competition "in spite of our youthful new Skylark line," so Buick felt "it should be brought to the attention of the market in the manner used by every intermediate car maker except Buick, with a car having strong visual identity and a performance image." The benchmarks were the GTO Judge, 4-4-2 W30, Charger R/T, and Torino Cobra.

The presentation showed the proposed GSX with front and rear spoilers, stripes, hood-mounted tachometer, and special ornamentation. Buick also benchmarked the GSX's performance against the W30, showing 0-60 and quarter-mile times of the 455 and the Stage 1, with the latter being a half-second quicker than the Olds, according to Buick engineers. "Base powertrain is that of 1970 GS 455 which, incidentally, compares favorably in performance with image cars of other makers.

"From this you can see that Buick already has the muscle, but needs the visual impact of our competition to get the attention of the market. The GSX will provide this attention. It is unmistakably a performance car, not only in action, but in appearance as well."

Buick gave an overview of each competitor, including its main features and the additions of each performance package. Also reported were 1969 production information and projected production for 1970. Even though the Torino Cobra had a "bold exterior appearance," Buick realized the Cobra was more of an econo-supercar in the vein of the Plymouth Road Runner that included "low level interior trim, grille and exterior moldings," but it functioned as Ford's mid-size image car.

The Charger R/T, on the other hand, was a premium performance car whose exterior appearance had "less individuality than other cars in this group and relies chiefly on trim items for identity."

Likewise, the 4-4-2 W30 was taken to task as it didn't "offer appearance modifications of the quality or scope found on the GSX. Spoilers are offered on the Olds only as an extra cost option, for example. This is probably the most important single appearance item for a car of this type in the eyes of the prospective purchaser."

In comparison, the Buick GSX had "everything to generate customer interest: appearance, performance, and popular features as standard equipment.

In magazine ads, the Skylark Gran Sport was characterized as "a howitzer with windshield wipers." (Photo Courtesy M. J. Frumkin Collection)

"GSX will function not only as a showpiece to build floor traffic, but will build Buick's image in the vital youth market."

Buick projected production volume at 875 units, which was approximately 7 percent of the projected GS 455 volume. However, when model year production was tallied, 678 GSXs had been built, and the market was crashing. Simply put, the GSX was too little, too late to improve Buick's performance image, but it succeeded in bringing people to the Buick showroom.

Advertising Program

Befitting its image as a purveyor of finer automobiles (a step above Oldsmobile, a step below Cadillac), Buick didn't have a strong high-performance image. Performance always seemed to be a part of the Buick equation, but not in the way performance was viewed in 1955 at the start of the "horsepower race." Still, Buick had a faint performance heartbeat between 1959 and 1965 because nailhead engines were popular with hot rodders and drag racers.

Buick promoted the GS but didn't seem to go out of its way to tout it as an alternative to the GTO. Rather, it appeared that Buick offered the GS just so kids from Buick families could drive something appealings.

Buick's was understated even when the market was becoming brasher. A 1967 GS 400 headline proclaimed, "Your father never told you there'd be Buicks like this" while a 1969 GS 400 ad said, "You asked for an enthusiast's machine from Buick. It's happened. The 1969 GS 400." Ho-hum.

In 1970, when the performance market was at its peak, Buick advertised the GS series as "Introducing automobiles to light your fire," which sounded like Dad trying to be hip three years after the Doors hit the charts with the song.

CHAPTER 5

OLDS JOINS THE FRAY

Oldsmobile fans like to think the Lansing, Michigan–based company invented the muscle car with the 1949 Rocket 88. Both model and engine were new for 1949, the combination a result of merging the low-line 76 with the high-compression 303.7-ci OHV V-8 from the 98. All of a sudden, flathead Fords began to look a bit old-fashioned.

By 1955, with the industry flush with V-8s, several brands surpassed Oldsmobile's performance reputation. The 1957–1958 J-2 tri-carb Golden Rocket 377 brought Oldsmobile performance up a notch, but after winning the NASCAR Cup Championship in 1958, Oldsmobile's performance chops subsided. Olds had the sporty 1961 Starfire and 1961 F-85 Cutlass Sports Coupe (a classy "senior compact" with bucket seats), but they were not performance cars. The Cutlass-based 1962–1963 Jetfire, with Buick's aluminum 215-ci V-8 paired with a turbocharger, was a step in the right direction, but 215 hp wasn't enough to make the Jetfire as fine as the 409.

The 1968 Chicago Auto Show featured this display showing the underpinnings of the redesigned 4-4-2 and how the unique Outside Air Induction (OAI) system worked. (Photo Courtesy Mitch Frumkin)

4-4-2 and W30

The Pontiac GTO burst onto the scene in the fall of 1963. The GTO was a new concept in the market, yet Oldsmobile was the first on the scene with a competitor: the 4-4-2. The name stood for *4-speed, 4-barrel, dual exhaust*, with ads proclaiming, "Police needed it . . . Olds built it . . . Pursuit proved it! Put this one on *your* WANTED list!"

The B09 4-4-2 package for the F-85 and Cutlass featured an upgraded 330 with 310 hp, 4-speed, and heavy-duty chassis components including a rear sway bar. The 4-4-2 was strong on balance, but fell short of cubic inches and, accordingly, straight-line performance when compared to the GTO.

Oldsmobile prepared a new 400 for 1965, which was basically a small-bore 425 from the big cars. The definition of the 4-4-2 package also changed: 400-ci, 4-barrel, dual exhaust. Simulated rear fender scoops and tri-color "442" badges were easy visual cues. With 345 hp, performance was on par with the GTO. Road testers specifically praised handling, thanks to the rear sway bar. Despite the GTO juggernaut, Oldsmobile managed to sell a respectable 25,003 4-4-2s.

By 1966, the market was much more competitive, but the 4-4-2 held its own quite well. The L78 4-4-2 Performance Package was available for F-85 and Cutlass two-doors and included a 350-hp 400, front fender vents, and the usual heavy-duty upgrades.

In December 1965, the L69 4-4-2 Performance Package with tri-carbs became available, bumping horsepower up to 360.

Several months later, Oldsmobile introduced something special for NHRA C/Stock: W30 Outside Air Induction (OAI), a high-performance package that required the L69 package and included 4.11 gears, special 308-degree camshaft, close-ratio 4-speed, trunk-mounted battery, and special chrome air cleaner with air induction system. Oldsmobile also made a Track Pack kit for owners to upgrade their cars to W-30 specs.

The 4-4-2 package returned for 1967, now based on the upscale Cutlass Supreme. In addition to a tough-looking

Inspired by the GTO and Oldsmobile's police packages, the 4-4-2 was introduced in April 1964 for F-85 and Cutlass models. The standard rear-sway bar was a unique trademark. (Photo Courtesy General Motors)

Baltimore's Anderson Oldsmobile campaigned this 1965 F-85 4-4-2 Club Coupe in B/S and BB/S. After a year, the two-tone 4-speed stripper was retired and sold on Anderson's used-car lot. (Photo Courtesy David Siltman)

The 1966 4-4-2 was restyled, with the 400 receiving a 5-hp bump. The tri-carb L69 was introduced in December and featured a mandatory manual transmission and more radical camshaft. (Photo ©TEN: The Enthusiast Network. All rights reserved.)

In June 1966, the L69 was joined by the W30 package that included several heavy-duty upgrades and a unique air induction system. Fifty-four W30s were built and approximately 93 Track Pack kits were sold through dealers. (Photo ©TEN: The Enthusiast Network. All rights reserved.)

facelift, a new louvered hood and tri-color badges were the easiest way to tell a 4-4-2 from a regular Cutlass. GM's three-speed Turbo-Hydramatic finally became available.

Thanks to a new corporate-wide edict from General Motors, multiple carburetion was discontinued on all cars except the Corvette, so the L69 became a thing of the past.

The facelifted 1967 4-4-2 package lost the tri-carb option but gained a new Rochester Quadrajet and TH400. (Photo ©TEN: The Enthusiast Network. All rights reserved.)

However, the W30 package returned with a Rochester Quadrajet 4-barrel with OAI routed to cavities between the headlights. The 360-hp engine also came with a W30 signature item: red plastic front fender wells. The Track Pack continued to be available from the parts counter.

In 1968 Olds brought a redesigned A-body with a semi-fastback body featuring a slight Toronado influence. Finally achieving model status, the 4-4-2 featured a notched rear bumper with flared exhaust extensions, louvered hood, and optional W36 Rally Stripe. A redesigned 400 (now with undersquare proportions) put out 350 hp with a manual transmission but only 325 with the TH400. A one-year option was the 290-horse 2-barrel Turnpike Cruiser package.

Oldsmobile was much more aggressive marketing the W30 Force-Air Induction System in 1968. Touted as factory blueprinted with "select-fit" parts, the W30's new 328-degree cam was so radical that power brakes were not available. OAI scoops were relocated to under the bumper, a visual treat complemented by a standard Rally Stripe. Also, for the first time, the W30 package was available for the convertible.

1968 Performance Offerings

If 400 ci wasn't enough for you, you were out of luck thanks to the GM rule limiting A-Body engine size. However, the problem could be solved courtesy of the 1968 Hurst/Olds.

Oldsmobile entered 1968 with a wide array of performers: a redesigned 4-4-2, a Ram-Rod 350 F-85/Cutlass S, and a W34 Toronado. Motion Performance teamed up with Markowitz Oldsmobile to work its magic the same way it had for Baldwin Chevrolet, but the partnership lasted less than a year. (Photo Courtesy Martyn L. Schorr, Co-Founder Baldwin-Motion)

Perhaps Oldsmobile was stifled by GM's cubic-inch limit, but Hurst was not. Hurst commissioned more than 500 1968 4-4-2s built with a specially prepared 455, Hurst Dual/Gate shifter, and custom two-tone paint. The Hurst/Olds was called the "Gentleman's Supercar" thanks to its 13-second ETs and high level of appointments. (Photo Courtesy Hurst Inc.)

Help from Hurst

It was a 4-4-2 modified by Hurst Performance and equipped with a 390-hp 455, special-order Peruvian Silver and Ebony Black paint, OAI, red fender wells, modified TH400 with Hurst Dual-Gate, and other heavy-duty upgrades. Designed for "uncompromising street performance that will exceed any vehicle of its type," the 1968 H/O carried a full Oldsmobile warranty. The first of the "Gentleman's Hot Rods," 451 H/O hardtops and 64 coupes were built.

Ram-Rod 350

The H/O wasn't the only new performance Oldsmobile for 1968; the Ram-Rod 350 was a high-performance small-block available for F-85 and Cutlass S two-doors. Order the W31 package and you received a 325-hp 350, special 2-inch intake and 1⅝-inch exhaust valves, special high-lift camshaft, OAI, and other heavy-duty upgrades.

The Ram-Rod was a tough entry in NHRA competition. It may have been the most impressive Oldsmobile performance car of all, but it was a big-block world and only 742 were built.

W34 Toronado

Another 1968 performance Oldsmobile worthy of note is the W34 Toronado. This package included an upgraded 455 with 400 hp thanks to a high-lift camshaft, recurved distributor, special TH400 with heavy-duty torque converter, and OAI with a single intake attached to the inner fender.

Dr. Oldsmobile Creates the W-Machines

Oldsmobile's game became more aggressive in 1969. The 4-4-2 featured new front and rear styling complemented by a dual-plane hood with GT hood pinstripes; W42 dual stripes were optional. The 400/350 remained standard, with horsepower down 25 when the TH400 was specified.

The W30

The W30 featured internal improvements but maintained its 360-horse rating. Now branded under the W-Machine moniker, the W30 package was tweaked slightly and included W42 stripes and front-fender exterior identification.

The W32

Oldsmobile introduced a new W-Machine for 1969 called the W32. Positioned between the base 4-4-2 and the W30, this package featured a 350-hp 400 with special camshaft, mandatory automatic transmission, special distributor, OAI, and exterior identification.

Olds positioned the W32 as having "excellent tractability, good idle quality, and superior 'stop light' performance," seizing upon a perceived

Oldsmobile began branding its top performers as "W-Machines" in 1969. At the 1969 Chicago Auto Show, Dr. Oldsmobile was brought to life as a crazy inventor who opened a shipping crate to reveal his W-Machine. (Photo Courtesy General Motors and Mitch Frumkin)

trend for hot street automatics. The trend must not have been as great as projected; only 297 4-4-2 W32s were built.

The W31

Oldsmobile's Junior Supercar was formally branded as W31 for 1969. An F-85 or Cutlass S equipped with this package was now available with the TH350 automatic, broadening its appeal and leading *Car and Driver* magazine to proclaim, "W31 stands for soul [and] what may very well be this country's best sport sedan."

The W31 package also featured standard W42 stripes and W31 identification to look the part, but only 913 buyers took Oldsmobile up on its offer.

A Hairier Hurst

And then there was the H/O. Despite its limited availability, the 1968 H/O was a rousing success and did wonders for Oldsmobile's image. Its

PROJECT W31

Late in 1969, the Michigan State University chapter of the Society of Automotive Engineers (SAE) received a gift from Oldsmobile. A 1969 Cutlass S W31 that was used as an engineering test vehicle was donated so "we could invest our practical mechanical know-how and engineering imagination," as Fred Bowen said in the May 9, 1971, *The Lansing State Journal*. Senior mechanical engineering major Paul Aurand was instrumental in getting Project W31 approved by the dean of engineering, including storage space on campus.

The October 1970 *Spartan Engineer* described how SAE club members prepared Project W31 to do battle in NHRA G/Stock for the spring 1970 season. The engine and transmission were removed and rebuilt, with Aurand removing the synchronizer clutches and springs from the 4-speed to grind "every other internal tooth from all forward gears and every other internal spline from the two shift sliders" for smooth, clutchless shifts.

The suspension was also tweaked. Front springs from a 6-cylinder Tempest replaced the factory units for better weight transfer. The rear springs were assisted by Air Lift air cylinders, using a pinion snubber to prevent wheel hop. To save weight, power accessories, sealer, undercoating, and sound deadener were removed. The only work the team didn't handle was blueprinting the heads.

Being broke college students, team members appealed to aftermarket manufacturers for donations to help the W31 be more competitive on the dragstrip. "Although we have expected and received a few turn-downs, the results of this endeavor have been gratifying," Bowen told *Spartan Engineer*.

Motor Wheel, Goodyear, Accel, and Kustom Equipment, among others, were notable for their kind donations.

In their first outing, the team headed to Onondaga Dragway and ran the 3,450-pound W31 in G/SS (thanks to borrowed slicks), winning its class with a best of 13.70 at 107 mph. A second outing at Tri-City Dragway, now with proper 7-inch slicks for G/S, resulted in 13.40s at 103 mph. The team was eliminated in the first round, and another run the next day resulted in transmission failure.

With a borrowed transmission, the team headed to Onondaga for a third trial, but they learned that the stock transmission couldn't shift fast enough to be competitive. They subsequently spent several hours making modifications before heading to Tri-City, netting a G/S trophy despite bugs that had cropped up. Subsequent visits to the drags resulted in a best of 13.15 at 105 mph (the national record was 12.05 at 115).

According to Project W31 member Al Wilson, "We had an oil control problem on both rear cylinders. The spark plugs were always oily and there was oil smoke upon launch. We never resolved this, as we assumed the expander ring was overlapped. We were going to build a new engine over the following winter, so we never addressed it.

"When the engine was completed, we eagerly took the W31 to a remote parking lot on Mt. Hope Road one evening for some test hits. I think it was the second hit that deposited the bottom of the engine on the pavement. What a disappointment! We then reinstalled the old engine."

Project W31 had a revolving door of participants through 1973. Beyond that, the fate of the W-Machine is unknown.

According to Project W31 team member Dennis Kline, "It was amazing that it ran because we used parts from several different brands, such as Chevy valves. We were a very ingenious bunch." (Photos Courtesy Al Wilson)

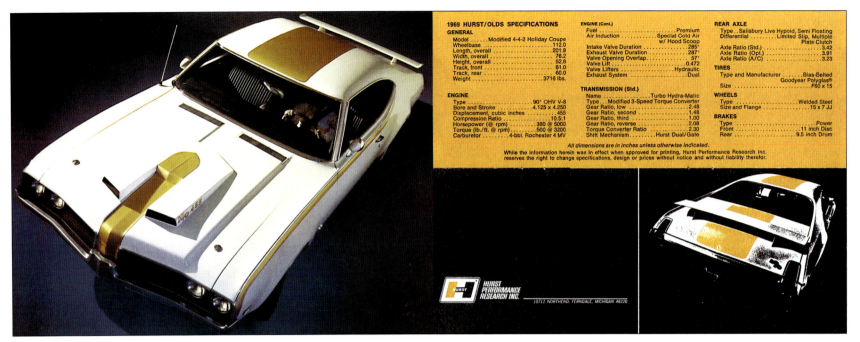

1969 HURST/OLDS SPECIFICATIONS

GENERAL	
Model	Modified 4-4-2 Holiday Coupe
Wheelbase	112.0
Length, overall	201.9
Width, overall	76.2
Height, overall	52.8
Track, front	61.0
Track, rear	60.0
Weight	3716 lbs.

ENGINE	
Type	90° OHV V-8
Bore and Stroke	4.125 x 4.250
Displacement, cubic inches	455
Compression Ratio	10.5:1
Horsepower (@ rpm)	380 @ 5000
Torque (lb./ft. @ rpm)	500 @ 3200
Carburetor	4-bbl. Rochester 4 MV

ENGINE (Cont.)	
Fuel	Premium
Air Induction	Special Cold Air w/ Hood Scoop
Intake Valve Duration	285°
Exhaust Valve Duration	287°
Valve Opening Overlap	57°
Valve Lift	0.472
Valve Lifters	Hydraulic
Exhaust System	Dual

TRANSMISSION (Std.)	
Name	Turbo Hydra-Matic
Type	Modified 3-Speed Torque Converter
Gear Ratio, low	2.48
Gear Ratio, second	1.48
Gear Ratio, third	1.00
Gear Ratio, reverse	2.08
Torque Converter Ratio	2.30
Shift Mechanism	Hurst Dual/Gate

REAR AXLE	
Type	Salisbury Live Hypoid, Semi Floating
Differential	Limited Slip, Multiple Plate Clutch
Axle Ratio (Std.)	3.42
Axle Ratio (Opt.)	3.91
Axle Ratio (A/C)	3.23

TIRES	
Type and Manufacturer	Bias-Belted Goodyear Polyglas®
Size	F60 x 15

WHEELS	
Type	Welded Steel
Size and Flange	15 x 7 JJ

BRAKES	
Type	Power
Front	11 inch Disc
Rear	9.5 inch Drum

All dimensions are in inches unless otherwise indicated.

While the information herein was in effect when approved for printing, Hurst Performance Research Inc. reserves the right to change specifications, design or prices without notice and without liability therefor.

HURST PERFORMANCE RESEARCH INC.
10711 NORTHEND, FERNDALE, MICHIGAN 48220

Dramatic white and gold paint, spoiler, and conspicuous hood scoops set the 1969 Hurst/Olds apart from 1968's H/O, if not other cars. Production increased by 80 percent. (Photo Courtesy Hurst Inc.)

understated styling did an about-face for 1969 as the H/O became one of the most outrageous cars of the year. All H/Os came with a 380-hp 455 and were painted Cameo White with Hurst Fire Frost Gold accents, racing mirrors, and flying spoiler. Hurst replaced Oldsmobile's unique OAI system with twin "mailbox" hood scoops that used an air cleaner assembly with a vacuum actuator.

Dr. Oldsmobile's Crowning Achievement

Oldsmobile stepped up its W-Machine effort even more for 1970. Stylists redesigned the A-Body with simulated rear fender arches that gave coupes a more muscular look. New for the 4-4-2 were mid-level pinstripes along the sides and over the wheel wells. But the big news was that General Motors lifted its cubic-inch limit, allowing Oldsmobile to install the 455. The standard 4-4-2 engine was rated at 365 hp and, for the first time, air induction was available for non-W-Machines via a new fiberglass W25 hood with twin stripes. The Indianapolis Pace Car package for the convertible had black/red-trimmed stripes that extended to the trunk lid.

The W30 package was rated at 370 hp and included thick side stripes and a standard W25 hood among its features. Oldsmobile now targeted two segments with the W30: 4-speeds, which continued to use a radical camshaft, while Olds felt TH400 buyers would appreciate the flexibility of a streetable W-Machine with a less rumpety-rump cam. That allowed the W30 automatic to be available with air conditioning and power brakes for

The 4-4-2 features a nice restyle, a newly available 455 with optional W25 fiberglass hood, and revamped striping. The WSO package included the hood and added thicker stripes in addition to the upgraded engine.

the first time. The addition of the optional W35 spoiler and W27 aluminum rear axle carrier produced a rather serious street machine.

Dr. Olds Scores Again

The W31 package returned for the F-85/Cutlass S for the last time, still powered by a 350/325 but now featuring 1970 W-Machine updates. It was joined in February 1970 by a youth-oriented insurance buster and showroom traffic-builder called the Rallye 350.

The Rallye 350's 310-hp 350 found a sweet spot between speed and insurance rates. The "budget supercar" also served as a beacon to draw customers to Oldsmobile showrooms. (Photo Courtesy General Motors)

Lowered compression caused the 1971 4-4-2's standard engine decline by 25 hp to 340. However, an attractive facelift and shuffled trim kept things fresh. (Photo Courtesy Thomas J. Uttke, Jr.)

Originally proposed as a 1970 H/O with the W31 minus the "select-fit" parts, Oldsmobile, added the regular-production 350/310, and created a "budget-pleasing all-action car" with Sebring Yellow paint with black/orange stripes and decals, matching urethane bumpers and SSII wheels sans trim rings, W25 hood, spoiler (later made optional), and several heavy-duty upgrades. Despite having more bark than bite, the Rallye 350 was a respectable performer, capable of easy low-15s. The Rallye 350X was a midyear promotional package that sold a decent 3,547 units.

Remember the W32? It was gone for the 4-4-2, but it became an option for the new SX Performance Package for Cutlass Supreme two-doors. Somewhat like the 1968's Turnpike Cruiser, the 1970 SX included a 2-barrel 455 (replaced midyear with a 4-barrel), dual exhausts with notched rear bumper and exhaust extensions, TH400 automatic transmission, and SX identification. The W32 engine, which was the same 455/365 from the 4-4-2, was optional.

A W32 SX was more of a powerful personal-luxury vehicle than an all-out performance machine so youth appeal was likely limited.

Dr. Oldsmobile Falls Out of Favor

GM's corporate-wide lowering of engine compression reduced the 4-4-2's 455 to 340 hp. The W30 fell 20 hp to 350. Still, there were bright spots.

The 4-speed was available with a W37 dual-disc clutch (shared with the Corvette). A new grille, parking lights, taillights, and standard hood stripe were easy visual cues for 1971. The pillared coupe disappeared for the first time. Sales fell to 7,580 units, including 920 W30s.

It became worse in 1972: The 4-4-2 now became the W29 Appearance and Handling Package available on four Cutlass/Cutlass S/Cutlass Supreme two-door models. Standard engine was now a 2-barrel 350. The package

lacked dual exhausts with the signature notched rear bumper and extensions. However, the 455 and W30 were still available, the latter now rated at 300 net horsepower.

The 4-4-2's sales rebounded for 1972: 9,845 cars, including 772 W30s, the last of the W-Machines.

Hurst Saves the Day

The H/O made a return in 1972, and it was chosen to pace the Indy 500. This time the H/O was based on the Cutlass Supreme hardtop and

The 1972 Hurst/Olds was now based on the Cutlass Supreme and came standard with a 270-hp 455; the 300-horse W30 was optional. An optional sunroof proved to be relatively popular. (Photo Courtesy Hurst Inc.)

convertible, all Cameo White with prominent Hurst Gold "laser" accents. Other standard features included 455 with dual exhausts, twin sport mirrors, Antique Gold landau vinyl roof, Hurst Gold Super Stock III wheels, power disc brakes, W25 hood, Dual-Gate automatic with console, and Rallye suspension.

Buyers could specify one of two available packages: W45 came with a 455/270 and W46 came with the 300-horse W30.

Dr. Oldsmobile: RIP

The 1973 Cutlass was completely redesigned with Colonnade styling. This was also the first year of government-mandated 5-mph front bumpers. Styling was compromised because the bumpers were required after the design began taking shape in GM's studios. But when a Cutlass or Cutlass S Colonnade Coupe was equipped with the 4-4-2 Appearance and Handling Package, it was likely the best-balanced 4-4-2 ever.

The package included striping on the louvered hood, deck lid, and wheel arches, plus special grille, Rallye suspension, and standard 350 4-barrel. When swiveling bucket seats and the 270-hp 455 4-speed were added, it was one of the more exciting cars for 1973.

Those who wanted more distinction could find it with the H/O, which was available in either white and gold or black and gold. The 455/270 was

standard with 250 hp for cars equipped with air conditioning.

Both the 4-4-2 and H/O continued off and on into the 1980s, but they were never anything more than stylish vehicles with performance pretensions. Considering that the Cutlass Supreme was Detroit's best-selling car in the mid-1970s, it was clear that the buying public's imagination had been captured by luxury more than performance.

Dealerships

A group of Oldsmobile dealers from around the country (Berejik, Dewey-Griffin, Chesrown, King, and Century) had a very special connection for 1969. Here's the story of how they got together.

One of the most popular television shows in the 1960s was *The Smothers Brothers Comedy Hour*. The Smothers brothers initially found fame as folk singers and comedians. They landed a variety show in 1967 that quickly developed a reputation for its irreverence and satire on topical issues such as the Vietnam War, drugs, politics, and religion. These were all issues popular with the under-25 crowd.

Their success allowed Dick Smothers to pursue his love of auto racing. He told *Popular Hot Rodding* in April 1969, "I dig it all. I don't care if it's Formula racing, Championship racing, Grand National racing, or drag racing, or even a little foolin' around on the mini-bike. I've been intrigued with engines, their sounds, and the feel of a piece of race machinery for as long as I can recall, and this is just another way that I can outlet my feelings.

"In fact, racing is the only thing I can think of that I do which requires 100 percent of me. In everything else I've tried, I've found that proficiency

The 1973 Hurst/Olds, designed "For the Man in Motion," was based on the all-new Cutlass S Colonnade and was available in either black and gold or white and gold. Hurst continued to offer distinctive options, including Super Air Shocks. (Photo Courtesy Hurst Inc.)

When TV star and racing enthusiast Dick Smothers joined forces with Oldsmobile in 1968, he was given this Cutlass S W31 for exhibition runs. His first outing was at the 1968 U.S. Nationals in Indy. (Photo ©TEN: The Enthusiast Network. All rights reserved.)

Berejik Oldsmobile was the East Coast representative of the Smothers Brothers Racing Team. Loyed Woodland raced this 1969 4-4-2 W30 in E/S. (Gene Horn Photo)

was not nearly as difficult to achieve as it is in auto racing. So it's my bag, and I'll dig it for as long as I can." Dick's enthusiasm eventually led to his own racing team with Oldsmobile.

That story begins with Carl Schiefer, Director of Marketing and son of the founder of Schiefer Manufacturing. Thanks to a collaboration with Hurst in 1968, Schiefer was introduced to Oldsmobile's head of public relations, Jim Williams, and Motorsports Manager Dale Smith. In the words of former *Hot Rod* editor Jim McFarland, Schiefer was known as a progressive advertising and marketing thinker, and Smith had a keen sense of the power of both marketing and racing. By combining everyone's competencies they came up with the idea of reaching out to Dick Smothers.

"The quickest way to establish an image for a high-performance model is to go stock car drag racing. It boils down to racing what you make without spending time and money for the modifications," related Smith in his book *Racing to the Past*. "I have observed factories that entered racing with big budgets and won big in NASCAR with highly modified production cars, but after the race was over

THE PARTIES TO THE PARTY

The team's five racers, dealers, cars, and racing classes were as follows:

- Loyed Woodland, Berejik Oldsmobile, Needham, Massachusetts: 1969 4-4-2 W30 4-speed coupe, E/S
- Pete Kost, Dewey-Griffin Oldsmobile, Bremerton, Washington: 1969 4-4-2 W30 automatic convertible, F/SA
- Ron Garey, Chesrown Oldsmobile, Columbus/Newark, Ohio: 1969 F-85 W31 4-speed coupe, F/S
- Jim Waibel, King Oldsmobile, Lakeland, Florida: 1969 Cutlass S W31 4-speed convertible, G/S
- Willard Wright, Century Oldsmobile, Van Nuys, California: 1969 Cutlass S W31 automatic convertible, G/SA

As a sponsor of the Smothers Brothers Racing Team, Valvoline featured the whole gang (including Don Garlits and Jim Busby) in this print ad. (Photo Courtesy Valvoline)

their production models could get their doors blown off by factories that had produced a hot model for drag and street competition."

Schiefer contacted Dick to discuss promoting Oldsmobile's performance models, in a new campaign focused on the newly branded W-Machines. Smith and Williams flew to Los Angeles and, together with Schiefer, met with Dick to propose a Smothers Brothers racing team with cars representing different divisions in NHRA drag racing, all financed by Oldsmobile.

Smothers had never been involved in drag racing, but his interest was piqued. On the surface, it was a win/win, as Oldsmobile would gain from Dick's name recognition and Dick would garner even more publicity for the TV show.

A team was assembled to represent the Oldsmobile/ Smothers Brothers brands. Five racers from around the country who had caught the eye of Dale Smith (several of whom had no Oldsmobile experience) were flown to Los Angeles in September 1968 and met with Smith and Dick Smothers at the Century Plaza.

According to Pete Kost, one of the racers who signed on, "They discussed what they wanted to do, everything that was going to transpire, and the models that were going to be raced. Everyone pretty much agreed at the meeting, but Dale wanted a commitment within a few days" because he wanted them to compete in February's Winternationals at Pomona.

Smith had a meager $100,000 budget to promote Oldsmobile's racing endeavors, all in a fund earmarked for Mobil and Union Oil fuel economy events (remember, General Motors had a no-racing policy). But there was another, more clever subversion: The TV show served as a front for the team. Some of the funds that sponsor Oldsmobile gave to *The Smothers Brothers Comedy Hour* were diverted to Dick's team. "In addition to the money, I intercepted usable parts, needed by the racers, from being scrapped. This consisted of engines, transmissions, and differentials, which are all high-attrition items in racing," Smith wrote.

Dick's first appearance was at an exhibition run at the 1968 NHRA U.S. Nationals in Indianapolis with a 1968 Super Stock Cutlass S Ram-Rod 350. "Man, I was completely stoked on the car. It was really nothing like herding a Formula rig, even though it required a lot of attention to driver requirement. But it's fun, and I figured it was time to see in what small way I could help a lot of people realize where drag racing's really at."

Although all five teams waited for their respective car builds, each received three crated engines and tricked-out transmissions. In the case of Pete Kost, heavy winter weather delayed shipment of his W30 convertible, and time was running out to prepare it for Winternationals. He flew to Lansing, picked up his 4-4-2 (painted in Smothers Brothers' regalia, no less), went

Pete Kost and the **Dewey-Griffin** *1969 4-4-2 W30 were Pacific Northwest representatives of the Smothers Brothers Racing Team. (Photo ©TEN: The Enthusiast Network. All rights reserved.)*

to the Uniroyal store across the street to buy studded tires, and drove all the way back to the Pacific Northwest. Much of the trip was in sub-20-degree weather that necessitated removing the ice from the OAI under the bumper.

All racers had a phone number for Smith if they ever needed replacement parts. Kost says he was very approachable and any part needed was available to him.

Sam Murray, who ran the Berejik Oldsmobile speed shop and later worked as a mechanic for the team, related a funny story: "Jim Waibel was a Chevy guy, so when he was preparing his W31 convertible, he did not machine the crankshaft for the pilot bushing to connect with the 4-speed's input shaft (Chevrolet had 4-speed-specific cranks, while Oldsmobile machined theirs when necessary). Waibel called Smith in a panic, as the Winternationals was rapidly approaching and something wasn't jibing with his build. After learning about Oldsmobile's crankshaft, he was forced to remove the engine and transmission from the Cutlass S and pull out the crank to have it properly machined."

Problems soon crept up, not on the dragstrip but in the TV studio. The Smothers brothers were in a constant battle with CBS censors over content, language, and sensibilities and sensitivities of the status quo. CBS bosses began to demand show previews for an "affiliate review" so viewers in certain markets wouldn't be offended. After catching an offending bit similar to one that had earlier angered viewers, the bosses immediately fired the Brothers in April 1969, despite the fact that the show had already been renewed for another season.

By the end of the race season, the Smothers Brothers Racing Team was disbanded.

Oldsmobile wasn't street racing, but to get the word out, it encouraged dealers to tempt young people (and the young at heart) to purchase a 1965 4-4-2 and, among other things, take it to the track.

"Make your move now in the booming high-performance market! Start fast . . . and stay ahead with 4-4-2. Here's how:

- Use lively local merchandising
- Use local advertising
- Use local promotions
  - Enter a 4-4-2 in local sports car rallies to give it visibility
  - Invite prospects for 4-4-2 quarter-mile demonstrations
- Appoint a performance expert to start a 4-4-2 club for young enthusiasts
- Display a 4-4-2 where crowds congregate

"Here's what Olds is providing to help you rev up prospect enthusiasm!":

- Oldsmobile "Hottest Number" stickers for immediate identification
- 4-4-2 Inside Track folder with technical data that enthusiasts demand
- Performance log
- Postcards"
- 4-4-2 Club
- 4-4-2 *Hot Line* brochure

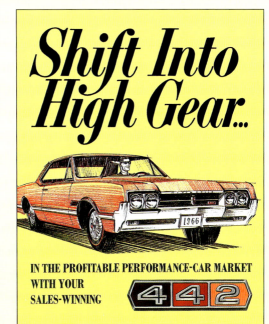

IN THE PROFITABLE PERFORMANCE-CAR MARKET WITH YOUR SALES-WINNING 442

Oldsmobile continued to provide its dealers with insight for catering to the youth market for 1966. The companion 4-4-2 Hot Line "direct mail prospect interest-rouser" included tune-up tips and info on new options. (Photo Courtesy General Motors)

By 1966, Oldsmobile marketers were aware of the rapid growth of the performance segment. Pushing dealerships to form a local Oldsmobile 4-4-2 Club was a way for them to realize the profit potential from enthusiasts and the youth market. (Photo Courtesy General Motors)

This brochure was developed to acquaint dealers with the 1965 4-4-2 and its promotion. The 4-4-2 Hot Line newsletter gave marketing ideas and demonstrated what worked for other dealers, such as the 4-4-2 Rally Drive-Away organized by 26 dealers in the Boston Zone that featured 54 4-4-2s. (Photo Courtesy General Motors)

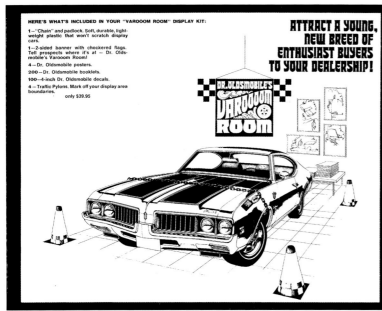

To attract "a young breed of enthusiast buyers," Oldsmobile developed the Varooom Room in 1969 to carry the Dr. Oldsmobile theme from the magazine pages to the showroom by turning a corner of the dealership into Dr. Oldsmobile's laboratory. (Photo Courtesy General Motors)

Marketing Strategy

Oldsmobile may not have been as popular as Chevrolet or have the racing equity of Chrysler, but the Lansing company competed for the same slice of the pie. Its place as a Tier 2 performance brand with Tier 1 aspirations put Oldsmobile in a distinct position that led to several unique strategies.

Varooom Room

The Varooom Room showroom display brought the Dr. Oldsmobile ad campaign to the car-buying experience. For $39.95, a dealership could opt for this kit that included:

- Plastic chain and padlock to restrain the W-Machine
- Four pylons to mark off the display
- A two-sided banner with checkered flags "to tell prospects where it's at"
- Four Dr. Oldsmobile posters
- 200 Dr. Oldsmobile booklets
- 100 4-inch Dr. Oldsmobile decals

Youngmobile Thinking

The Varooom Room's purpose was to bring performance-minded prospects ("a young, new breed of enthusiast buyers") to the showroom and get them thinking Oldsmobile (while getting others to think young things about Olds). W-Machines were promoted as the "in thing," and the Varooom Room could create excitement because "the special-performance business is becoming big business."

Dealerships were urged to make performance *their* business, especially during the spring sales push.

The Olds Pit Crew

Oldsmobile highlighted the "special performance" advertising (the Dr. Oldsmobile insert that appeared in several magazines) as a way the division supported participating Varooom Rooms. Olds promised that W-Machine orders would be given special attention to help make "this spring a going thing in your dealership's VAROOOM ROOM."

Green's For Go

This promotion included a "special green-edged car order form" to help expedite W-Machine orders because "production lines are all geared" for W-Machines to receive preference.

THE COMPLETE AUTOMOTIVE PERFORMANCE CAR "SCENE"

Oldsmobile created a document subtitled "As presented to Oldsmobile Zone Personnel, April, 1969," for zone managers to "discuss in considerable detail the complete automotive performance scene, how we fit into the performance business, to become familiar with our own performance products, and to gain perspective for this very interesting, highly emotional aspect of our industry." Because performance buyers were quite different from the average prospect, Oldsmobile drafted this overview on the state of the market and its place in it.

Performance Car Buyers

Oldsmobile described performance car buyers like this.

- They already know the similarities and differences between various performance models.
- The need for transportation was secondary to their enthusiasm for cars, which was more of an emotional experience.
- An enthusiast who talked cars could be seen as an authority. When laymen consulted one for opinions, the enthusiast became an "influence buyer."
- A manufacturer could "contrive a marketing strategy to influence the influence buyers" if an influence buyer's "word-of-mouth" opinions influenced sales.
- Influencing an influence buyer was done "through proper product execution," with product concepts starting in the street "and [taking] shape in agencies and marketing rooms" before being "passed back to the drawing board." The Plymouth Road Runner was the best example of "this new form of product planning," with the H/O being another "in a limited way."
- In a change from several years before, manufacturers released "publicity, advertising and promotional programs before engineers have finalized engineering orders to production." The GTO Judge was given as a contemporary example.
- Racing was often used by manufacturers to impress enthusiasts and achieve the desired impact. "Without such credentials," a performance car may suffer from a weaker image.

1968 Performance Car Production

This section examined how much enthusiasts influenced domestic car production for the 1968 model year. Based on sales of the 25 leading sporty/performance cars, their market penetration was 8.07 percent. Of that, the 4-4-2 represented 4.8 percent of the specialty market, which Oldsmobile felt was "respectable" considering the model's premium status.

Here's how Oldsmobile categorized the segment:

- Super Cars
- Sporty Cars
- Junior Supercars (stripped-down price-leader intermediates with a high-performance engine of slightly less displacement than supercars, such as the 1968 Plymouth Road Runner. Oldsmobile believed that junior supercars could displace supercars in the marketplace)
- Compact Street Machines
- Sports Cars
- Group II/Trans-Am

The expanded W-Machine lineup reflected a belief that there still was room for growth in the performance segment, and "fractional gains could profoundly affect the demand for our entire A-Body line; indeed, for full-size cars as well."

1969 Performance Car Availability

Oldsmobile sought to demonstrate how the different performance categories had shifted over the past year. The division admitted it could be confusing, yet a pivotal question begged to be asked: "Most automotive enthusiasts readily recognize all the makes and categories we have been discussing. With so many performance cars, what is their real significance or importance, and why should Oldsmobile be concerned with a small aspect of the industry that is so selective, so competitive, so complex?"

Answer: These cars were designed for the "influence buyer," and Oldsmobile felt the segment (as small as it was) wielded enormous influence.

The specialty market was the product of the times since these "product trend-setters" forced product planners to stay up-to-date with "various appearance items, options, accessories, and even significant product engineering improvements."

Many features originally introduced on sporty and performance cars had impact throughout the industry, including bucket seats, disc brakes, custom wheels, consoles, tachometers, sports steering wheels, vinyl tops, seat belts and shoulder harnesses, padded instrumentation, and ultra-high-compression and multiple-carbureted engines.

Lightweight vehicle components were estimated to be the next trend in car design thanks to greater use of "plastics, aluminum, and other exotic materials contributing specifically to vehicle performance."

Performance cars features also influenced industry styling, including fastbacks, stylized wheel openings, blacked-out trim, wider front ends, low-slung body silhouettes, stripes, emblems and decals, flush door handles, and spoilers.

In sum, "The impact of today's performance offerings contribute substantially to the most basic reason for the dynamics of domestic auto production, sales, industry profits, which is the frequency and appeal of model change."

Olds' Concept of the Performance Car

"Our strongest engineering objective since the introduction of the 4-4-2 back in 1964 has been to design balance into our production offering. This approach makes Oldsmobile unique in the industry." The 4-4-2's rear stabilizer bar and level of insulation, isolation, and general comfort was an example of how Oldsmobile did not sacrifice or compromise product for the sake of performance. In contrast, enthusiasts who bought cars with a "driver-passenger environment created to simulate a race car" tended to experience impressive "initial reactions." However, after several months of tolerating a truck-like ride and noise, the appeal "wears thin and the car 'grows off you' not 'on you.' As a result, owner loyalty is affected."

Oldsmobile felt the 4-4-2's "product sophistication" generally appealed "to the successful enthusiast rather than a 'teeny-bopper' Dodge Swinger 340-type of prospect."

Competitive Products

Next, Oldsmobile looked at the competition to determine the strongest and then speculated why. Within General Motors, Olds felt that the GTO was the most vulnerable because "GTO street and strip performance has generally not kept pace with the 4-4-2."

Outside General Motors, the Torino GT initially appeared to be a top competitor but the "GT is basically a 'doll' package with several engine options." Cars such as the Corvette, Road Runner, Charger, Camaro Z/28, and GTO were trend-setters "with subtle distinguishing features that set [themselves] apart *from* competition rather than *against* competition."

Oldsmobile felt the 4-4-2 was in an exclusive class thanks to its "unique suspension (with rear stabilizer bar), passenger-car comfort, and sophistication."

W-Machines for Car Lovers

So what did Oldsmobile have for hard-core enthusiasts? Oldsmobile offered testimony from *Car and Driver*, which fell in love with the Cutlass S W31: "Lansing has managed to build a car America has been waiting for."

Street recognition was very important for enthusiasts, which was why front fender identification and (in the case of W30 and W31) prominent stripes on the hood were introduced for 1969 W-Machines. Although W-Machines generally shared continuity in their appearance, their respective purposes were different: W31 was the Junior Supercar for the street/strip, W32 was the high-performance street automatic supercar, and W30 was the Banzai supercar for strip competition.

Personalizing the W-Machine

Oldsmobile was cognizant that enthusiasts were interested in personalizing their cars with custom steering wheels, consoles, and mag wheels with white-letter tires, "particularly if they are going to be used as street machines." For the W31, Oldsmobile felt that enthusiasts should be advised of the FE-2 suspension package, and they also "will nearly always want a tachometer" and tinted glass (the latter for appearance).

Oldsmobile also recognized that, "among young enthusiasts, a trend has been developing for performance appearance packages aside from powertrain considerations as evidenced by Torino GT sales." A basic Cutlass S could receive a "doll package" by ordering it with hood stripes, Super Stock mags, and Wide Oval tires.

Servicing the W-Machine

"What becomes of our so-called influence buyer after the sale? When properly handled, the enthusiast becomes a walking-talking ad man, promoter, merchandiser, and even salesman for the product, dealer, and his service operations. [And] when mishandled or overlooked, he becomes all these things in reverse." Hence, Oldsmobile determined the most important consideration for the enthusiast was pre-delivery.

An enthusiast was much more inclined to take pride in ownership than the general automotive consumer, so he or she also required more attention and consideration from the dealership. Enthusiasts understood that their cars required more maintenance to perform at their peak. If a W-Machine was ordered and "proper get-ready was not performed," a customer "may instantly lose respect for a dealer's capability and never come back."

Verbally informing new customers about the factory warranty was an important part of customer relations, especially because drag racing would invalidate the warranty. "He must know, in no uncertain terms, that if he so much as adds a spacer plate between the manifold and carburetor it will void his warranty. This merely sets the record straight, and an enthusiast will appreciate where he stands if he is told sympathetically 'Telling it like it is' with respect to warranty will normally not deter a decision to go racing, but it will eliminate entirely customer relations problems."

Making the W30/W31/W32 Run

Oldsmobile produced a special product information release detailing super-tuning information, blueprinting and balancing engines, suspension modifications, and complete specifications and parts numbers for full or partial aftermarket conversions.

But because performance cars and options constituted less than 10 percent of Oldsmobile's business, some questioned how important it was to cater to this segment.

Perspective

Oldsmobile recognized that, despite its small market segment penetration, consumers who bought performance cars were influential to both the market and manufacturers. Although many performance cars were highly impractical or even unattainable for most consumers, they had a glamorous appeal. "We know the average customer who is attracted to the showroom by performance offerings really wants something else, but he is in the showroom. And once he is there, he becomes very practical and will probably buy conventional transportation out of stock rather than order a performance machine. "The low-volume performance car demands a disproportionate amount of exposure and recognition."

For this reason, Oldsmobile asked its representatives "to participate in this aspect of our business, to involve yourselves in the development of this specialty market, to get to know our performance products through first-hand experience, to drive them and have fun with them, to demonstrate them to your dealers and talk about their rub-off value, to educate yourselves and your dealers regarding this aspect of our business, to become proficient and sophisticated with respect to marketing these products as we are with other aspects of our business."

The upcoming "Dr. Oldsmobile's Va Rooom Room" kit was mentioned as an "imaginative merchandising approach [that] will act as a calling card to car buffs" and make them feel at home in the showroom.

Advertising Program

Although the first to respond to the GTO, Oldsmobile never garnered a strong, youthful image compared to Pontiac and Chevrolet.

Innovative Ads

For 1968, Oldsmobile catered to the young-at-heart while de-emphasizing the "old" in Oldsmobile through its Youngmobile campaign: "Young in the way they look. Young in the way they feel. Young in the way they move." Oldsmobile's general manager Harold Metzel reit-erated the company's position in the August 26, 1968, *Automotive News*: "The youth market is almost bound to grow, and young people have a lot of influence on their elders. That helped our Eighty-Eight and Ninety-Eight along," adding that the Toronado had generated a lot of youth interest that often led to sales of other cars.

One of those youths was a University of Wisconsin student named Marc D. Kaufman. He didn't like the ads he saw in college newspapers, so he formed a company and a team to reach his peers, then scored Oldsmobile as a client. "We know how to reach ourselves. You cannot expect a man of 30 or 40 years of age to reach a market that changes spontaneously, and thinks and operates on its own wave lengths," Kaufman related to the January 25, 1969, *Oshkosh Daily Northwestern*.

With Oldsmobile's agency of record, D.P. Brother & Co., serving as counsel, Kaufman Associates produced 4-4-2 and Cutlass S ads that ran in 140 college newspapers plus supporting ads in college communities. "People don't associate the Olds as a college kid's car. We had to orient it to the college market."

A University of Wisconsin student felt he could do a better job reaching the youth market and hooked up with Oldsmobile's D.P. Brother & Co. to produce ads that ran in 140 college newspapers. (Photos Courtesy General Motors)

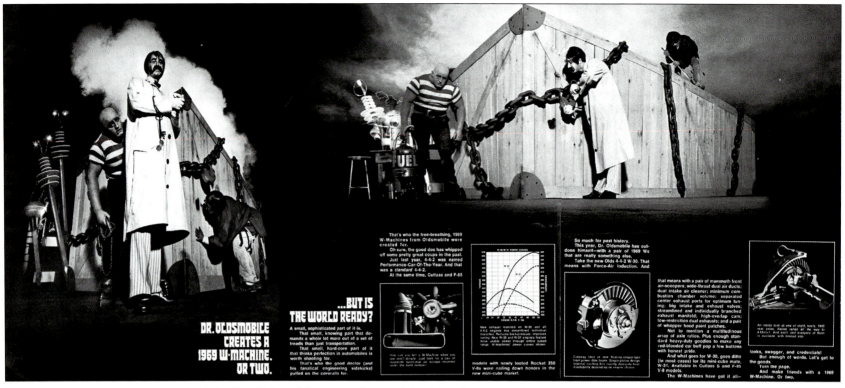

This multi-page brochure launched the Dr. Oldsmobile campaign and the branding of W-Machines. The mad scientist's henchmen were Elephant Engine Ernie, Shifty Sidney, Wind Tunnel Waldo, and Esses Fernhill. (Photo Courtesy General Motors)

Dr. Oldsmobile

During that time, D. P. Brother introduced the Dr. Oldsmobile campaign featuring the "fanatical engineering genius" of Dr. Oldsmobile and his Performance Committee. Their W-Machine creations made their first appearance in December 1968 in an eight-page insert in *Hot Rod, Motor Trend*, and other periodicals. The 4-4-2 W30 and Cutlass S W31 were shown, plus equipment to make the W-Machines hot and hotter, such as a selection of eight beefy axles with ratios up to 4.66:1.

Throughout the model year, the campaign featured other W-Machines including the introduction of the 4-4-2 W32, touted as "The W-Machine a mother could learn to love." All used a tagline "Make your escape from the ordinary" borne from the Youngmobile Thinking 1969 campaign.

The good doctor and his crew continued to be active in 1970, and represented all of Oldsmobile's performance models. Dr. Oldsmobile continued into the 1971 model year, but the campaign was put to rest by the end of 1970 when Oldsmobile lost interest in promoting performance.

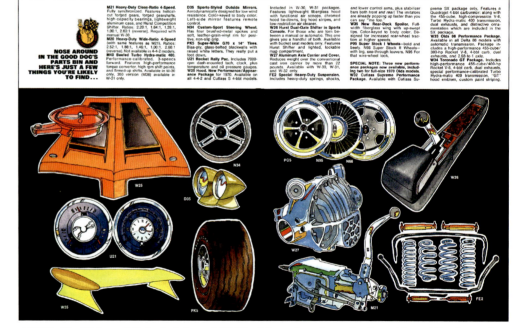

1970's Dr. Oldsmobile's 4-4-2 and W-Machines brochure featured less kitsch, and the Doctor represented all of Oldsmobile's performance cars. The W27 aluminum axle carrier/cover was a unique option. (Photo Courtesy General Motors)

CHAPTER 6

FORD FIGHTS BACK

At the start of the 1950s, Ford was the hot rodder's best friend. The flathead V-8 was plentiful, cheap, and proven. In contrast, Chevrolet and Plymouth (two of the "Low-Priced Three") never had an eight-cylinder engine to compete with the Blue Oval since the flathead was introduced in 1932.

But the advent of the small-block Chevy in 1955 was such a revelation to enthusiasts that the flathead's replacement, the 1954 Y-block, never really stood a chance. Ford didn't really turn up the heat until the 1957 312 (the E-code with dual-quads and the supercharged F-code with 4-barrel). That improvement continued into 1958 with the new FE series, the baddest 352 with 300 hp, but subsequent 1959 models didn't improve from there.

Beginning in 1960, Ford began a performance effort that was not compromised until government regulations squeezed compression and power from it more than a decade later.

Ford Finally Makes a Move

The 360-hp High Performance 352 was (on paper) the most powerful American high-performance car next to the Chrysler 300-F. However, the only transmission available with this solid-lifter engine was a column-shifted 3-speed manual, which was hardly the best way to compete against 4-speed Chevrolets and Pontiacs and TorqueFlite-equipped Mopars. Ford bored and stroked the FE to 390 ci in 1961, available with 375 or 401 horses, the latter with three 2-barrel carbs. A BorgWarner 4-speed manual, delivered in the trunk for dealer installation, became available later in the year.

The solid-lifter 390s continued into 1962 but were eventually joined by a 406. It was available with the same induction choices but rated at 385 and 405 hp, and the optional 4-speed was factory-installed. The 406 carried over into 1963 until it was replaced midyear by the new Thunderbird 427, available in both High-Performance 410-horse and Super High Performance 425-horse guises (the latter with twin 4-barrels). Ford introduced these engines at the same time as the new Galaxie Sports Hardtop that featured a slicker roofline than the Thunderbird-inspired one that had been introduced for 1962.

Midyear 1963 also marked the introduction of the solid-lifter Challenger High Performance 289, which ads claimed had "a violent urge to

The 1970 Performance Buyer's Digest *showed Ford entering the decade with new style and verve. Despite new pony cars from Chrysler and General Motors, Ford held its own with the successful Mach I. (Photo Courtesy Ford Motor Company)*

The slick roof of the 1960 Galaxie Starliner was the perfect comple-ment for the 360-hp 352, which would have given Ford the upper hand in the horsepower sweepstakes if not for its clumsy column-shifted 3-speed. (Tom Shaw Photo)

The solid-lifter 390 carried over into 1962, eventually joined by a 406 with up to 405 hp. In January 1963, the 406 (shown) was replaced by the 427. (Tom Shaw Photo)

In some respects, the 1963 Fairlane with the 271-hp 289 was the first midsize muscle car. The high-winding small-block was available only with a manual transmission but was saddled with a single exhaust. (Tom Shaw Photo)

For Ford's Winner's Streak Hardtop Sale, dealerships could opt for a Total Per-formance kit to dress up a 1964 Galaxie to resem-ble vehicles victorious at Riverside, Daytona, and elsewhere. (Photo Courtesy Ford Motor Company)

Ford's 1964 427 Galaxie drag car featured a high-rise intake shrouded by a fiberglass teardrop hood. Bob Spears raced this one in AA/S. (Photo ©TEN: The Enthusiast Network. All rights reserved.)

show up larger powerplants." This 271-hp small-block was available only for the midsize Fairlane. Both the High Performance 289 and 427 marked the beginning of Ford's Total Performance era, an organized global assault on racing around the world.

Every 1964 Ford model, including the lowly Falcon, Fairlane, and full-size cars, had a sporty version available, but only the latter two were available with true high-performance engines. They were joined midyear by the Mustang, which eventually had the High Performance 289 available as an option.

Ford's NASCAR and drag racing exploits were at the forefront of Ford's Total Performance efforts. Several dedicated drag cars were built in 1964, perhaps the most famous being the Fairlane 500-based Thunderbolt. Detroit Steel Tubing was commissioned to handle the high-rise 427, so the

Total Performance was a world-wide onslaught in just about every form of automotive racing. This 1964 advertisement suggested that Total Performance was a laboratory to develop great cars. (Photo Courtesy Ford Motor Company)

Ford felt there was a bit of Ford GT in the 1965 Mustang GT, including a stripe that was Ford's "badge of America's greatest total performance cars!" (Photo Courtesy Ford Motor Company)

Ford described the 1964 Fairlane Thunderbolt as "uncorking answers on high-performance transmissions, acceleration, weigh transfer and traction." This Thunderbolt was sold new at Ed Martin Ford in Indianapolis and campaigned as White Tornado. (Tom Shaw Photo)

The full-size 1965 Custom 500 with the 427 was perhaps Ford's best contender against the GTO, as Ford still had no direct response to the Pontiac. Note the NASCAR-inspired headlight covers. (Tom Shaw Photo)

front suspension components were modified and relocated to accommodate the 425-hp engine. A teardrop hood helped clear the intake and allowed the engine compartment to breathe, while two tubes mounted from the inboard headlights to the intake helped the 427 breathe. To keep weight down, several fiberglass and Plexiglas body components were used. With Gas Rhonda at the wheel, Ford won the 1964 NHRA championship.

By 1965, America was Mustang-crazy. With more than a half-million built in 18 months, there was no bigger success story in Detroit, but a High Performance 289 Mustang (or the same engine in the Fairlane or Falcon, the latter Canada-only) simply wasn't competitive with the GTO. Hence, the brunt of Ford's high-performance lineup continued to fall upon the full-size cars. They had been redesigned with handsome knife-edged styling complemented by vertical headlights. These big flyers continued their NASCAR success but they were rarely seen on the street or the strip. Production of 427s fell severely from a couple thousand to a couple hundred.

How to Cook a Tiger

Finally in 1966, Ford came out with a "proper" muscle car. The Fairlane was completely redesigned, moving up a slight notch in size so it could handle a big-block. The Fairlane GT came decked out in high-line XL trim and included a chrome-trimmed 335-hp Thunderbird Special 390, racing stripes, simulated hood intakes, buckets, and console. Opt for the 3-speed automatic and the GT turned into the GT/A, which included a console-shifted Cruise-O-Matic that allowed the driver to hold a gear manually. The Fairlane GT was a snazzy effort, but the 390 was not up to the task of beating GTOs despite advertising to the contrary.

Later in 1966, Ford built 57 Fairlane 500 hard-

Ford didn't fall short with the 1966 427 Fairlane 500, but all 57 were built for the NHRA with little regard for the street. All were white with a fiberglass hood feeding air to the 427. (Stephanie Davies Photo)

HOW TO COOK A TIGER

On the hunt for "Tigers," Ford touted the 1966 Fairlane GT as just the recipe for muffling the GTO's roar. But the truth was that Ford had trouble discerning between racing and performance, and the 390 simply was not enough. (Photo Courtesy Ford Motor Company)

tops for NHRA homologation. All were white with the 425-hp 427, fiberglass hood with air induction, 4-speed, and not much else. However, due to their rarity on the street, they failed to establish Ford as a serious competitor in a market that now included Chrysler's 426 Hemi. Full-size 427 Fords were slightly more numerous, but the market had moved toward midsize cars, and the new 345-horse 428 was not for the performance crowd.

Considering that the 1966 Fairlane GT acceleration received lukewarm reviews, it was odd that Ford downgraded the 390's horsepower to 320 *and* made the engine optional for 1967. The 427 returned for pedestrian Fairlanes, including a 410-horse 4-barrel variant, but the 230 built made little impact on the street.

Both 427s were available for full-size Fords as well, which were redesigned with rounder styling and, for coupes, a sleeker semi-fastback roofline. However, the single-traction rear axle, weight, and rarity (only 89 built) made even less impact than the Fairlane. The Galaxie 500/XL with the 7-Litre package was as sporty as it got, but the 428/345 still wasn't pure muscle.

Ford Falters on the Street

And the Mustang? It was redesigned for 1967, with *Hot Rod* stating in March, "When Ford decided to change the Mustang, everybody held their breath. But it's okay people, everythin's gonna be all right."

The Mustang was heavier, but it now was capable of holding the 390 between its shock towers. The 390 should have been a fine way to move the Mustang up the ranks in the high-performance market, but road testers found the 390 Mustang a "stone." The High Performance 289 was still available, but only 489 were built (compared to almost 30,000 390s), suggesting that America was more interested in cheap, easy horsepower and torque rather than an expensive, high-strung solid-lifter engine.

If 1967 proved to be exciting yet disappointing for Ford fans, 1968 was a year to rejoice. The facelifted full-size Fords, now featuring horizontal headlights, relied on the 340-hp 428 as the top offering, something that paled in comparison to Chevrolet's Impala SS 427. The 7-Litre package was replaced by the new GT Equipment Group, which featured a 390, Wide-Oval tires, heavy-duty suspension, low-restriction exhausts, full-length GT, and simulated mag-style wheel covers, among other items.

The Fairlane was redesigned for 1968; the GT moved to the new, upscale Torino series. The Torino GT was available as a hardtop, convertible, and all-new fastback. As before, the GT was more sporty than sport, with standard 289, Wide-Oval tires, styled steel wheels, and GT stripes.

A Ranchero GT also joined the roster. The top engine was a 390-hp 427 with a hydraulic cam and available only with an automatic, but Ford never installed one. That left the 325-horse 390 as the best Ford could offer.

Indeed, Ford continued to face the same problem: its street cars were not competitive in an arena with several 400-plus-hp monsters. This was reflected in sales compared to the GTO and SS 396. Ford certainly was dotting its Is and crossing its Ts in all forms of racing, but on the street it was a different story. That is, until April 1968 when the 428 Cobra Jet was introduced.

Cobra Jet: Ford's Saving Grace

The Cobra Jet had its origins with Tasca Ford. The CJ initially was the successor to the advertised-but-unreleased 427. The March 1968 *Hot Rod* featured a test of a Cobra Jet Mustang with editor Eric Dahlquist proclaiming, "The CJ will be the utter delight of every Ford lover and the bane of all the rest because, quite frankly, it is probably the fastest regular production sedan ever built." He proceeded to rip 13.56 at 106.64 mph, "the fastest-running Pure Stock in the history of man." That Mustang was among the first 50 CJs built, all Wimbledon White Model 63A fastbacks with 4-speed, 3.89 rear gears, F70-14 Wide Ovals, hood scoop with Ram Air, and little else.

All were built on December 27, 1967, just in time for the 1968 NHRA Winternationals. Of the 50 built, 20 were "trick" without seam sealer or sound deadener.

The redesigned 1967 Mustang was able to handle the big-block 390. Alas, the Camaro's solid-lifter 396 made mincemeat out of the Mustang. (Richard Truesdell Photo)

The redesigned 1968 Fairlane featured a new sporty model called Torino GT. Few cars looked faster than the fastback but, thanks to empty 427 promises, the 390 continued to be a weak link until the 428 Cobra Jet appeared in April. (Photo ©TEN: The Enthusiast Network. All rights reserved.)

Like the Torino, the Mustang advertised a 427 that never manifested itself. Thanks to the efforts of Rhode Island's Tasca Ford and Hot Rod *magazine, Ford got the hint and introduced the 428 Cobra Jet, leveling the playing field. (Photo ©TEN: The Enthusiast Network. All rights reserved.)*

On January 28, 1968, Hubert Platt introduced the 428 Cobra Jet to the racing world at the AHRA Winter Nationals at Lions Drag Strip. Several days later, six CJ Mustangs showed up at the NHRA Winternationals in Pomona, all prepared by Holman-Moody-Stroppe for C/SA, SS/E, and SS/EA classes. Four made it to their respective class finals, with Al Joniec winning both his class and Super Stock Eliminator.

For the rest of America, the Cobra Jet Mustang made its debut on April 1, 1968. Regular-production CJs were available in all three body styles, required the GT package, and included a functional fiberglass hood scoop with black stripe. The same engine was available for the Fairlane/Torino, but it was available only with an automatic and didn't have air induction.

Unlike the stillborn 427, however, both models were readily available with the CJ. Ford's reputation on the street changed completely. Plus, the CJ was the perfect showcase for the Torino GT convertible that paced the 1968 Indy 500.

With newfound vigor, Ford began 1969 on a now-even playing field. The Torino GT continued to be Ford's midsize sporty car, although buyers were still required to spec out the right equipment for high performance. Air induction was now available with the Cobra Jet, plus a new Drag Pack (3.91 or 4.30 gears, external oil cooler, and heavy-duty engine upgrades) turned the Cobra Jet into a Super Cobra Jet. For more modest performance aspirations, a new 290-hp 351 Windsor was the first performance option for the Torino GT, followed by the stalwart 390 (now with 320 horses).

Ford Hits Back Some More

The success of the 1968 Plymouth Road Runner meant that Ford *needed* a response. This time, Ford was quick to the draw and countered with the Cobra (sometimes referred to as the "Fairlane Cobra"). As Ford's new midsize image car, the Cobra was more austere than the Torino GT and was available ony as a SportsRoof (Ford Marketing's name for fastback) or

coupe. The 428 Cobra Jet was standard, giving the Cobra a distinct advantage over the base 383 Road Runner.

The Cobra was also the basis for the Torino Talladega, Ford's NASCAR homologation special and a direct response to the Dodge Charger 500. All 750 built were Cobra SportsRoofs with the 428 CJ, oil cooler, automatic, and aerodynamic modifications to the nose, front fenders, and rocker panels.

The Cobra Jet wasn't available in the redesigned big Fords; they received the new 385-series big-block. At 429 ci, the torquey 360-hp Thunder Jet was most at home in the sporty Galaxie 500 and XL SportsRoof. For a sportier flavor and more flash, the XL's GT package included the standard 390, mag-like wheel covers, suspension upgrades, and stripes, among other items.

The Mustang Matures

The redesigned Mustang was bigger, lower, and wider yet didn't suffer from its new-found maturity. A luxurious Grandé joined the hardtop but, for performance fans, the new Mach I SportsRoof was one of Ford's "better ideas."

Par for Ford, the Mach I's standard 2-barrel 351 Windsor wasn't on enthusiasts' radar, but the 4-barrel upgrade, 390, and 428 Cobra Jet did the

The redesigned 1969 Mustang featured a new image version called Mach I. Standard for the striped SportsRoof was a mild 351 2-barrel, but the Cobra Jet made it one of the most popular cars on the street scene. (Tom Shaw Photo)

The Cobra was Ford's answer to the Plymouth Road Runner but featured a trump card: 428 Cobra Jet. The 428 was much stronger than the 383, and the Cobra was available as a super-sleek SportsRoof fastback. Only 14,885 Cobras were built, not enough competition against more than 80,000 Road Runners. (Photo ©TEN: The Enthusiast Network. All rights reserved.)

After two years with the Camaro Z/28 in the spotlight, Ford introduced the 1969 Mustang Boss 302. Special black-out trim, distinctive side stripes, filled-in side scoops, functional front spoiler, and fat tires mounted on Magnum 500s were some of its unique features. (Richard Truesdell Photo)

The 1970 Torino Cobra was trimmed like the low-line Fairlane 500, so neat Torino GT options such as hidden headlights, stripes, and full-width taillights were absent. Not missing was a high-spec standard engine: the 360-hp 429 Thunder Jet. (Lee Lundberg Photo)

job. A new Ram Air option called "Shaker" was attached to the air cleaner and poked through a hole in the hood. Like the Fairlane/Torino, the Drag Pack was available for the CJ. With more than 72,000 built, the Mach I was a rousing success.

The GT package continued, available for all three body styles. The Mustang GT shared much of the same equipment with the Mach I, other than the GT stripe along the rockers. However, with 6,694 built, the Mustang GT couldn't match the popularity of the Mach I and was discontinued after 1969.

Two special Mustang models were built for homologation purposes: Boss 302 and 429. For the SCCA Trans-Am series, the Boss 302 featured a reengineered 302 with special heads without gaskets, solid-lifter cam, aluminum intake, big Holley carb, and mandatory 4-speed, among other equipment. Rated at 290 hp, the Boss 302 was a direct shot at Chevrolet's successful Camaro Z/28.

The Boss 429 took the opposite approach. Completely unadorned except for small "BOSS 429" decals on the front fenders, it had presence like no other Mustang. The 375-hp 429 featured semi-hemi aluminum heads, forged steel crank, trunk-mounted battery, heavy-duty front and rear springs, front spoiler, huge hood scoop, mandatory 4-speed, F60 x 15s mounted on Magnum 500s, and more. Kar Kraft was contracted to make the big 429 fit, resulting in 849 builds. All that effort was to make the Boss 429 engine legal for NASCAR.

1970 Rolls On

Ford redesigned its midsize Fairlane/Torino series and introduced a new small-block for 1970. The Torino GT was now available only as a SportsRoof or convertible. Rear-fender louvers with GT badges could be

complemented with Laser stripes; hidden headlights were another new appearance option. The standard hood with non-function scoop could be replaced by the newly available Shaker. Out back, full-width honeycomb taillights distinguished the Torino GT from other Fairlane/Torinos.

Available engines weren't interesting until the 351 Cleveland 4-barrel, a new design with big-valve heads and 300 hp. Next up were several 429s replacing the 428: 360-horse Thunder Jet and 370-horse Cobra Jet (with the Drag Pack adding five horses); the Boss 429 was advertised but never released.

The Ranchero GT also received a similar performance treatment.

The Cobra evolved into the Torino Cobra for 1970, now available only as a SportsRoof. Featuring a standard 429 Thunder Jet and blacked-out hood, the only engine upgrade was the 429 Cobra Jet with Ram Air and the Drag Pack as options. However, intrepid racers ordered the CJ for the 1970½ Falcon two-door sedan, a low-line model introduced for the mid-year spring sales push.

Full-size Fords continued to lose their performance luster; the XL's GT package and 4-speed were relegated to history. However, a buyer could specify enough sporty options to fake it quite well, including the 429/360 and new Dualtone blackout paint.

The 1970 Mustang received a facelift that eliminated the outboard headlights and the SportsRoof's rear fender scoops. The Mach I lost its side stripes but gained a hood stripe in black or white, grille lamps, and distinctive rocker trim for a tougher look. With the optional 351/300, it indeed was tougher than the previous year's Windsor. Both the 428 Cobra Jet and Drag Pack returned; a Detroit Locker rear was included with 4.30-geared Drag Pack cars after December 1969.

A more refined Boss 302 returned for 1970, featuring new stripes, colors, and an available Shaker hood scoop. The Boss 429 came back, although

The Boss 429 Mustang was introduced in 1969 to homologate the engine for the NASCAR-spec Talladega. It returned for 1970, remaining the antithesis of the Boss 302 thanks to understated identification. (Richard Truesdell Photo)

Ford's Z/28-fighter continued into 1970 with revised striping and new options, including a Shaker scoop. Unlike the Camaro, the Boss 302 remained true to its purpose and featured a solid-lifter small-block under 5.0 liters. (Richard Truesdell Photo)

The 1971 Torino GT featured a revised grille, new rocker trim, and a shuffled engine lineup. The Shaker was available with the 351 and 429 CJ, but the Drag Pack was gone. (Lee Lundberg Photo)

The redesigned 1971 Mustang looked nothing like its predecessors. The Mach I remained the core performance model, but its standard engine was downgraded to a 302. The Drag Pack was available for the 429 Cobra Jet, but the Boss 351 was arguably faster.

its changes were more subtle, including a black hood scoop and a new palette of colors.

Holding On by Holding Out

Unlike General Motors, Ford continued to produce high-compression engines for 1971, but it was clear that high performance was being deemphasized.

The Torino and Ranchero GT featured a new grille, restyled Laser stripes, and new rocker panels with GT identification. The 429/360 and the Drag Pack were gone, and the 351 4-barrel fell 15 hp to 285, thanks to a slight compression drop. The Torino Cobra lost its standard big-block and relied on the 351/285 with the 429 Cobra Jet optional; the Shaker was optional

for both. Reshuffled trim included a blacked-out tail panel, restyled hood blackout, and Laser stripes.

A redesigned Mustang for 1971 grew in size and weight, but the engine bay now had room for the 429 Cobra Jet to replace the 428 CJ. All three body styles were still available. The Mach I continued to carry the performance torch, somewhat, as the standard Mach I engine was now a 302 with a flat hood. Engine upgrades included a hood featuring NACA scoops that could be made functional. The 351 4-barrel was the first true step toward performance (which was quietly joined midyear by a regular-gas 351 Cobra Jet with 280 hp), with the 429 CJ at the top. Unlike the Torino, 429 CJ-equipped Mustangs were available with the Drag Pack, which included 3.91 or 4.11 gears.

A new Boss replaced the 1969–1970 302 and 429: Boss 351. This new Boss arguably exploited the redesigned Mustang best, thanks to a 330-hp 351, Ram Air, 4-speed, front spoiler, Competition Suspension with

The 1972 Gran Torino Sport was Ford's new midsize performance car, but performance was almost dead in Dearborn. Incredibly, the 429 was less powerful than the 351 CJ. An air induction system was offered but was soon discontinued. (Photo ©TEN: The Enthusiast Network. All rights reserved.)

Tasca Ford was the second-largest Ford dealership in the United States. The combination of Bob Tasca's early embrace of drag racing, his vision, and his ability to surround himself with expert technicians had enormous influence in Dearborn. (Photo Courtesy Tasca Ford)

staggered rear shocks, High Back buckets, F60-15 tires, and more. It was the whole shebang at a time when the bang was beginning to wheeze.

351 HO: Ford's Last Stand

Ford was, perhaps, the weakest of the Big Three when it came to high performance in 1972. The Torino was completely restyled; the Gran Torino Sport (GTS) replaced the Torino GT and Torino Cobra.

The GTS carried on the Torino GT's style but without the strong engine offerings. The 248-hp 351 Cobra Jet was as good as it got, but the 429 4-barrel had 40 *fewer* horses. The Mustang's CJ was rated higher at 266 horses, and a 275-horse 351 HO was introduced. A spiritual successor to the Boss 351, the HO required 3.91 gears and a 4-speed and, unlike the Boss, the HO was available for any Mustang body style.

The Mustang and GTS continued for one more year with the 351 CJ, but the glory days were gone. After that, poseurs like the Mustang II carried Ford through the 1970s until Fox-bodied Mustangs revived the 5.0 and led a new breed of performance cars.

Dealerships

No other Ford dealership demonstrated the credo "Win on Sunday, Sell on Monday" better than Tasca. The East Providence, Rhode Island, dealership got into drag racing in late 1961 when Bob Tasca and one of his mechanics were chatting with a local whose 406/405 Galaxie was struggling against Brand X competitors.

Tasca Ford commissioned Detroit's Alexander Brothers to build a 427-powered Candy Apple 1964 Thunderbird featuring contemporary Cibie headlights. The brothers also built Tasca a Kelly Green 1966 Fairlane GT/A. (Photo Courtesy Tasca Ford)

As recounted in Bob McClurg's *The Tasca Ford Legacy*, Mr. Tasca asked what was needed to make the Galaxie competitive, and then proceeded to supply a new set of tires, high-performance engine parts, and sponsorship. Tasca eventually wanted to convert the Galaxie into a dedicated race car, but the owner wanted to keep it as his daily driver. In response, Tasca ran a 406-powered 1962 Galaxie Club Sedan of his own. "Teenagers have brought

After campaigning a 427 SOHC A/FX Mustang in Experimental Stock, Tasca commissioned Holman-Moody to build a Mustang match racer for the Unlimited class. *Mystery 9* ran 9.82 ETs on gasoline and later served as the template for Ford's own 1966 match racers. (Photo Courtesy Tasca Ford)

Tasca may have created the prototypical Cobra Jet, but Ford created the 428-powered Mustang that Hubert Platt drove in the 1968 Winternationals. Tasca driver Bill Lawton piloted this one. (Photo Courtesy Tasca Ford)

in their parents to the tune of 41 sales in our first six weeks in racing," he said in the May/June 1962 *Ford Crest News*.

Tasca soon scored one of 11 1962 Super Stock lightweights, naming it *Orbiter-1*. The Galaxie was refactored to A/FX, but the experience helped the dealership develop *Challenger II*, a 1962 Fairlane stuffed with a 406, courtesy of Detroit Steel Tubing.

Tasca Ford was a key player in promoting Total Performance seminars, complete with a huge hauler that converted to a stage displaying the latest in Ford and Autolite high-performance parts. The seminars also included a traveling machine shop featuring a workbench, grinder, and more. Throughout 1969, Tasca ran seminars in 23 sales districts, including an All-Ford Dealership Drag Race at Capitol Raceway where area dealerships were encouraged to bring their demonstrators and race each other.

Tasca Ford's place in muscle car history has been enshrined thanks to ingenuity that Ford failed to use. Tasca was all too familiar with the 390's lackluster performance, even with a supertune. Tasca Performance Manager Dean Gregson told *Hot Rod* in November 1967, "We found the [390 Mustang] so non-competitive for the supercar field, in a sense we began to feel we were cheating the customer. He was paying for what he saw advertised in all the magazines as a fast car, but that's not what he was getting. The 1968 looked like more of the 1967's poor performance, but worse because the cars were heavier."

Hot Rod editor Eric Dahlquist did not disagree. "When we went to Ford for various briefings or previews, usually the subject of Ford's lack of street muscle came up. Invariably, someone from Ford responded by saying they had plenty of good pieces [from the parts department]; they

just weren't packaged in an appropriate car. By far, the greatest percentage of potential muscle car buyers were looking to buy, not build, their own cars."

Gregson continued, "We had to do something about it. We began to offer the customer little packages of stock pieces to make his machine like it was supposed to be." The impetus was a 1967 Mustang GT/A demonstrator with a 390 that had accidentally exploded, so a 428 Police Interceptor short-block was installed. Tasca mechanic Bill Gilbert suggested using 1964 427 medium-riser heads; a medium-riser aluminum intake with a pair of 735-cfm Holleys (later replaced by Holley 780s) were also thrown in, and a special-grind cam.

After suspension and transmission tweaks, the GT/A was rechristened KR-8 (King of the Road-428). Added Gilbert, "If you put your foot to it, and once it passes 7,000 rpm, you say, 'Whoa, what have we got here?' We took an absolute dud, and made it into an absolute winner.'"

At the behest of several Ford engineers, Dahlquist visited Tasca to "see what one dealer was doing to market and sell high performance the way it should be done." The timing couldn't have been any better: after a day of driving the KR-8 and running 13.39 ETs on street tires, Dahlquist remarked, "It was fast; faster than any GTO, Chevelle, or GTX and was totally tractable to boot.

"Bob [Tasca] laid out how all the KR-8 performance modifications were over-the-parts-counter pieces. It was the same mantra that the Ford engineers had been singing for many years. The KR-8 seemed a no-brainer for the factory to do itself. They just had to push the right button."

He returned to California and wrote up the story for the November

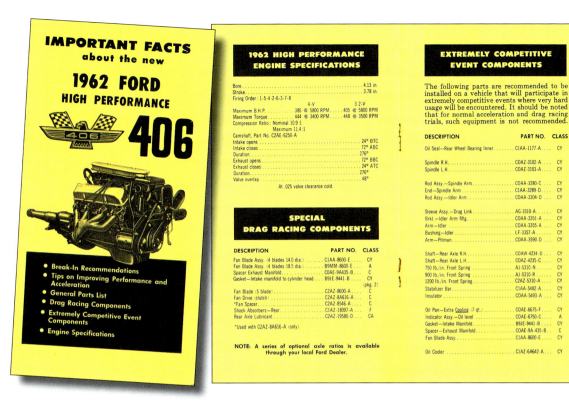

Far Left: *The 406, introduced in November 1961, marked the first of Ford's true Super Stock warriors as the Total Performance program began to take hold. (Photo Courtesy Ford Motor Company)* **Left:** *Right out of the box, Ford offered 406 buyers components for "extremely competitive events where very hard usage will be encountered." (Photo Courtesy Ford Motor Company)*

Get a Corner on Performance

Ford primed its dealers for 1969 with a brochure to show them how to garner attention and profit by establishing themselves as performance headquarters. "A good way to build traffic is to set up a special Performance Corner in your dealership featuring a hot Mach I or Cobra and kick it off with a second introduction," along with a designated performance specialist.

A national advertising campaign supported the Performance Corner. Its announcement was spearheaded by TV commercials appearing during *The FBI* (with 22 million potential viewers) and on NFL telecasts (20 million per game). Follow-up ads later appeared on *Laugh-In* and the 1969 Summer Olympics. Total impressions were projected at 488 million.

issue, which included a poll urging readers to circle yes or no and send it to Henry Ford II.

Ford got the message: On December 26, 1967, Ford Racing director Jacque Passino sent a telegram to Ford regional and district sales managers announcing the availability of the 428 Cobra Jet Mustang for ordering.

Marketing Strategy

Ford may have had trouble translating its racing success to success on the street, but that was not for lack of trying. Ford's marketing department put a lot of energy into producing material for consumer and sales organizations.

Important Facts about the 406

With the introduction of the 406 during the dawn of Super Stock racing, Ford produced a brochure filled with information and support for more performance-inclined 406 owners: break-in recommendations, tips on improving performance and acceleration, general parts list, engine specifications, special drag racing components such as rear shock absorbers, spacer exhaust manifold, gaskets, rear axle ratios, and a number of fan assembly items. It also discussed extremely competitive event components, not recommended for "normal acceleration and drag racing trials;" the equipment ran the gamut from spindles, rear axle shafts, and an extra-cooling oil pan.

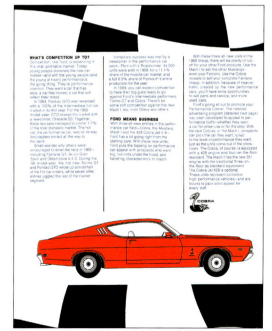

Ford acknowledged the competition and how performance cars had escalated in popularity, so "in 1969, you can expect competition to have their big guns ready to go against Ford's intermediate performers, Torino GT and Cobra." (Photo Courtesy Ford Motor Company)

Ford Performance Handbook

After the introduction of the 406, *Hot Rod* published the *Ford Performance Handbook* in conjunction with Ford. Edited by Ray Brock, this special issue was a book of information for Ford enthusiasts.

At the front, Brock explained: "Several top automotive technical experts were called upon to assist in the writing of this book. We sincerely hope that the following pages will give the information you need to get the most enjoyment from your Ford automobile. Tips on tune-ups, economy

Ford Times was a monthly Reader's Digest-*style publication that also featured promotional articles on Ford products. This one urged readers to "take a look at your Ford dealer's Performance Corner." (Photo Courtesy Ford Motor Company)*

Want To Add Muscle To Your Ford?

Take a look at your Ford dealer's performance corner

Ford dealers across the land are making their showrooms headquarters for performance-minded drivers throughout this year.

This is understandable when you consider the impressive Ford championships earned in rough NASCAR, USAC, and ARCA competition during the past year. All Ford dealers are putting the spotlight on high performance in the Ford Division car lines, and many of them are really getting into the spirit of the thing by setting up special areas called "performance corners."

What is a performance corner? It's a special part of the showroom where Ford's 1969 muscle cars—the Mustang Mach I, the Torino GT, the Ford XL and the Fairlane Cobra—are displayed. You'll recognize it by the racing flag checkerboard design of the carpeting, banners, and posters that set the area apart.

Visit the performance corner and you'll learn about the great variety of engines, transmissions, and other options that are available for these high-performing cars. You'll also learn about the race-bred Autolite-Ford Hi-Per parts your Ford dealer can provide.

The Hi-Per parts have been developed during Ford Motor Com-

pany's active participation in nearly every major segment of automobile racing, and are designed exclusively for Ford engines.

The performance corners also offer many personal accessories such as men's and women's racing jackets, medallions, key chains, cigarette lighters, and tie tacks.

Ask your Ford dealer for a free copy of the "1969 Performance Buyer's Digest," containing information on high performance cars, engines and parts.

Performance will be underscored by two two-man drag racing teams, one headed by Hubert Platt of Atlanta, Georgia, and the other by Ed Terry of Hayward, California,

Fairlane Cobra—a high performer.

58   FORD TIMES—MAY 1969

Here is a typical Ford dealer's Performance Corner display

which will campaign at various drag strips. Each team will use a specially modified 428 Cobra Jet Mustang and a 428 Fairlane Cobra.

These teams will also appear at various Ford dealerships across the country, and will aid in forming a series of Ford dealership-sponsored Ford Drag Clubs. They will conduct drag clinics, and demonstrate their driving skills at local tracks on the weekends.

Ford Total Performance Shows will present another facet of the program. Two traveling shows in 40-foot vans will crisscross the country carrying displays of high-performance parts, engines, and cars. Stars of the shows will be the Ford Mark IV (which won at Sebring and Le Mans in 1967), the specially modified Fairlane/Torino that carried David Pearson to his NASCAR 1968 championship, and Mustang "funny cars."

Like the drag teams, the Total Performance Shows will headquar-

ter at Ford dealerships during the week and then go on display at local tracks on weekends.

Local Mustang Clubs will set up "corrals" at the various tracks. These clubs, which have chapters throughout the country, are open to Mustang owners, and owners of other makes as well. If you're interested in joining, write National Council of Mustang Clubs, P. O. Box 4321, Dearborn, Michigan 48126.

The new "Lotus Simulator" is a performance feature that will attract attention at the major automobile shows. A rear projector beams a picture of a race track on a screen, and a "driver" sits in the cockpit of a Lotus racer. The device is so realistic that the driver can accelerate or brake as he negotiates the turns, and go full bore on the straightaways.

The machine times each driver to give an idea of how he compares with racing professionals. ☐

FORD TIMES—MAY 1969   59

Bonneville Salt Flats, September 19, 1968

All-new Mustang runs 24 hours nonstop at 157.663 m.p.h.

1969 Mustangs shatter 295 speed and endurance records.

No American production car has ever gone so far so fast. In a single 24-hour run—the engine never stopped turning—the specially prepared and modified canary yellow 1969 Mustang SportsRoof screamed its way around the rutted 10-mile course at an average of 157.663 miles per hour. Driven by professional record-breaker Mickey Thompson and co-driver Danny Ongais, the sleek new Mustang, powered by a 302-cubic-inch Ford V-8, went a distance of 3,783 miles in the 24 hours. Thompson's average speed was 17 miles per hour faster and the distance driven was 405 miles farther than the previous record. In the 24-hour period the yellow 1969 Mustang set over 100 American stock car records in the Class "C" Division for engines between 183 and 304 cubic inches as prescribed by the United States Auto Club. In another specially prepared 1969 Mustang SportsRoof, Thompson went on to break all standing and flying start records from 25 to 500 miles in Class B (305 to 488 cubic inch displacement). All these records make an undeniable statement about the new 1969 Mustang . . . never before has any car combined the performance to go so fast and the durability to do it for so long. What this means to you: The 1969 Mustangs are winners—at the track or on the turnpikes. See them in your Ford Dealer's Performance Corner.

NEW MUSTANG RECORDS
(Partial listing)
Class B (305 to 488 cu. in. displacement)
Flying Start—25, 50, 75, 100, 200, 250, 300, 400 and 500 kilometers
Flying Start—25, 50, 75, 100, 200, 250, 300, 400 and 500 miles
Standing Start—25, 50, 75, 100, 200, 250, 300, 400 and 500 miles
Standing Start—25, 50, 75, 100, 200, 250, 300, 400 and 500 kilometers

Class C (183 to 305 cu. in. displacement)
Flying Start—25, 50, 75, 100, 200, 250, 300, 400, 500, 1000, 2000, 3000, 4000, 5000 kilometers
Flying Start—25, 50, 75, 100, 200, 250, 300, 400, 500, 1000, 2000, 3000, 4000 miles
Standing Start—25, 50, 75, 100, 200, 250, 300, 400, 500, 1000, 2000, 3000, 4000, 5000 kilometers
Standing Start—25, 50, 75, 100, 200, 250, 300, 400, 500, 1000, 2000, 3000, 4000 miles
Flying Start—1-hour, 3-hour, 6-hour and 24-hour endurance
Standing Start—1-hour, 3-hour, 6-hour and 24-hour endurance

FORD
IT'S THE GOING THING!

USAC   MUSTANG   Ford

The place you've got to go to see what's going on—your Ford Dealer!

A three-page announcement for the Performance Corner highlighting the Mach I and Cobra was featured in seven major car magazines for October 1968. Life, Sports Illustrated, and eight buff magazines featured an ad celebrating Mickey Thompson's record-breaking run at Bonneville. By January, the 1969 Performance Buyer's Digest appeared in seven buff magazines for more than 2.6 million hits. (Photo Courtesy Ford Motor Company)

build a display like this with the basic performance corner kit...and additional items you can order

You can build a sharp display with any number of cars, using materials available through Ford. The basic kit items are illustrated here, in addition to the extra materials. They include:

K. Checkered black and white rug. Easy-to-handle 9' X 12' size. Durable, long-wearing nylon. A very attractive way to add extra zing to your performance corner.

L. Literature stand. A rigid, durable display that becomes part of the vehicle when in place. An attractive

way to offer catalogs (G), brochures, postcards (O), etc., in your Performance Corner.

M. Complete lighted sign. Shows Cobra and Mach I symbols. May be ordered as a complete sign, or sign face only. (Designed to replace "Ford Country" face on signs originally ordered by many dealers.)

O. Postcards. Jumbo size. Shows Mach I and Cobra SportsRoof and gives highlights. Order in packs of 100.

The Performance Corner Kit contained everything a dealer needed to identify itself as a performance headquarters, including a giant 2 x 18–foot banner, circular floor stands, acetate window trim, and a stack of 1969 Performance Buyer's Digests. (Photo Courtesy Ford Motor Company)

Ford teamed up with Hot Rod *magazine to produce this special issue that* *covered Ford's engine roster and other mechanical topics to help Ford* *enthusiasts find more performance success. (Nikolas Kolenich Photo)*

driving, engine modifications, gear ratio selection, parts interchangeability, and speed equipment are all ideas we've picked up from your letters."

The chapters included:

- Evolution of the Ford Engine: From Henry Ford's *999* racer to the advent of the FE V-8, Ford showed its advancements from 20 hp at 1600 rpm to 405 hp at 5,800.

- A Look at the Ford Engines: A summary of cylinder blocks, connecting rods, cylinder heads, camshafts, and more.

- Engine Modifications: Written to bring the reader up to date on available performance equipment for late Ford Motor Company engines.

- Clutches, Transmissions and Overdrive: An overview of how Ford equips its various models and what further changes might be needed for all-out competition.

- Rear Axle Ratios for Competition: Wayne Thoms discussed appropriate rear axle ratios

Because of economic and demographic differ- *ences, Ford's Canadian dealer network some-* *times grouped Ford and Mercury together, as* *demonstrated by this 1967 brochure spotlight-* *ing sporty and performance vehicles. (Photo* *Courtesy Ford Motor Company)*

for competitive drag racing, including variables such as transmission, differential, and peak horsepower.

- Chassis Tuning for Competition: Most Ford products were built with ride and handling that was suited for most situations but, for competition, the potential is there.

- Engine Tune-ups: A little thought, a lot of effort and persistence can make a winner out of your car by optimizing carburetion, ignition, spark plug, and valve settings.

- Ford Success Stories: Profiles on Bonneville racer Karol Miller, drag racer Les Ritchey, and NASCAR specialists Holman and Moody.

- Speed Shops and Parts Suppliers: A state-by-state listing where to find Ford hop-up gear.

Action Cars for '67

In 1967, Ford of Canada produced the *Action Cars for '67* brochure that presented sporty full-size Fords, Fairlanes, Mustangs, Falcons, Rancheros, and Mercury Comets and Cougars. Each section highlighted a model with information on spec'ing out a performer, from modest (the "fun" Falcon Futura) to magnificent (the "hot set-up" 427 Galaxie). Additional details for the enthusiast included summaries of the 289, 390, 428, and 427, plus Cobra high-performance and racing equipment to "squeeze more performance from your new or used Ford product"; axle ratios; engine/model availability; horsepower-to-weight ratios for combinations of models; body styles; and a NASCAR/NHRA Stock Car Classification Guide.

1969 Performance Buyer's Digest

Ford released the *1969 Performance Buyer's Digest*, saying "the cars… the engines…the parts…Ford has everything you need to build your kind of machine." Inserted in several buff magazines at the end of 1968 (and later distributed at dealerships), the digest pointed out that engineers responsible for Ford's winning ways in motorsports were the same folks who were "involved in designing performance cars and parts you can buy."

The following models were featured:

- Cobra: Raised in a tough neighborhood (Daytona, Riverside, Atlanta), the Cobra was touted as the "nearest thing to a NASCAR stocker you can bolt a license plate onto."
- Torino GT: Puts a lot of class into the quarter mile that happened to share a lot with the car that won the 1968 NASCAR Manufacturer's Championship, but "we've cooled them down for street use and added enough style and comfort to make them America's plushest performance cars."
- Mustang Mach I: Holder of 295 land speed records, this Mustang shared "the same wind-splitting sheet metal as the specifically modified Mach I that screamed around Bonneville, clocking over 155, hour after hour . . ."
- Mustang GT: Stack extra performance on the Mustang you fancy with "three sporty shapes that [have] made our specially prepared Mustangs the big Trans Am gun over many a rough road course."
- Ford XL GT: The Michigan Strong Boy with 480 pounds of torque that "could move a mountain" thanks to the optional 429 Thunder Jet.

Every Ford can be a winner with Ford performance parts, including "the same parts bin that Dan Gurney, A. J. Foyt, and Dave Pearson use." The following items were readily available:

- Cam and Lifter Kit: "A relatively mild grind for street or strip," especially for a 289 or 302 with hydraulic lifters.
- Induction Kit 4V: Included air cleaner with carburetor and intake manifold for all 260, 289, and 302 engines.
- 428-ci V-8: "This is the hauler that took the 1968 Winternationals at Pomona, winning both SS/E and Super Stock Eliminator Classes."
- Induction Systems 4V: For certain FE engines, it combined an equal-runner aluminum manifold with a center pivot 735-cfm carburetor. "Off-set carburetor location gives equal runner length for tuned induction, better high-speed flow, plus good low-end torque."
- Dual Point Distributor Assembly: Two sets of points to increase effective cam dwell by 7 degrees, plus high-pressure springs to help prevent bounce.
- Heavy-Duty Oil Pump: This 427 item could pump 22 gallons per minute at 70 to 80 psi at 4,000 rpm for other FE engines.

1970 Performance Buyer's Digest

Ford created this marketing piece, which touted, "The cars…The engines…The parts…Ford has everything you need for your kind of performance driving."

It began with "Ford's had a corner on performance . . . since your grandfather learned to drive," which waxed historic on Ford history-makers such

The 1969 Performance Buyer's Digest brochure was a part of Ford's new high-performance marketing effort that demonstrated the division had a strong contender to satisfy every segment of the performance market (with the right parts to make them run faster). (Photo Courtesy Ford Motor Company)

as the flathead V-8 and GT40 at Le Mans. Ford's "latest achievements" could be found at "your Ford Dealer's Performance Corner for 1970. Why not turn the page and take a look at what they've put together?"

The following models were featured:

- Mach I: Quickest pony of them all! Ford touted the new 351 Cleveland but left no doubt that the 428 Cobra Jet with Shaker was the fastest way to go.
- Boss 302: Son of Trans-Am. After an auspicious start in 1969, the Boss 302 was back with new style yet "designed to go quick and hang tight."
- Torino Cobra: This one makes tracks! As Ford's new top-gun car that puts a lot of muscle in your driveway at a reasonable price, the Cobra now had the same cubes as the hot Cobras that run Riverside and Daytona.
- Torino GT: Beautiful way to go! As the Cobra's "luxury-lovin' cousin," the Torino GT put an extra emphasis on style; the kind of car "you take to the strip Saturday afternoon, then use to make the scene Saturday night."
- Fords: For the fun of it. Dedicated to Ford's other sporty vehicles such as the Ranchero GT, add the 429 Cobra Jet with Shaker and you'd have "the haulingest vehicle this side of a space rocket booster." The "big Daddy of Ford's fleet," the XL "makes luxury a sporting proposition" with hideaway headlamps and available 429.

Muscle Parts Program

Ford's performance parts were now grouped under the Muscle Parts banner. "We took what we'd learned from running Ford-powered cars in competition around the world and applied it to our stockers:"

These components were part of the program:

- Carburetors, air cleaners, and intake manifolds: "The first stage on your way to more power is better breathing" with several bolt-ons, including a 31-hp upgrade for the 289/302/351.
- Camshafts: "To take advantage of better breathing carbs and manifolds, add a performance cam to open valves higher and longer" for up to 35 to 40 additional horses.
- Mechanical cam: The same cam that helped Ford win Le Mans, this "solid lifter cam will achieve a peak horsepower gain of 59 hp at 6,000 rpm" for 289 or 302 V-8s.
- Traction and stabilizer bars: "Improve cornering power on your Mustang with a 1-inch stabilizer bar. Keep your rear wheels on the ground when the green light comes on. Bolt-on traction bars will do it."
- Cast aluminum valvecovers: "After you've built up your new mill to new specs, brag a little with aluminum rocker covers [to show] 'eyeballers' you're running the hot setup."
- Deep-sump oil pan: "Resist high-rev oil frothing and run cooler" with this filter for FE-series engines, which "has a scraper to resist oil surge."

High Performance Data Book: Ford versus Competition

Imagine 1970: The performance market had grown and was now at its most competitive. Ford designed this brochure to cut through the clutter and "help [salesmen] sell performance cars and options" because "comparison knowledge is especially valuable when selling performance cars."

The comparisons were drag-oriented because drag racing "sells more cars than all other types of racing combined. A win at Indianapolis, Le Mans, or Daytona can increase customer identification toward Ford" but, in a hard lesson learned over the years, "those winning engines and cars bear no resemblance to anything they can buy." Drag racing offered something tangible, something that could be bought in the showroom.

Ford's revamped Muscle Parts program for 1970 featured "regular service parts that might do the job," and if they didn't, Ford "didn't quit until we had bulletproof pieces across the board." (Photo Courtesy Ford Motor Company)

Do your own thing—with Ford Muscle Parts.

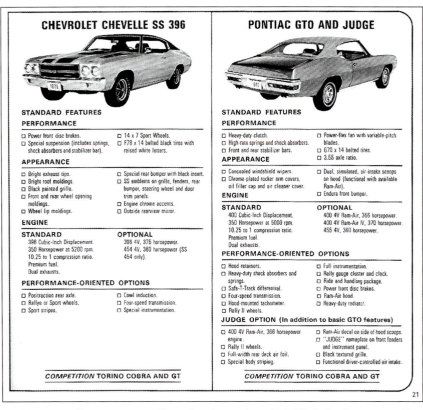

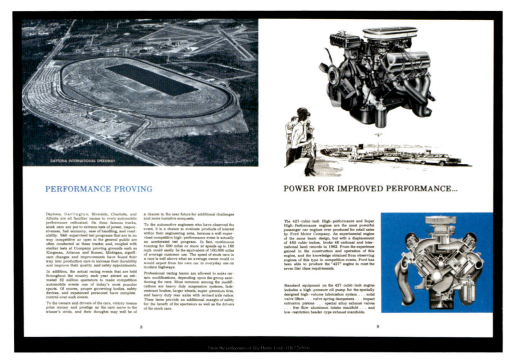

Two "intermediate super car" entries from the 1970 High Performance Data Book *described their vital statistics and the Ford model they competed against. (Photo Courtesy Ford Motor Company)*

Concluding was a word on insurance: "Many companies have recently announced rate hikes for performance vehicles. This may negatively affect your sales to some extent, but remember, all performance cars are in the same boat."

Ford grouped vehicles among several categories, with each listing their respective features in *Performance, Appearance, Engine,* and *Performance-oriented Options* sub-categories: Trans-Am–type cars, pony cars, super pony cars, and intermediate super cars.

Ford also dedicated a Chrysler Corporation Optional Performance Packages section to sort through Mopar terminology such as "Track Pak" and "Performance Axle Package."

Advertising Program

Ford's global Total Performance program spanned many years and brought Le Mans victory to Dearborn. But to millions of American enthusiasts, Total Performance meant victory on the paved ovals and the 400-meter strips. Drivers running Fords were among the world's greatest: Dan Gurney, A. J. Foyt, Jim Clark, and others.

Total Performance

In 1962, *Motor Trend* called Total Performance "a universal commitment (from president Henry Ford II down) that the company would develop the cars, engines, and/or teams it took to win in the world's most significant racing series." By 1970, Ford and Ford-powered vehicles had won or made their mark in just about every competition there was.

Ford Total Performance 1903-1963 described Total Performance as more than a marketing program. It brought benefits to the consumer such as acceleration and speed, plus:

- Roadability: Provides built-in features to help resist skidding and to hold the road
- Braking power: Permits smooth, straight-line stops
- Steering: For effortless directional control
- Instruments and Controls: Easy to read and operate
- Visibility: Reduces blind spots

Ford Engineering produced the 1963 Total Performance brochure to chronicle products and features that benefitted from the high-performance program, including improved safety, comfort, convenience, and durability. (Photo Courtesy Ford Motor Company)

The Ford Dealer Magazine *distributed to Ford dealers gave an over-view of the large-scale Total Performance effort, from racing around the world to custom car shows that catered to the burgeoning youth market. (Photo Courtesy Ford Motor Company)*

- Suspension: Provides a smooth ride without wheel-bounce
- Riding comfort: Scientifically designed seats that reduce travel fatigue

Ford Engineering created *The Advancement of the Ford V-8* brochure to chronicle Ford's performance products because "performance will continue to play an ever increasing part of all human endeavor." In the pages of the brochure were these sections:

- Stock Car Events and Safety Development: Ford's 1954 Y-block quickly became "one of America's favorite all-around engines." But it was in 1955 that Ford's stock car racing efforts "proved to be a prime factor in the research and development of more reliable and safer cars for the general market."
- Performance Proving: Fords "are put to extreme tests of power, responsiveness, fuel economy, ease of handling, and roadability" on the racetracks, but Ford's proving grounds were the locus for increased durability, quality, and safety. Racing gave Ford engineers "a chance to evaluate products of interest because a well-supervised competitive high-performance event is actually an accelerated test program," with a 500-mile, 160-mph race being equivalent to 100,000 miles of customer use.
- Power for Improved Performance: Ford's 427 offered "many special features which made it withstand the stress of high-performance operation and for long life in everyday driving" such as cross-bolted main bearing caps, impact extrusion pistons, and special connecting rods.

The Total Performance Design of the 1963½ Ford Galaxie warranted special mention:

- The aerodynamic design of Sports Hardtop models "has been proven in competition at several of the nation's most difficult road and track events and under conditions that duplicated normal driving on modern freeways."
- The sleek Sports Hardtop required less horsepower to reach the same speed as a Galaxie sedan with the forward roof.

This 1966 Total Performance ad suggested that Ford's world-wide competitive exploits helped make its passenger cars "safer, better-handling, more efficient, more fun to drive." (Photo Courtesy Ford Motor Company)

Carroll Shelby's association with the Mustang was the perfect situation for both Shelby American and Ford Motor Company: the "Total Performance" company wanted the Mustang homologated for SCCA B/Production but was having little success getting it done. Hiring a subcontractor to handle the job was a logical step. Carroll Shelby already had connections to both Ford and the SCCA world; the union was a no-brainer.

SCCA rules required 100 production vehicles to be ready for inspection by the first of the New Year to be approved for the racing season. The rules also allowed a choice of modifying the suspension or the engine. Shelby had four months to figure this out and build 100 cars before the dawn of 1965.

Shelby decided to keep the engine stock except for some bolt-on parts (bringing the Hi-Po 289 from 271 to 306 hp), and went to work on the front and rear suspensions plus everything else required for preparation. Partially built Mustang 2+2s were sent for completion to Shelby American's Venice, California, facility where Ford's little secretary's car, er, pony car became a bona fide sports car. Both the 521 GT350 street cars and the 34 GT350R competition versions (plus four GT350 drag cars) were Wimbledon White with blue rocker panel stripes, with overhead Le Mans stripes optional.

To the untrained eye, the 1966 GT350 looked the same, but it presented a new grille, side scoops, and a Plexiglas C-pillar replaced the louvers. Shelby made it a more civilized vehicle based on customer feedback, but increased production required a less labor-intensive vehicle.

Enthusiasts had the choice of several options that were not available in 1965, including an automatic transmission (which mandated a smaller Autolite carb) and five paint colors. Most significantly, the 1966 GT350

Carroll Shelby engineered enough changes to turn the Mustang into something that caught the attention of the sports car cognoscenti, yet gave red-blooded American performance enthusiasts something to desire as well. (Tim Costello Photo)

was more family friendly thanks to a rear seat. For even more horsepower, a Paxton supercharger could be specified for $700.

A special partnership with Hertz for the Hertz Sports Car Club resulted in the creation of the Shelby GT350 H. All told, 2,364 GT350s were built (including 999 Hertz cars), plus another four drag cars and four special-order convertibles.

Shelby American followed suit with the Mustang's first redesign for 1967, but did Ford one better. For more distinction, the Shelby GT utilized several fiberglass pieces, including an aggressive-looking hood, nose, trunk lid with integral spoiler, and side scoops. Large high beams in the grille and taillights borrowed from the 1967 Mercury Cougar made the Shelby GT look like a Mustang that had been customized for the show circuit. The High-Performance 289 was carried over, with a supercharger still available.

Although the Mustang made do with the new 390, Shelby American took advantage of the enlarged pony car and created the

For four weeks starting in November 1965, Carroll Shelby toured the United States and visited Ford and Shelby dealerships in 12 major cities with the Cobra Caravan. (Photo Courtesy of the AACA Library & Research Center, Hershey, Pennsylvania)

The redesigned 1969 Mustang meant the even sleeker Shelby GT was riding on its coattails. The GT500 returned for 1969 with the Cobra Jet; the GT350 featured a new 290-hp 351. (Bill Cook Photo)

Big news for 1968 was the introduction of the Shelby GT350 and GT500 convertibles, but Ford wrestled control from Carroll Shelby and the operation moved from Venice, California, to metropolitan Detroit. (Photo ©TEN: The Enthusiast Network. All rights reserved.)

355-hp GT500, complete with 428 Police Interceptor and dual-quads on an aluminum intake. Ford's race-bred 427 also was an option, but only two 427-powered GT500s plus the GT40-inspired Super Snake were built. Shelby American's gamble to make the GT a more street-friendly car continued to pay off with 1,175 GT350s and 2,048 GT500s built.

The year 1968 was one of transition for Shelby American. Ford Motor Company pushed for control, resulting in Shelby American being split into three separate organizations. The main operation was rechristened Shelby Automotive, Inc., and was based in metropolitan Detroit, but final assembly was handled by subcontractor A.O. Smith in central Michigan. That wasn't the only mainstreaming of the Shelby brand: the GT350 lost the Hi-Po 289, relying instead on a 250-hp 302 with aluminum intake, and the GT500's 428 PI now used a single Holley atop an aluminum intake (gaining 5 hp in the process).

Styling was cleaned up, and enthusiasts had the choice of a production convertible with integral roll bar.

In April 1968, Ford introduced the 428 Cobra Jet. This engine became the first 428 ever installed in the Mustang but, when installed in the Shelby GT500, the model was renamed GT500 KR (King of the Road). Although the 335-hp rating appeared to be a downgrade, the CJ was clearly stronger than the previous 428s. As Ford's showcase for the CJ, the KR was the most popular recipient of the Cobra Jet: 1,571 GT500 KRs were built, plus another 1,448 GT500s and 1,431 GT350s.

A redesigned 1969 Mustang was both bigger and more muscular. The Shelby GT's modifications, including the addition of fiberglass front fenders, made for a sleeker-looking Mustang thanks to a combination grille/bumper that surrounded dual headlights. Of course, this being a Shelby GT, there were scoops galore, including several NACA ducts on the hood. The traditional Shelby GT racing stripes were replaced by more prominent longitudinal stripes below the beltline.

The 1969 GT350 was the recipient of Ford's new 351 Windsor small-block with 290 hp, a nice bump from the tepid 302. The GT500 returned, now equipped with the 428 Cobra Jet. An optional Drag Pack added 3.91 or 4.30 gears, oil cooler, and upgraded heavy-duty equipment.

Even though 1968 was a strong year sales-wise, the market was headed in another direction so the decision was made to end Shelby GT production after 1969. Certainly the Shelby GT was no slouch, but Ford already offered interesting alternatives such as the Mach I, Boss 302, and Boss 429. All unsold and unfinished 1969 Shelby GTs received twin black stripes on the hood, Boss 302 front spoiler, and 1970 serial numbers. For 1969–1970, 1,281 GT350s and 1,896 GT500s were built.

Of course, this wouldn't be the last we'd hear from Carroll Shelby.

A running change for the 1967 Shelbys was the repositioning of the high beams. They initially were positioned in the middle of the grille, but their proximity ran afoul of laws in several states, so they were moved to the grille's outer edges. (Richard Truesdell Photo)

"The Going Thing" for Dealers

Ford introduced an integrated high-performance marketing guide/training manual for 1969–1970 titled *Performance: It's the Going Thing!* to support dealers. The guide covered the performance market, the performance dealer, Ford performance products, U.S. motorsports activities, and performance merchandising and materials.

The contents of the guide are summarized here:

Section 1: Introduction

The reasons for this book . . . the reasons why Ford has gone all-out to be Number One in racing.

Part 1 – Welcome to the World of Performance
Part 2 – Why Ford is in Racing

Section 2: The Performance Market

What it is, who it is, where it is . . . the plus sales and profits performance represents . . . the people who are selling against us and how well they're doing.

Part 1 – What is Performance?
Part 2 – The Performance Market is the Youth Market
Part 3 – Size and Growth of the Performance Market
Part 4 – Competition in the Performance Market

Section 3: The Performance Dealer

Where and how you begin to become a performance dealer . . . finding sales and service specialists, insurance for performance cars, used cars, race car sponsorship, much more.

Part 1 – What is a Performance Dealer?
Part 2 – How to Become a Performance Dealer
Part 3 – Performance Dealer Activities
Part 4 – Dealer Experiences in the Performance Market

Ford considered performance a state of mind that could be expressed in active qualities or in appearance, with both pointing "to the dominance of youth and the young at heart among automobile buyers" whose influence was felt all over. "Thus we see that the performance market is the youth market." (Photo Courtesy Ford Motor Company)

This section related the history of the American performance scene and how it had grown to more than six percent of the industry by 1968. "Add to these the 'appearance' performance cars, the ones whose owners specified smaller engines but a full helping of stripes, hood scoops, mag wheel covers, etc." and the segment approached 17 percent. (Photo Courtesy Ford Motor Company)

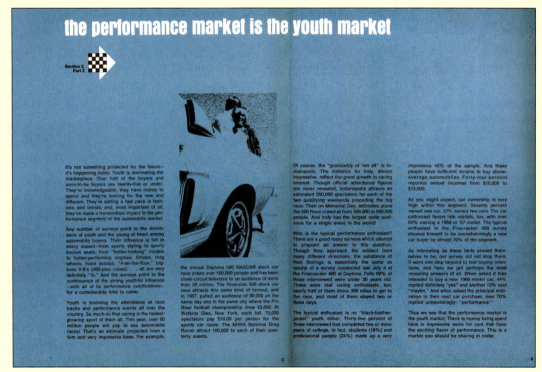

what is a performance dealer?

The typical performance dealer is, first of all, a man who has watched with great interest the emergence and growth of this market since its first appearance. And he has carefully noted its steady "growth month after month. He has noted, too, that the buyers in this market are young and knowledgeable and that they have the financial resources to pay for the cars they favor, the ones offering extra performance. And he has come to the conclusion that in the performance market there is very much the same kind of profit opportunity which came with the introduction of the Mustang.

If the "qualifications" of a performance dealer up to this point sound like those of any Ford Dealer, it's no coincidence. The performance market is an opportunity wide-open and waiting for every Ford Dealer.

Section 3, Part 1

"Kids are smart! No one's going to fool them with some banners saying he's a performance dealer...they know what's happening."
—Ed Schoenherr

dealer experiences in the performance market

Section 3, Part 4

Edward J. Schoenherr, president and owner since 1956 of Stark Hickey Ford in Royal Oak, Michigan, didn't become a performance dealer overnight. His suburban Detroit dealership has been tuned to the Motor City's zeal for muscled machinery for more than a decade. In many ways, his success as a performance dealer reflects his early love of boat racing.

In 1946, a Ford Six powered one of his boats to a world record. His Allison-engined hydroplane, "My Sweetie," brought him the National Sweepstakes, the President's Cup and the 1949 Gold Cup. At the time Ed sold "My Sweetie," it was considered the Number One boat on the U.S. Harmsworth Team.

Ed was general manager of another Detroit Ford dealership for eight years before becoming the owner of Stark Hickey Ford. His business instinct and great interest in performance aimed his dealership toward Detroit area dragways, where it began cutting its performance teeth in 1957. That year, Stark Hickey-bannered cars began competing for racing laurels and enthusiasts' loyalties and have never stopped.

Currently, a Stark Hickey Shelby challenges the best in local Detroit sports car racing. A Mustang Cobra Jet keeps the dealership in the forefront of the national drag world; the car shattered a world's record in its class in 1968 and has been a consistently impressive performer.

Ed sums up his dealership's competitive activity this way: "If the kids see a Stark Hickey Ford car shut down everything else and win, they know Stark Hickey must know something about performance." That kind of put-your-money-where-your-mouth-is philosophy, as other dealers have found, is hard to argue with. "But," he emphasizes, "you've got to go all the way. You've got to be ready with service and parts —the performance hardware. And you've got to show genuine interest in performance the same way the youngsters do." In this latter area, Ed's two sons Rick and John are special assets to the dealership. Both young men are active in their father's business; they know performance—have done some race driving— and can speak authoritatively to performance prospects.

Being a performance dealer meant more than simply selling high-performance cars. Among other things, dealers needed to be an authority on performance, including having service and parts specialists (plus inventory) to support enthusiasts. (Photo Courtesy Ford Motor Company)

Section 4: Ford Performance Products
The full range and individual advantages of the hot line you have for sale . . . cars, engines, parts.

Part 1 - Mustang Mach I
Part 2 - Fairlane Cobra
Part 3 - 428 Cobra Jet V-8
Part 4 - Torino Talladega
Part 5 - Mustang Boss
Part 6 - Shelby Products
Part 7 - 351 V-8 Bolt-On Kit
Part 8 - Autolite Performance Parts
Part 9 - Autolite Performance Parts Kits

Section 5: U.S. Motorsports Activities
The entire world of racing: the cars, the drivers, the events that make it so fascinating . . . who sponsors what events . . . how to know what the buffs are saying . . . where to go to see the races this year.

Section 6: Performance Merchandising and Materials
Here are the tools and suggestions for making the best use of them . . . programs, plans, tips, suggestions – all the selling help you need to launch yourself into the world of performance.

This section featured competitive comparisons based on value, engines, and performance; how to optimize performance cars for Street Only, Street/Strip, and Dragstrip Only (C-Stock); Axle Ratio Selector for CJs; and General Tips: "Though slightly heavier, Sports-Roof models have a slight advantage in static weight distribution over Hardtops." (Photo Courtesy Ford Motor Company)

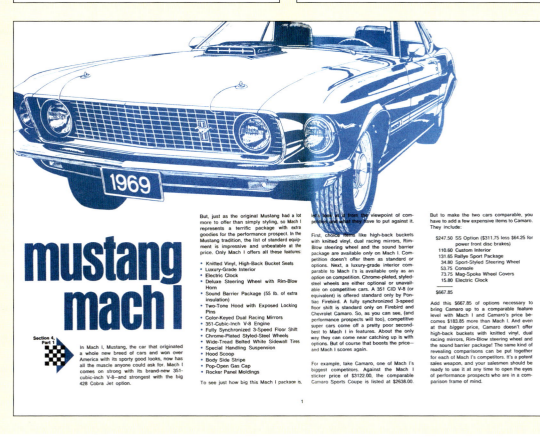

1969

mustang mach 1

Section 4, Part 1

In Mach I, Mustang, the car that originated a whole new breed of cars and won over America with its sporty good looks, now has all the muscle anyone could ask for. Mach I comes on strong with its brand-new 351-cubic-inch V-8—and strongest with the big 428 Cobra Jet option.

But, just as the original Mustang had a lot more to offer than simply styling, so Mach I represents a terrific package with extra goodies for the performance prospect. In the Mustang tradition, the list of standard equipment is impressive and unbeatable at the price. Only Mach I offers all these features:

- Knitted Vinyl, High-Back Bucket Seats
- Luxury-Grade Interior
- Electric Clock
- Deluxe Steering Wheel with Rim-Blow Horn
- Sound Barrier Package (55 lb. of extra insulation)
- Two-Tone Hood with Exposed Locking Pins
- Color-Keyed Dual Racing Mirrors
- 351-Cubic-Inch V-8 Engine
- Fully Synchronized 3-Speed Floor Shift
- Chrome-Plated Styled-Steel Wheels
- Wide-Tread Belted White Sidewall Tires
- Special Handling Suspension
- Hood Scoop
- Body Side Stripe
- Pop-Open Gas Cap
- Rocker Panel Moldings

To see just how big this Mach I package is,

let's look at it from the viewpoint of competition and what they have to put against it.

First, choice items like high-back buckets with knitted vinyl, dual racing mirrors, Rim-Blow steering wheel and the sound barrier package are available only on Mach I. Competition doesn't offer them as standard or options. Next, a luxury-grade interior comparable to Mach I's is available only as an option on competition. Chrome-plated, styled-steel wheels are either optional or unavailable on competitive cars. A 351 CID V-8 (or equivalent) is offered standard only by Pontiac Firebird. A fully synchronized 3-speed floor shift is standard only on Firebird and Chevrolet Camaro. So, as you can see, (and performance prospects will too), competitive super cars come off a pretty poor second-best to Mach I in features. About the only way they can come near catching up is with options. But of course that boosts the price— and Mach I scores again.

For example, take Camaro, one of Mach I's biggest competitors. Against the Mach I sticker price of $3122.00, the comparable Camaro Sports Coupe is listed at $2638.00.

But to make the two cars comparable, you have to add a few expensive items to Camaro. They include:

$247.50	SS Option ($311.75 less $64.25 for power front disc brakes)
110.60	Custom Interior
131.65	Rallye Sport Package
34.80	Sport-Styled Steering Wheel
53.75	Console
73.75	Mag-Spoke Wheel Covers
15.80	Electric Clock
$667.85	

Add this $667.85 of options necessary to bring Camaro up to a comparable feature level with Mach I and Camaro's price becomes $183.85 more than Mach I. And even at that bigger price, Camaro doesn't offer high-back buckets with knitted vinyl, dual racing mirrors, Rim-Blow steering wheel and the sound barrier package! The same kind of revealing comparisons can be put together for each of Mach I's competitors. It's a potent sales weapon, and your salesmen should be ready to use it at any time to open the eyes of performance prospects who are in a comparison frame of mind.

Representing the West Coast, Ed Terry raced this Cobra Jet–powered 1969 Mustang for the Ford Drag Team. The "Going Thing" track promotion was inspired by Ford Drag Team vehicles. (Photo ©TEN: The Enthusiast Network. All rights reserved.)

Randy Payne represented the East Coast by driving this 1969 Cobra for the Ford Drag Team. (Photo ©TEN: The Enthusiast Network. All rights reserved.)

The May/June 1963 *The Ford Dealer Magazine* featured the headline, "Ford's bold new image: The only car with 'Total Performance Quality!'"

Total Performance meant different things to different people, from product durability to fuel economy, but "in the final analysis the car is capable of top performance in all the areas where a car is expected to perform" like in the Daytona 500, Monte Carlo Rallye, and Pikes Peak Hill Climb.

Ford's performance image and victories were "the talk of the nation," giving dealerships a way to capitalize on the Total Performance story, especially in competition. Romy Hammes Ford in Indiana had achieved success in the Rebel 300 and the Winternationals with two cars driven by salesmen. "To be real truthful, we win most of them. It not only helps to convince people we have a good car, but it helps our dealership image to be in racing," said dealer vice president Jerry Hammes.

Added North Carolina-based Lafayette Motor Sales, "Since we entered racing several years ago, our sales have increased about 40 percent. We think the image it has built for us is responsible. People like to associate with a winner; and the more we win the more we sell."

Ford also was "the only manufacturer with major representation" in hot rod and custom car shows around the United States. In a bid "to capitalize on youth interest in performance vehicles and customized cars," Ford created the Custom Car Caravan that toured with production and customized versions of its current lineup such as the Thunderbird Italien and Fairlane Starburst. Several of the country's top builders attended "to discuss the latest in customizing techniques." For performance enthusiasts, Performance Advisor Ak Miller talked about Ford's performance vehicles and equipment.

Ford also sponsored events directed at the youth market such as the Ford Fashion Fair, where the division joined forces with several youth apparel manufacturers to hold fashion shows at teenage fairs in New York, Boston, Detroit, and Los Angeles. In 1962, 233,000 attended the latter; The Custom Car Caravan joined the show in 1963. At the Ford-Aurora Grand National Motoring Competition, more than one million were in attendance. This electric slot car competition in 1962 was sponsored by Ford and Aurora Model Car Company, with attendance forecasted to double for 1963.

By 1966, Ford was on top of the world with perhaps its greatest Total Performance achievement: sweeping Le Mans.

Performance: It's the Going Thing

In the twilight of 1968, Ford began an campaign that touted the brand as "The Going Thing." The company created a Sunshine Pop group organized by a duo who also wrote, arranged, and produced music for the Partridge

Family. Organized by the J. Walter Thompson agency, The Going Thing supported Ford's youthful marketing efforts through 1970 with three LPs.

Ford Drag Club

This component was promoted as "Extra sales, bigger profits for *you!*" With racing attracting more than 800,000 participants and 20 million spectators a year, the idea was to convert the enthusiasm into car and parts sales.

Ford Muscle Parts

Ford Muscle Parts was more than just an integrated resource for components. It was an important ingredient in attracting high-performance market sales and profits. Bonneville veteran Danny Eames, and NHRA co-founder Ak Miller were responsible for this program.

With sections titled "The Nitty Gritty of Performance" (engines, exhaust pressure, and traction) and "Modification Tips, Blueprinting Specs, and All That Stuff" (camshafts, ignition, and compression), the Muscle Parts catalog was a comprehensive compendium to show "how to do it from scratch, in detail, by steps. Nobody tells you that you can invest a ton and only get a pound of performance, if you buy the wrong pieces. So Ford got the idea to do it. And did. We tell it all, straight out."

The "Staged Performance" section featured a step-by-step guide to systematic performance modifications with kits in several performance levels. "You want to give your machine more sock and you've got the bucks to make it happen. Maybe it's mild: such as adding a 4-barrel induction setup for better acceleration. Or something wild: such as a high-lift long-duration mechanical cam, special heads, valves, and pistons, high-ratio locking axle, traction bars, slicks, etc. Or, is it in between?"

Several kits were offered through this program.

The Impressor kits "generally include induction goodies, a HP hydraulic cam and valvetrain pieces, hot ignition setup, and headers. Strictly bolt-on stuff. As our first performance level, this kit might be considered a 'sleeper.' Until you get on it. Then its big horsepower increase over stock tells you exactly what it is: the Impressor."

Except for minor valvetrain differences, the Controller Kit built upon the Impressor and added "bigger cylinder heads, 'pop up' pistons, and in some cases, optional valves. About all it takes to develop this extra muscle is a few more tech specs and your Impressor Kit wrench. Heavy on this one, however, does more than just impress: it makes you the Controller."

The Dominator kit included all the pieces from the Controller "plus a gutsy-grind mechanical cam. This big stick adds the really big muscle to

Shown here conducting a seminar are Hubert Platt (left) and Ed Terry (right), captains of the East Coast and West Coast Ford Drag Teams, respectfully. Platt and Terry typically conducted these in the days prior to scheduled racing events. (Photo ©TEN: The Enthusiast Network. All rights reserved.)

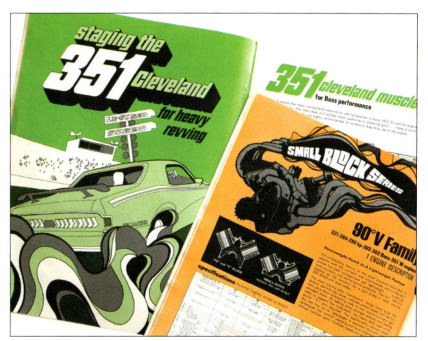

Part of Ford's unified effort in chasing the high-performance dollar was the Muscle Parts program. The program (and catalog) sought to streamline information on parts interchangeability for different engine series, competitive pricing (Ford's initial pricing structure offered no incentive over speed shops), and the best parts for a particular need. (Nikolas Kolenich Photo)

your machine. The kind of sock that tells the other guy: Big Breather Is Watching You: the Dominator."

Ford's advice was, "Don't try to short-cut the system. Take Ak's advice: 'Install all recommended kit parts for a performance level and you'll add the total horsepower rating to your engine.'"

Ford even showed how to maximize kit installation by staging the 289-302 to "Boss the Avenue," staging the 351 to "Rev 6001," staging the 390 to "Turn a Low ET," staging the 428 CJ to "Get Out of the Gate," and staging the 427 for "Strip 'n Track."

The Mustang Sidewinder Special

Mustangs may have been everywhere, but there were plenty of unique regional promotions (some factory-backed, others created by district sales offices) that helped keep consumers interested. Among the 1968 California Specials and 1970 Twister Specials lies one surrounded by an enigma: the Sidewinder Special. Most Ford folks haven't heard of it, but it's an honest-to-goodness high-performance regional special.

According to Michael Baze, Ford encouraged regional promotions as part of its 1970 high-performance marketing plans. Ford approached several district offices in the Midwest about a sales contest. Each office created a fleet of high-performance vehicles and Ford determined which office best met the objective of highest sales penetration. The Omaha district office was one of the few that signed up.

The Omaha district merchandising manager normally was responsible for handling the duties of this competition, but he wasn't terribly interested in performance. However, assistant Bill Willis remembered a young college graduate in the office who had expressed interest in hot cars in his interview.

Willis reeled Baze in for the project, which he seized with aplomb. "The [high-performance] cars we cared about were unimportant because they didn't represent value for the company. There wasn't any enthusiasm in the offices at Ford; they were the black sheep of car merchandising. Ford devoted a lot of money because the youths were into performance, and that was the way to get to them. The everyday enterprise bored us to death: Mom and Pop sedans, pickups, and the usual transportation boxes."

The logical choice for the competition would have been an image model with a big engine, such as a Mach I with the 428 Cobra Jet. Willis' directive was to undercut what they were expecting others to do, so Baze went ahead and ordered approximately 48 Mustang SportsRoofs (*not* the Mach I) with the 300-hp 351, automatic, 3.50 gears with Traction-Lok, Competition Suspension, and Goodyear Polyglas tires, all available in a palette of Ford's brightest colors. Not only did a 351 SportsRoof cost less than a Cobra Jet Mach I, Baze also estimated the 351 may have an advantage off the line with the tires of the time. The Sidewinder name was chosen due to Ford's association with Cobras.

For identification, Ford's Sports Performance Information Center offered several stripes for promotional purposes on any level. Baze chose a design inspired by the 1969 Boss 302's, then topped it off with a Sidewinder decal of his own design. Only two or three Sidewinders were dressed like this until Ford began to deliver cars with a broad black stripe (similar to the Twister Special's), so Baze moved the Sidewinder decal to the rear fender.

A trip to Lake Tahoe was in store for the office that managed the best sales penetration and, yes, the Omaha office was the winner. Alas, Baze was not allowed to travel because he was not part of the original managing team that headed the project. Willis generously gave Baze his spot in the trip.

The 1970 Mustang Sidewinder Special, developed by Ford's Omaha sales district, is a notable example of a regional high-performance special. Unlike the more famous Twister Special Mach I, the Sidewinder was based on a standard SportsRoof with a 351 Cleveland engine.

MERCURY TAKES FLIGHT

Ford Motor Company was never really certain about Mercury's position during its 1939-2011 existence. Initially created as a brand between Ford and the Lincoln Zephyr, Mercury evolved into a junior Lincoln by 1949, soon to become a darling of the hot rod set.

In 1952, the Lincoln shrunk, almost looking like a premium Mercury. Mercury regained its own identity in 1957, upping the horsepower wars in 1958 with the industry's first 400-horse engine.

Then, in 1961, Mercury moved down-market, functioning as a deluxe Ford instead of a mid-level competitor to Olds and Chrysler. Although Chrysler would never have dared to offer a compact, Mercury was only too happy to sell the Falcon-based Comet.

Back in the Saddle

Beginning in 1962, Mercury began to find harmony with itself thanks to the new 406 engine and Monterey Custom S-55, which gave enthusiasts the buckets and consoles they demanded.

The FE-based 427 and the semi-fastback Marauder sub-series made their first appearance in January 1963. The 427 was an important development for both NASCAR and NHRA, although Mercury didn't benefit from lightweight and factory experimental full-size models as Ford did. For performance enthusiasts, the Marauder offered a slipperier alternative to the Breezeway roofline with its reverse-slant retractable backlight. These two updates helped Mercury garner five checkered flags in NASCAR Grand National races in 1964.

The compact Comet was redesigned for 1964, complemented by a sporty 225-horse Cyclone variant with a 271-hp High Performance 289 as an option. It was a fun, fast car, but not much competition to the GTO in speed or sales. However, it was the perfect basis for the A/FX 427 Comet.

To clear the heads and exhaust manifolds, Detroit Steel Tubing was recruited to lower the shock towers before stuffing in a 427 High-Riser. Cold air to the two 780-cfm 4-barrels was routed from the cowl by a huge blister on the fiberglass hood. Don Nicholson had a 63-race winning streak with his 10-second A/FX Comet.

For 1965, the Comet was revamped with vertical headlights; the Cyclone received a unique grille plus an optional non-functional fiberglass hood midyear. The 289 High Performance was used as the basis for the factory experimental B/FX Cyclone, which was capable of mid-11-second ETs.

Full-size Mercurys were touted as "Now in the Lincoln Continental tradition." Any semblance of sportiness that was exploited in 1963–1964 was out the door, although a handful of 427s were built.

The Cyclone Grows Up

Better things came for 1966 after the success of the Pontiac GTO. The redesigned Comet grew into an intermediate; the Cyclone carried the weight for enthusiasts. The base Cyclone was rather tepid, equipped

Don Nicholson raced an A/FX 427 Comet in 1965, but this time it was sporting an SOHC. A 289-powered B/FX was also produced. (Photo ©TEN: The Enthusiast Network. All rights reserved.)

with a 2-barrel 289 but sporty nonetheless with bucket seats. The GT package provided a 335-hp 390 with engine dress-up kit, non-functional twin-scooped fiberglass hood, console, handling package, and lower-body racing stripes. Order the 3-speed automatic and you *automatically* received the Sport Shift Merc-O-Matic that delivered "unusual driving flexibility; fully automatic when left in the 'D' position, or a completely manual 1-2-3 shift."

Officials at Indianapolis Motor Speedway were justifiably impressed and chose a red Cyclone GT convertible as the pace car for the 1966 Indy 500.

With Dyno Don Nicholson piloting a Cyclone funny car, Mercury seemed poised to take on the GTO except for one problem: the 390 could not compete with the Tri-Power 389. An April 1966 *Car Life* road test said, "It's just possible that Ford/Mercury haven't gone far enough with the 390. Perhaps some of those high-rev, quick-bleed hydraulic lifters (like those used by Pontiac and Chevrolet to get more than 6,000 rpm from the HP engines) and a hotter camshaft would give it some excitement." The magazine also pointed out that the 390's main problem was cylinder heads with "restrictive valve passages [that] hinder the engine's 'breathing.'"

The new Monterey-based S-55 gave full-size fans something sporty, but it was more of a showcase for the new 345-hp Super Marauder 428 rather than a full-size performance car.

Sign of the Cat

The big news at Mercury for 1967 was the unleashing of the Cougar. Created as an upscale pony car (based on the Mustang), the Cougar was "untamed elegance, America's first luxury sports car at a popular price." The Cougar distinguished itself from other pony cars thanks to "European flair" and a standard V-8; hidden headlights and sequential rear turn signals were two other items that made the Cougar stand out. To cater to performance enthusiasts, Mercury offered the GT package featuring a 320-hp 390 with low-restriction dual exhausts with acoustically tuned mufflers, chrome dress-up kit, Performance Handling Package, and other performance items.

Mercury offered the GT package for the 1967 Cougar, which included a 4-barrel 390. The 390 was also available without the GT package. (Photo ©TEN: The Enthusiast Network. All rights reserved.)

The GT-E package for the 1968 Cougar featured special trim and badging plus an exclusive 390-hp 427. In April, the 427 was replaced by the new 428 Cobra Jet, which included a functional ram-air hood. Of the 394 GT-Es, only 37 were built with the CJ. (Richard Truesdell Photo)

Dan Gurney, Parnelli Jones, and Ed Leslie were part of Mercury's Trans-Am team. At a press junket in Carmel, California, from October 31 to November 2, 1966, they stumped for the Cougar and introduced the Group 2 Cougar racer to members of the media. Fifty Cougars were made available to the press for driving impressions, and reporters were treated to rides in the Group 2 Cougar and Mercury GT40 (Ford had two GT40s competing as Mercurys).

In the spring, Mercury introduced the 1967 Cougar Dan Gurney Special. Nothing more than a dolled-up Cougar to boost sales, the DGS didn't have any sporting pretensions but simply borrowed from Gurney's racing equity.

The Cyclone changed little for 1967; the most noticeable revisions were a new grille and taillights. The base Cyclone remained the same and the GT's standard 390 was detuned to 320 hp. Horsepower wasn't the only thing that was missing for 1967; the console was demoted to the option list for the GT.

On the upside, Mercury introduced two 427s for all two-door Comets: 4-barrel with 410 hp and dual-quads with 425 horses. With only 60 427 Comets built (27 of them Cyclones) and the 390 simply not measuring up, Mercury's street reputation remained dull at a time when GTO sales were ten times as strong.

1968: Evolution All Around

A year of maturation came in 1968 for the performance segment and Mercury. The Cougar evolved to offer several performance versions and engines to drive home the message that Mercury was committed to high performance.

The Marauder 390 GT engine was up 5 hp to 325, and still included with the GT package. However on January 1968, the $1,311 GT-E package was added to the Cougar lineup. Not only was the Cougar GT-E loaded for bear with stylistic and performance bells and whistles, but it also was the only 1968 Ford product (as well as the final one) built with the 427 from the factory: a hydraulic cam and single 4-barrel. The GT-E also included a mandatory automatic transmission, Super Competition Handling Package, FR70 x 14 radials, quad chrome exhaust tips, simulated hood scoop, Styled Steel Wheels, and unique taillights, and blackened grille (with horizontal trim), among other items.

The redesigned 1968 Cyclone's strength was on NASCAR racetracks. Its influence on the street, however, was dampened by uncompetitive engines, which may have explained mediocre sales: 12,260 fastbacks and 1,368 coupes. (Photo ©TEN: The Enthusiast Network. All rights reserved.)

The 427 was replaced in April 1968 with the 428 Cobra Jet, giving the GT-E a functional air-induction system with black hood scoop and stripe. Not only was a 4-speed now available for the GT-E, but the CJ could also be ordered for regular Cougars.

The quasi-custom Cougar XR7-G was introduced in March. Originally a project headed by Shelby Automotive, the G (reflecting another Gurney inspiration) included many premium features such as a Talbot racing mirror, fog lights, simulated hood scoop (shared with the GT-E), and hood pins, among other items.

The Comet was completely redesigned for 1968. For the performance oriented Cyclone, the convertible was gone, but a new fastback joined the hardtop. The base Cyclone engine was a 302, but the 325-hp 390 and 390-horse 427 were suited for enthusiasts. A lower-body racing stripe was standard; the GT (now a stand-alone model) featured an additional upper beltline stripe, standard bucket seats, handling package, wide-tread tires, and more. In April, the 428 Cobra Jet replaced the 427 (which was never installed at the factory), giving Mercury's street rep a big boost. On the track, Cale Yarborough and LeeRoy Yarbrough assisted Mercury's rep on the oval.

Mercury Hits the Streep

The Cougar received its first redesign in 1969, and included a convertible. Standard power was upgraded to a new 351 small-block with 290 hp available from the optional 4-barrel.

The 320-horse 390 and 428 Cobra Jet were optional, the latter available with Ram Air.

The CJ was available with the new Drag-Pak, which included 3.91 or 4.30 gears, oil cooler, and several heavy-duty engine components.

Trans-Am fans were not left out; the new Boss 302 was available exclusively with the Eliminator package, which included a standard 351 4-barrel, hood scoop, complete instrumentation, high-back buckets, spoiler, styled steel wheels, and stripes, among other items.

The 351 Performance Group was another new package for enthusiasts. It included the 351/290 plus hood scoop with identifying stripe, F70 x 14 Polyglas tires, and stiffer springs and shocks.

The Cyclone was given a mild facelift for 1969, but the series was fine-tuned for the evolving market. The Cyclone hardtop was relegated to history, leaving the fastback as the only body style. The 302 was again standard, but enthusiasts could satisfy their appetites with the new 351/290 or move up to the 320-horse 390 or 428 Cobra Jet, the latter now available with Ram Air. The GT model was gone, replaced by the GT Appearance Group that added buckets seats and other sporty trim. New dual stripes that ran along the Cyclone's beltline were an option. Cobra Jet buyers who had racing on their minds could opt for the Drag-Pak, which included digger gears and other heavy-duty equipment.

So what about that evolving market? The 1968 Plymouth Road Runner made other automakers realize that there was a segment to be tapped, so Mercury created the Cyclone CJ, which came with fewer frills than the base Cyclone but also came standard with the 428 CJ plus white-sidewall F70 x 14 Polyglas tires, Handling Package, hood stripes, and identifying decals. "Cyclone CJ with its CJ 428 engine provides top performance, yet has full warranty coverage, and is not in the highest insurance coverage class," claimed Mercury. The Cyclone continued to struggle in the market. Only 5,882 Cyclones and 3,261 Cyclone CJs were built.

The redesigned 1969 Cougar featured the new Eliminator performance package, which included a standard 290-hp 351 with options including a 390, 428 Cobra Jet, and Boss 302. (Richard Truesdell Photo)

Mercury's response to the Plymouth Road Runner was the 1969 Cyclone CJ with a standard 428 Cobra Jet. Not a bad way to start! The base Cyclone, which featured a higher level of equipment, was also available with the 428. (Photo ©TEN: The Enthusiast Network. All rights reserved.)

The Cyclone Spoiler Cale Yarborough and Dan Gurney (shown) Specials were the basis for the NASCAR-inspired Spoiler II. The Spoiler II's nose was 4 inches longer and more steeply sloped than its Talladega cousin's. (Richard Fleener Photo)

The Cougar Eliminator was offered again in 1970 with new colors, stripes, and a revamped 351 featuring 10 more horsepower. Color choices were Competition Orange, Gold, Blue, Yellow, Green, and Pastel Blue. This is one of the very few special-ordered in a non-standard color.

To NASCAR with Love

Midyear, a new Cyclone performance package was introduced: the Cyclone Spoiler. The Cyclone Spoiler was a striped-and-spoilered performance car with standard 351/290 (with 390 and CJ optional). It was inspired by the vehicles of two NASCAR drivers: the Cale Yarborough Special, painted white and red, and the Dan Gurney Special, painted white and blue.

Mercury also produced the Cyclone Spoiler Sports Special (sometimes known as the Spoiler II), which was the division's NASCAR homologation special. Inspired by the Dodge Charger 500, the Spoiler II featured a flush nose extending over 19 inches from the stock Cyclone's plus a few other subtle modifications for better aerodynamics. Only 503 were built, all with the 351/290.

Also for 1969, a sporty full-size model joined Mercury's performance lineup : the Marauder. A semi-fastback design with long-hood/short-deck proportions, segmented taillights, and hidden headlights, the Marauder featured a standard 2-barrel 390; the only engine worth its salt was the 360-hp 429.

Those who wanted more athleticism could opt for the Marauder X-100, which came with the 429 4-barrel standard and low-gloss matte "sports-tone" finish on the trunk and flying buttresses. With mid-15-second ETs, it was no stormer, but it sold about as well as the Cyclone.

Mercury Sets Its (Gun)sights

The biggest year yet for Mercury performance was set to be 1970. Never before had Mercury offered so many performance engines to enthusiasts. A facelifted Cougar harkened back to the 1967–1968 grille. For enthusiasts, a new 300-hp 351 Cleveland was a good start, but if you wanted more power you could opt for the 428 Cobra Jet. The Drag-Pak and Ram Air were available for the CJ.

The Eliminator's appearance became much more aggressive for 1970 especially when equipped with one of the bright Competition colors. Still based on the base Cougar, the package included the 351/300 (with the Cobra Jet or Boss 302 optional), new black longitudinal stripes, new rear-quarter identification, and a stripe on the spoiler.

The Montego line was redesigned for 1970 with the Cyclone showcasing a controversial styling thanks to a gun-sight grille. Its line-up included three models with different purposes and equipment.

The Cyclone was the value leader of the Cyclone line, functioning somewhat as the replacement for 1969's Cyclone CJ. The 360-hp 429 was standard; the 370-horse 429 Cobra Jet was optional.

Standard for the Cyclone GT was a 2-barrel 351 but the 351/300, 429/360, and 429 Cobra Jet were fine upgrades. The GT was distinguished by standard bucket seats, hidden headlights, scooped hood, and lower-body trim.

The Cyclone Spoiler was now a complete performance package with standard 429 Cobra Jet with Ram Air and a full complement of equipment including high-back buckets, full instrumentation with dials canted toward the driver, 4-speed, and bright Competition colors.

The Drag-Pak and Ram Air were available for all 429 CJ-equipped Cyclones, with the Detroit Locker available when 4.30 gears were specified.

Mercury reconfigured the redesigned Cyclone series for 1970. As one of three Cyclone models, the Cyclone GT was targeted at the "luxury-sport" segment with standard hidden headlights, lower-body trim, and 351 2-barrel. This GT has the 429 Cobra Jet with Drag-Pak (Super Cobra Jet) and deleted lower-body blackout. (Richard Truesdell Photo, Courtesy M. J. Frumkin Collection)

The 1970 Spoiler was reconfigured as the ultimate Cyclone, equipped with standard 429 Cobra Jet with Ram Air and all the gewgaws that had been making an impression on the street. (Lee Lundberg Photo)

The redesigned 1971 Cougar continued to be the Mustang's cousin, but it was clear that the cat was moving in a personal-luxury direction. Nevertheless, the GT package included several heavy-duty items plus a hood scoop, which functioned only when Ram Air was ordered for the newly available 429 Cobra Jet. (Photo Courtesy Ford Motor Company)

The Marauder and Marauder X-100 were back for 1970 with few changes. This was the last appearance for the sporty Merc.

The Cougar Fattens Up

After mediocre high-performance sales in 1970, it was a daunting time for Mercury in 1971. The Cougar were all-new, but the emphasis was on luxury more than ever before. The Eliminator package and anything resembling stripes and spoilers were eliminated. The trademark hidden headlights were also gone. The 351 4-barrel was a carryover, but a slight cut in compression resulted in a loss of 15 hp.

But all was not lost for the Cougar. The 429 Cobra Jet replaced the 428, offering 370 hp plus the availability of Ram Air, although the Drag-Pak was discontinued. Interestingly, the GT Package made a return, but in standard form it was clearly more about handling than performance. Included in the package were hood scoop, gauges, Competition Handling Package, heavy-duty cooling, and other equipment.

With crippled momentum, most 1971 Cyclones had their standard engines downgraded. For the Cyclone, the 285-hp 351 became standard, with the 429 Cobra Jet optional. For the Cyclone GT, the 351 2-barrel remained standard, with the 351/285 and 429 CJ as options. New "GT" insignia appeared inside the crosshairs of the gunsight grille. For the Cyclone

Although the Cyclone's three-tiered marketing strategy made sense for 1970, it was completely out of step for 1971. The Cyclone Spoiler lost its standard big-block but displayed new beltline stripes for a fresh look. (Tom Shaw Photo)

Although performance was practically dead for 1972, sportiness was not. The redesigned Montego GT replaced the Cyclone, but an unusual Cyclone Performance Package featured air induction, stripes, fat tires, limited-slip differential, and either the 351 CJ or 429. (Photo Courtesy Mitch Frumkin)

Spoiler, new, bolder stripes ran along the beltline and shouted "CYCLONE SPOILER" up front. The 351/285 became the new powerplant, with the 429 Cobra Jet as an option.

Ram air was optional for the CJ, but the Drag-Pak was no longer available. In the depressed market, only 444 Cyclones, 2,287 GTs, and 353 Spoilers were built.

Mercury Matures with the Market

Thanks to a government mandate, compression was lowered on all 1972 engines, and they now were measured in net horsepower. The new 351 Cobra Jet (available with the 351 CJ Performance Group) was rated at 266 horses, with the regular 351 4-barrel a few horses less. Surprisingly, Mercury continued to offer the GT Package, still standard with the 2-barrel 351.

The new 1972 Montego GT was much sportier, but the performance loss was even more glaring. This replacement for the Cyclone had a stylish new figure but the 351 Cobra Jet in this application was rated at 248 hp, which was actually more than the available 429. A Cyclone Performance Package was available for both engines and included air induction and stripes, but it wasn't enough to relive the good ol' days and it was canceled early.

Both the Cougar and the Montego GT were available with the 351 Cobra Jet for 1973, but the fun was clearly over. Horsepower continued to drop and government-mandated front bumpers added weight. By the end of the year, the Montego GT was gone and the Cougar moved up to the Montego platform as a true personal-luxury coupe.

Mercury performance for the street may have died, but performance success in NASCAR was as close as a click of the remote control.

Dealerships

Ford had Tasca to promote Total Performance, but what about Mercury? Mercury was strong in NASCAR and NHRA, but the division had few dealerships that were successful in promoting high performance, and Mercury's performance-car sales were always toward the bottom of the pack.

Fortunately, one dealer stood out: Kumpf Lincoln-Mercury in Denver, thanks in part to its association with Kenz & Leslie.

Bill Kenz and Roy Leslie joined forces in 1938 in the heyday of midget racing. Kenz's technical strengths and Leslie's driving acumen led to many championship wins and records into the 1950s.

They ran a speed shop in Denver in those early days, but it was their efforts at Bonneville that established their national reputation. After Bill Kenz's *Odd Rod* exceeded 140 mph at Bonneville in 1949, the duo put their noggins together to develop the twin-flathead *777 Streamliner*. This vehicle was the first of its kind to reach 200 mph, and exceeded that marker by 10. They returned in 1951 to set a new 230 mph record, then shattered that two years later with a 256 mph run. After adding a third flathead in 1956, the *777 Streamliner* became America's fastest car for the fifth time with a 270-mph run.

By then, Kenz & Leslie had already begun dabbling in drag racing for several years, running flathead roadsters and dragsters into the 1960s when they switched to more modern Ford FE power. Kenz, ever the ingenious

Kenz & Leslie campaigned the Kumpf-sponsored High Country Cougar funny car in 1968 complete with SOHC 427 and Cougar GT-E trim. Tens of thousands of kids built plastic replicas courtesy of AMT. (Photo Courtesy Kenz & Leslie)

Moving the 1966 Comet into the midsize segment meant the Cyclone was better prepared to compete with the GTO. Dyno Don was killing it on the dragstrips, so Mercury was poised to exploit the high-performance equity with the This is no ordinary Mercury Comet brochure. (Photo Courtesy Ford Motor Company)

one, developed a manifold for the new-for-1961 390 so it could handle a supercharger. Next came a Top Fueler with SOHC 427 power until the team graduated to Funny Cars with a 1966 Mercury Cyclone, followed by a 1967.

Their nitro-burning SOHC 1968 *High Country Cougar* GT-E funny car brought them to the forefront once again. A year later, the updated 1969 *High Country Cougar II* became familiar to kids when AMT introduced a plastic model kit.

During Kenz & Leslie's Mercury years, they were sponsored by Kumpf Lincoln-Mercury. In November 1968, Kumpf president Florian Barth

announced a special 1969 Cougar "performance engineered" by Kenz & Leslie. Not much is known about these cars, but it is believed that around 10 white and red 428 Cobra Jet Ram Air Cougar XR-7s were ordered by Kumpf and modified by Kenz & Leslie with red stripes on the front fender tops, F70 tires, Cragars, and a host of other special equipment and options that included Kenz's tuning expertise.

Marketing Strategy

In retrospect, there was a profound imbalance between Mercury's high-performance marketing and sales. With Dyno Don, Dan Gurney, and Cale Yarborough, among others, Mercury had all of the right ingredients on the track, but the folks on the street were not impressed. Mercury patched things up

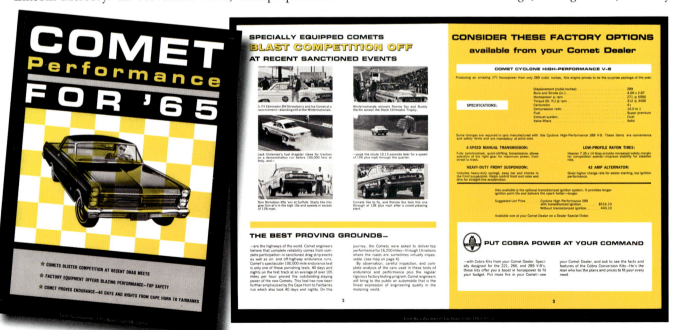

Mercury developed this brochure to tout the 1965 Comet's performance credentials in both endurance runs and drag racing. The Cyclone High Performance 289 was also featured. (Photo Courtesy Ford Motor Company)

Catering to performance enthusiasts meant profits from sales and service. Mercury wanted its dealerships to be aware of and receptive to the increased popularity of drag racing by including a special complementary What Makes Drag Racing? brochure with the tagline "This is no ordinary Mercury Comet." (Photo Courtesy Ford Motor Company)

This section of the brochure explains Mercury's recognition of drag racing's significance and the marketing push to the performance market. That push included a 1966 Comet Specifications/NHRA Classes brochure, conversion kits, periodic drag racing newsletters, and more. (Photo Courtesy Ford Motor Company)

with the midyear 1968 introduction of the 428 Cobra Jet, but by that time the performance segment began a rapid decline.

Comet Performance Brochures

Mercury had some fine drivers on its team in the 1960s. However, despite the pull of "Win on Sunday, Sell on Monday," Mercury's racing success didn't pay off in high-performance sales. It certainly wasn't for lack of trying, as the Comet Performance for 1965 brochure demonstrates.

With the Comet all grown up for 1966, Mercury produced a dealer-targeted promotional brochure titled This Is No Ordinary Mercury COMET, with the following page proclaiming "This Is No Ordinary PROMOTION!"

The purpose of the brochure was to educate dealerships on the sport of drag racing and "to show you how you can make the most of this activity to sell more new and used Comets and high-performance parts to the young people who dominate your market."

Mercury Comet Drag Performance

With 40 percent of the American population under 25, dealers were encouraged to cater to this demographic. Hence, "now, more than ever before." Comet "has the image of a sporty, high-performance car that a young man can be proud to drive" and offered "high-performance options and sporty styling, but we still need to show what Comet can do." The drag racing scene was the perfect place to showcase Comet's high-performance potential.

With more than 300,000 entrants at NHRA-sanctioned events, drag racing had increased 689 percent since 1955. Attendance at the 1965 NHRA Nationals in Indy hit an amazing 100,000. "To make a contest of it, there are classes, depending on weight and horsepower, and categories, depending on the special equipment a car might have. But the purpose is the same in all cases: to get there first in the least amount of time."

What the Division is Doing

"The Lincoln-Mercury Division was quick to recognize the significance of drag racing and what it could do for the performance and durability image of Comet."

For 1966, four Comet Cyclone GTs equipped with 427 SOHC engines were made available for sponsorship, and four Comet Cyclone GTs equipped with 390s were campaigned in stock classes.

"To help you familiarize your prospects and customers with the basics of drag racing, the What Makes Drag Racing? brochure is being produced in quantity along with the 1966 Comet Specifications/NHRA Classes brochure that shows how Comet qualifies for drag competition."

For customers interested in building competitive cars, dealers offered a High-Performance Conversion Kits brochure that included a parts catalog with high-performance items from Holman-Moody, Shelby American, and others.

Support also came from periodic newsletters "to keep you informed of what is happening around the drag circuit" including coverage of technical developments to "give you new ideas for promoting the high-performance capabilities and drag racing potential of the Comet."

What You Can Do

- Begin to make your dealership the performance headquarters by making it *look* like the performance headquarters.
- Designate one corner of the showroom "for the distribution of performance and drag racing literature" and one area in the service department "for the building and tuning of high-performance cars."
- Assign one salesman to handle all high-performance activities and appointing at least one mechanic as the performance specialist.
- Start featuring new and used high-performance cars in your newspaper advertising.
- Hold a series of performance clinics and have "some Comet performance kits on hand to show the group how they work, and how they can be used for maximum results."
- Show winning drag cars on the lot, plus feature the Comet Cyclone GT and other high-performance Comets in stock.
- Put a high-performance Mercury on display at the local dragstrip, and include spec sheets and a salesperson who knows the product. Set up a stand to sell emergency parts.

Mercury dealerships were able to keep a pulse on the division's racing successes with Mercury/Comet Performance News. The September 22, 1966, issue featured a match race between Eddie Schartman and Don Nicholson, with Nicholson setting an all-time-low ET of 7.96. (Photo Courtesy Ford Motor Company)

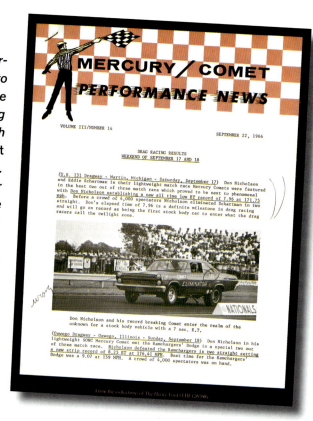

NHRA STOCK CAR SECTION S and SA

Here are the N.H.R.A. stock car classes.

CLASSES S Manual Trans.	CLASSES SA Automatic Trans.	WEIGHT-TO-POWER RATIO (lbs. shipping weight to Advertised hp.)
S/S	S/SA	0.00 to 6.99 lbs.
AA/S	AA/SA	7.00 to 8.69 lbs.
A/S	A/SA	8.70 to 9.49 lbs.
B/S	B/SA	9.50 to 10.59 lbs.
C/S	C/SA	10.60 to 11.29 lbs.
D/S	D/SA	11.30 to 11.88 lbs.
E/S	E/SA	11.89 to 12.49 lbs.
F/S	F/SA	12.50 to 13.99 lbs.
G/S	G/SA	14.00 to 14.99 lbs.
H/S	H/SA	15.00 to 15.59 lbs.
I/S	I/SA	15.60 to 16.99 lbs.
J/S	"	17.00 to 18.99 lbs.
K/S	"	19.00 to 21.49 lbs.
L/S	"	21.50 to 24.99 lbs.
M/S	"	25.00 to 27.99 lbs.
N/S	"	28.00 or more lbs.

HERE'S HOW DRAG CARS ARE CLASSIFIED IN THE STOCK CAR SECTION:

A 1966 Comet 202 2-Door Sedan with 200-hp. Cyclone 289 V-8 engine and 3-speed manual transmission weighs 2936 lbs. (Shipping). Dividing shipping weight (2936) by the horsepower (200) gives the weight-to-power ratio—14.68 lbs. per hp. This falls in Class G/S.

Here are the classes where 1966 Comets can run...

POWER TEAMS	COMET 202 2-door sedan	COMET 202 4-door sedan	CAPRI 4-door sedan	CAPRI Hardtop	CALIENTE 4-door sedan	CALIENTE Hardtop	CALIENTE Convertible	CYCLONE Hardtop	CYCLONE Convertible	CYCLONE GT Hardtop	CYCLONE GT Convertible	WAGONS Voyager	WAGONS Villager
COMET 200 "6" (1V) — 3-Speed Manual	L/S	L/S	L/S	L/S	L/S	L/S	M/S					M/S	M/S
— Multi-Drive Merc-O-Matic	I/S	I/SA	I/SA	I/SA	I/SA	I/SA	I/SA					I/SA	I/SA
CYCLONE 289 V-8 (2V) — 3-Speed Manual	G/S	G/S	H/S	H/S	H/S	H/S	I/S	H/S	I/S			I/S	J/S
— 4-Speed Manual													
— Multi-Drive Merc-O-Matic	G/SA	H/SA	H/SA	H/SA	H/SA	H/SA	I/SA	H/SA	I/SA			I/SA	I/SA
CYCLONE 390 (2V) — 3-Speed Manual	E/S	D/S	E/S	E/S	E/S	E/S	E/S					F/S	F/S
— 4-Speed Manual	E/S	E/S	E/S	E/S	E/S	E/S	F/S						
— Multi-Drive Merc-O-Matic	D/SA	D/SA	E/SA	E/SA	E/SA	E/SA	E/SA					F/SA	F/SA
CYCLONE GT 390 (4V) — 3-Speed Manual								B/S	C/S				
— 4-Speed Manual								B/S	C/S				
— Sport Shift								B/SA	C/SA				
427 V-8 (8V) — 4-Speed Manual	AA/S	AA/S	A/S	A/S	A/S	A/S	AA/S	AA/S				AA/S	AA/S
— Multi-Drive Merc-O-Matic	AA/SA	AA/SA	AA/SA	AA/SA	AA/SA	AA/SA	AA/SA					A/SA	A/SA

1966 Mercury Comet V-8 Power Teams Available for Drag Cars

	Cyclone 289 V-8	Cyclone 390 V-8	Cyclone 390 V-8	Cyclone GT 390 V-8	Cyclone 427 (8V)
Displacement	289 cu. in.	390 cu. in.	390 cu. in.	390 cu. in.	427 cu. in.
Bore & stroke (in.)	4.00 x 2.87	4.05 x 3.78	4.05 x 3.78	4.05 x 3.78	4.24 x 3.79
Adv. hp.@ rpm.	200 @ 4400	265 @ 4400	275 @ 4400	335 @ 4800	425 @ 6000
Adv. torque lb.-ft. @ rpm.	282 @ 2400	401 @ 2600	405 @ 2600	427 @ 3200	480 @ 3700
Carburetor	2-bbl.	2-bbl.	2-bbl.	4-bbl.	Dual 4-bbl.
Compression ratio	9.3:1	9.5:1	9.5:1	10.5:1	11.1:1
Fuel	Regular	Regular	Regular	Premium	Super Prem.
Exhaust	Single	Single (a)	Single (a)	Dual	Dual
Valve lifters	Hydraulic	Hydraulic	Hydraulic	Hydraulic	Mechanical
Transmissions: 3-speed manual	X	X	X	X	
4-speed manual				X	X
Multi-Drive Merc-O-Matic	X		X	X(b)	X

(a) Dual exhaust standard on convertible and available as dealer-installed accessory on other models. Accessory dual exhaust weighs 31 pounds additional.
(b) Sport Shift Merc-O-Matic

Here are Comet weight ranges with manual transmissions...

CLASSES Manual Trans.	WEIGHT-TO-POWER RATIO (lbs. shipping weight to Advertised hp.)	Shpg. Wt. Range Comet 200 "6" 120 hp.	Shpg. Wt. Range Cyclone 289 V-8 200 hp.	Shpg. Wt. Range Cyclone 390 V-8 265 hp.	Shpg. Wt. Range Cyclone GT 390 V-8 335 hp.	Shpg. Wt. Range Cyclone 427 V-8 (8V) 425 hp.
S/S	0.00 to 6.99 lbs.					
AA/S	7.00 to 8.69 lbs.					2975–3697
A/S	8.70 to 9.49 lbs.					3698–4033
B/S	9.50 to 10.59 lbs.				3182–3550	
C/S	10.60 to 11.29 lbs.				3551–3785	
D/S	11.30 to 11.88 lbs.				3786–3980	
E/S	11.89 to 12.49 lbs.					
F/S	12.50 to 13.99 lbs.			3313–3709		
G/S	14.00 to 14.99 lbs.			3710–3974		
H/S	15.00 to 15.59 lbs.		3000–3119	3975–4131		
I/S	15.60 to 16.99 lbs.		3120–3399			
J/S	17.00 to 18.99 lbs.		3340–3799			
K/S	19.00 to 21.49 lbs.					
L/S	21.50 to 24.99 lbs.	2580–2999				
M/S	25.00 to 27.99 lbs.	3000–3399				
N/S	28.00 or more lbs.	+3360				

Here are Comet weight ranges with automatics...

CLASSES Automatic Trans.	WEIGHT-TO-POWER RATIO (lbs. shipping weight to Advertised hp.)	Shpg. Wt. Range Comet 200 "6" 120 hp.	Shpg. Wt. Range Cyclone 289 V-8 200 hp.	Shpg. Wt. Range Cyclone 390 V-8 275 hp. (A/T)	Shpg. Wt. Range Cyclone GT 390 V-8 335 hp.	Shpg. Wt. Range Cyclone 427 V-8 (8V) 425 hp.
S/SA	0.00 to 6.99 lbs.					
AA/SA	7.00 to 8.69 lbs.					2975–3697
A/SA	8.70 to 9.49 lbs.					3698–4037
B/SA	9.50 to 10.59 lbs.					
C/SA	10.60 to 11.29 lbs.				3551–3785	
D/SA	11.30 to 11.88 lbs.				3786–3982	
E/SA	11.89 to 12.49 lbs.			3270–3437		
F/SA	12.50 to 13.99 lbs.			3438–3849		
G/SA	14.00 to 14.99 lbs.			3850–4124		
H/SA	15.00 to 15.59 lbs.		3000–3119			
I/SA	15.60 to 16.99 lbs.		3120–3399			
"	17.00 to 18.99 lbs.		3400–3799			
"	19.00 to 21.49 lbs.					
"	21.50 to 24.99 lbs.	2580–2999				
"	25.00 to 27.99 lbs.	3000–3359				
"	28.00 or more lbs.	+3360				

This 1966 brochure laid out the specs for all Comet models so a car could be strategically built to win a certain drag race class. (Photo Courtesy Ford Motor Company)

Go with the Green Now!

"In drag racing, many races are won or lost at the starting line. Since many cars are very closely matched, the winner is frequently the car that gets off first by a fraction of a second. If you want to win the lion's share of the growing performance-minded youth market, you can't waste a minute."

The complementary *1966 Mercury Comet Preliminary Drag Specifications and NHRA Stock Car Classifications* showed both dealers and customers how NHRA stock car classifications worked, and where different Comets fit in based on weight, horsepower, and transmission.

These topics were covered:

- NHRA Stock Car Section S and SA
- The classes where 1966 Comets can run
- 1966 Comet V-8 Power Teams available for drag cars
- Comet weight ranges with manual transmissions
- Comet weight ranges with automatics
- Manual transmission gear ratios
- Regular production and special-order axles
- Curb weights and weights of accessories and equipment

Drags Pay Off in Profits

The performance emphasis will "account for an ever increasing percentage of your sales, not just of the GT or big-engine cars, but of the entire line of Comets which will reflect the new performance image." Plus, "people who are competing in drag races need more service work than the average driver" and high-performance equipment purchases "can be charged for [sic] at a higher labor rate."

The Streep Scene tour's specialty car display highlighted this pearlescent orange Cougar Eliminator show car that featured the 428 Cobra Jet, Dana-Spicer 2-speed rear, American Racing mags, and custom interior. The production Eliminator included a conventional spoiler, paint job, interior, wheels, and rear axle. (Photo ©TEN: The Enthusiast Network. All rights reserved.)

As part of Mercury's 1969 product planning directive, Streep Scene was a cooperative effort with Coca-Cola and Car Craft. The magazine built this Super Cat Cobra Jet project car (with involvement from Don Nicholson), then toured at races and shows. After its retirement, Coca-Cola used the Super Cat as a giveaway. (Tom Shaw Photo)

A brief from Lincoln-Mercury Marketing Product Plans Office meeting on May 3, 1968 outlined the Division's "youth/performance" efforts past and present. The document included a list of observations on how Mercury should "exploit the new performance hardware."

Performance Emphasis

- Mercury oval-track racing in 1963–1964.
- Introduction of the Comet Cyclone in 1964.
- Drag racing presence since 1964 with big names, although Sox and Martin were wooed by Chrysler with much success on the track and with Performance Clinics.
- The sale of approximately 300 Comets with the Hi-Po 289/271, although "it was necessary to cancel about 50 of these when the total could not be filled within reasonable time limits."
- Offering the 390 as an option for the 1966 Comet, and standard for the 1966–1967 Cyclone GT.
- Dan Gurney leading the Mercury Sports Panel "with the primary objective of associating the Division and, more specifically, the Cougar car with Performance leadership."
- "The Cyclone as a performance image model has lacked appearance and feature differentiation and specific promotional support to compete effectively with GTO."
- "Our drag racing efforts have been worthwhile but have suffered by not supplying the necessary supporting hardware to those who want to run their own performance cars."

Mercury concluded that the division had made "a very small inroad in the youth/performance market," with the Cougar doing the most in attracting a younger demographic. "We *have* achieved some progress in building a *performance image*, although seriously hampered by availability of performance hardware."

Lincoln-Mercury Performance Image Objectives in Relation to Engine Programs

- Mercury wasn't keeping pace with the growth of high-horsepower engines, with the combined market of 390-equipped Comets and Ford Fairlanes being half of Chrysler's 300+-hp intermediates and 7 percent of General Motors'.
- The competition had more choices in both small- and large-displacement high-performance engines.
- "Performance-oriented customers have not chosen Ford's 289 and 390 engines. This is a long-standing situation that has seriously depreciated the reputation of our engines among car buffs."

- In discussions with performance-oriented kids, Chevrolet engines were perceived to breathe better, and "you can get more plus performance with a camshaft and carburetor change on a Chevy than a Ford."

Mercury concluded that it needed to maximize the impact of the high-performance version of the upcoming 351, especially for the Cougar. "In light of the growing mid-range engine market," Mercury's preliminary solution for 1969 was to "emphasize that the new 351-ci engine would be materially strengthened by some form of 'image'" package that included the 351-4V, upgraded suspension, and hood stripe, with improved Cleveland heads for 1970.

Lincoln-Mercury Performance Product Programs

"The 428 Cobra Jet engine is our best to create maximum impact in the performance market. We need both image and the best competitive price position possible and should use the Cyclone fastback with 428 CJ or which faces off against GTO's top engine, and a low end model (the Comet Sports Coupe) to provide 428 CJ performance at the lowest possible prices. The need for a low-end/high-performance model will become even more critical as larger engines are introduced in smaller (and lower base price) cars in upcoming years." 428 CJ plans for the 1969 Cougar "will parallel 1968 practice."

"To dramatize this new, lightweight and responsive engine and its suitability to the Cougar product, a 351 performance/handling package has been developed that will combine 351-4v engine, handling package, and hood tape stripe with '351' identification."

Lincoln-Mercury Performance Merchandising Program

Dealer programs were introduced to identify and establish a close working relationship with 25-50 performance-oriented dealerships and encourage them "in formulating, testing, and carrying out specific promotional programs." This also helped Mercury "stay closely meshed with the performance customer."

Image models were available to exploit the full performance potential of the new 351 and Cobra Jet.

The Gurney-inspired Cougar XR7-G was suggested as a special model for 1969 but with less custom equipment: 351-4V, special handling package including rear track bar, special wheels and Polyglas Wide Ovals, and unique exterior trim such as hood pins, black-out paint, and identification.

A Nicholson-inspired extension of the upcoming Cyclone CJ called *Eliminator* was "designed with features that appeal to the drag racing oriented customer": unique hood and spoiler, trunk-mounted battery, Hurst shifter, aircraft-type seat belts, 8,000-rpm tach, and Wink wide-angle mirror.

Race Participation

Mercury planned to use Nicholson's racing "as the image platform on which to build Cougar/Cyclone visibility" at dragstrips. And the 1968 Cyclone 500 drive-away programs in the South were believed to have provided product visibility and generated impressive incremental sales.

Promotion and Advertising Programs

Several promotional/advertising programs were under consideration, based on competitive performance hardware, racing personalities, and competitive racing achievements.

Dealer Promotions

Using "Performance Headquarters" dealers, Mercury planned to develop appearance tours with its racing personalities (and their cars, when possible).

Performance Clinics

Beginning with the September 1968 Summernationals, Mercury planned to conduct Performance Clinics at major NHRA events, with Nich-olson conducting a clinic emphasizing the 428 CJ. Mercury also worked with Performance Headquarters dealers for publicity tie-ins.

Increased Road Test Coverage

Mercury planned to specially prepare a roster of performance models "to provide excellent 'press' for the new performance hardware and the new 1969 cars and provides visibility in media that are targeted squarely at the youth market."

Increased Auto Show Participation

The division planned to increase its "performance" emphasis in the three major auto shows, plus others like Autorama.

As it turned out, the 1969 Cougar XR7-G never materialized, but the 351 Performance Group did. The Cyclone CJ Eliminator didn't see production, but the name was applied to a striped-and-spoilered Cougar package with standard 4-barrel 351.

Newsletter

The *Mercury/Comet Performance News* newsletter, which helped keep dealerships in the loop of Mercury's competitive exploits, was another component of this 1966 marketing push.

In the September 12, 1966, edition, Don Nicholson "established an unofficial world's record for the stock-bodied cars with a speed of 173.74 mph with an ET of 8.31." On day four, "the fourth and final round was won by Ed Schartman over Don Nicholson, setting a new ET record of 8.28 and a new speed record at 174.41 mph" in front of a crowd of 60,000.

In the September 29, 1966, edition, a Bud Moore–prepared Comet driven by Darel Dieringer won the Old Dominion 500. And the Kenz & Leslie SOHC Comet defeated the Golden Commandos' 1966 Hemi Plymouth with a best of 9.04 ET at 161 mph.

Streep Scene

Mercury's 1969 performance marketing program bore a slight resemblance to the May 1968 product planning brief. Christened "Streep Scene," this hybrid program catered to the enthusiast who drove every day ("Street") yet enjoyed competing on the weekend at the drags ("Strip"). The NHRA and the AHRA had developed their own respective "stock" classes and the Streep Scene was Mercury's way of showing enthusiasts what they could buy from the factory and how they could take advantage of these classes with modifications and tuning tips. If a Mercury owner wanted to move into Super Stock territory, the Streep Scene program had him or her covered as well.

Four different Mercurys were marketed under the Streep Scene banner: Cougar 351-4v, the Sure-footed Cat; Marauder X-100, the Scene Stealer; Cyclone CJ, the Street Sweeper; and Cougar CJ 428, The Prowler.

Don Nicholson toured the United States with an 18-wheeler, stopping at dealerships and car shows touting Mercury's street and strip entries. Two special features were Dyno Don's *Eliminator* Cougar funny car, and a miniature Streep Simulator dragstrip where visitors could sit inside, operate the controls, and experience the simulated sensation of navigating *Eliminator* down the dragstrip with a 190-mph 7-second blast.

Coca-Cola's sponsorship resulted in the National Thirst Eliminator campaign tied to the Streep Scene, which included a giveaway of *Car Craft*/Nicholson's Super Cat CJ Cougar.

Advertising Program

Mercury had the great luck of having Ford as a parent, so Total Performance trickled down to Marauders, Comets, Cyclones, and Cougars. How Mercury approached the consumer gave the brand distinct prominence compared to Ford.

L-M Woos Youths at the Dragstrip

Mercury did more than jump on the GTO bandwagon with the advent of the 1966 Cyclone. The division was intent on wooing youths via the

Cougar kit!

OPTIONAL HIGH
PERFORMANCE EQUIPMENT

Mercury Cougar—America's first luxury sports car at a popular price—offers excellent opportunities for plus-profits from the sales of performance parts and accessories. The very nature of the car makes it attractive to sports car types who will want to add more "sizzle and scat" to the basic model. This will, of course, unleash new merchandising opportunities for you as a Mercury dealer—and make you more competitive in the profitable high performance field. '67 is the year to put extra sizzle in your selling—with Mercury Cougar high-performance options . . . sharpening the claws of untamed elegance! Full information on Cougar performance options will be sent to you very soon.

dual-point distributor kit
9000 rpm tachometer
tuned exhaust headers
wood-rim steering wheel
cast aluminum wheels
extruded aluminum cam-ground pistons
high-lift cam
Weber carburetor induction kit

COUGAR

When it introduced the 1967 Cougar, Mercury sent this How to Sharpen a Cougar's Claws *folder to dealerships. Equipment designed by Shelby American gave dealerships merchandising opportunities to augment Mercury's high-performance image. (Photo Courtesy Ford Motor Company)*

dragstrip. "The way to the heart of the fast-growing youth market is through escalation of the performance image, Lincoln-Mercury is telling its dealers," read the March 21, 1966, *Automotive News*. Mercury had built up the Comet with the 100,000-mile Durability Run and factory-experimental racers, and now Comet's performance image was burnished on a more tangible level on the dragstrip.

According to Thomas Daniels of Lincoln-Mercury's sales promotion and training department, 200 of the division's 2,500 dealerships were active in drag racing in some capacity. "Naturally, California is the hottest bed of activity. That's where drag racing got its start in the late 1940s. It's a very popular sport and it's still in its infancy. Denver is another good spot, and so are the Northeast and the Southeast, particularly in the Atlanta area.

"Our objective is to show dealers how they can make the most of this activity to sell more new and used Comets and high-performance parts to the young people who dominate their market." If a dealership didn't have performance enthusiasts on staff, Daniels recommended that it "hire specialists rather than attempting to train some of his present employees."

Walker Motor Sales of Dayton, Ohio, was one of those dealerships. Jack Walker said, "I had one of the first drag cars that the factory built. We got a lot of trophies and publicity and a lot of exposure to the younger set. This eventually paid off in sales of both high-performance parts as well as Comet hardtops. I think our performance image has definitely sold cars."

Illinois-based Tom Coward Lincoln-Mercury reported that it sold 50 cars through drag racing over the past year. "Drag racing is bringing the 18-, 19-, and 20-year-olds to look at the Cyclone and other high-performance cars, but it's not limited to the younger people. This year the older generation, people in their 30s, 40s, and even 50s, are coming in because they are more conscious of speed and high performance."

Daniels mentioned that *Super Stock & Drag Illustrated* chose the Cyclone as its Performance Car of the Year, and a red Cyclone GT convertible was chosen to pace the Indianapolis 500. In anticipation of the race, dealers were encouraged to display replica pace cars in showrooms April 1–May 30. And to reach teenagers and youths who could influence their parents' car-buying decisions, these dealerships had slot car tracks for give-aways and purchase. "The 171 dealerships in the six-state Memphis district have ordered 16,000 of the 1/25-scale model slot cars," added Daniels, with each dealership conducting "racing demonstrations and competitions for the public."

This program was also used to gauge public reaction for a possible national promotion for 1967.

How to Sharpen a Cougar's Claws

Lincoln-Mercury dealerships received an October 27, 1966, letter highlighting merchandising opportunities for high-performance parts and accessories for both Cougars and Comets. "The folder *How to Sharpen a Cougar's Claws* has been made available to dealers in conjunction with special displays of typical high-performance equipment designed by Shelby American for use on Cougar and Mercury intermediates." Several performance kits could be ordered wholesale direct from Shelby.

Kit I featured a cast aluminum intake with 600-cfm Holley, 14-inch chrome air cleaner, hydraulic camshaft kit, tuned exhaust headers, extensions,

The 1967 Cougar's introduction coincided with increasing popularity of the Trans-Am series. Bud Moore's 1967 Cougar, driven by Parnelli Jones, won the first Revere 250. (Photo Courtesy Hurst Inc.)

Youths' interest in sports and Mercury's participation in motorsports led to the creation of the Mercury Sports Panel in 1967. A number of outstanding performers across different sports sat on the panel to help build "an identification between their own personal brilliance, prowess, and versatility and Lincoln-Mercury's car lines and sales organization." (Photos Courtesy Ford Motor Company and Mitch Frumkin)

and straight-through mufflers for the 289. Expected horsepower increase was 50 to 60.

Kit II was similar, but for high-RPM applications. A 715-cfm Holley, solid-lifter camshaft, and heavy-duty clutch gave 60 to75 additional horses.

Kit III combined a dual-quad high-riser intake, solid-lifter camshaft, dual-exhaust system, high-performance dual-point distributor, and heavy-duty clutch for an increase of up to 90 horses.

Kit IV featured a fiberglass hood with functional air induction, racing mirror with high-resolution glass, and five cast-aluminum wheels including hubcaps and chrome lug nuts.

Kit V included a wood-trimmed stainless steel steering wheel, transistorized 270-degree speedo, 9,000-rpm tachometer, and racing mirror.

The valvecover kit featured die-cast aluminum valvecovers with a black crinkle finish, which decreased rocker arm and tappet noise while keeping the oil cool.

The cast aluminum oil pan with polished fins added 6.5 quarts of oil capacity and aided cooling.

The Weber Carburetor Induction System with cast aluminum intake bumped horsepower up 60 to 65.

MERCURY WINS ATLANTA 500

Mercury's Atlanta district devised a regional drive-away promotion for the 1968 Atlanta 500 that displayed specially prepared Cyclone 500 models. The promotion was later repeated for the World 600 at Darlington and included a companion Cougar 500. (Jim Pinkerton Sticker. Photo Courtesy Ford Motor Company)

The 160 Mercury Cyclones get ready for some "parade" laps around the Atlanta track.

two for the money
and
one for the road

Above are two stocks worth holding onto—good bets for the long pull. Like 500 miles flat-out at Daytona and Atlanta where track-modified Montego Cyclones finished 1-2, turning each place into a kind of outdoor showroom. If you'd like a piece of the action in a road version, we recommend our Montego Cyclone GT "500" with a list of goodies as long as your arm. A 390 GT V-8 for openers, 325 horses strong (or, for quicker effects, our 428 Cobra Jet V-8!). Dual pipes. Whitewalled wide treads and GT (turbine) wheel covers. A suspension system with one of driving's biggest handling charges. Blackout grille and taillight panel. Tinted rear window. Twin buckets in a vinyl that "breathes" to help you keep your cool. Deluxe vinyl-wrapped steering wheel. Wood-grained instrument panel and authoritative gauges. Nylon carpeting. Even the body is striped for action. You won't miss the racing numerals. Especially when you hit the road!

Mercury's got it . . . the "Competitive Edge!" MERCURY Ford

19

This ad from the 1968 Carolina 500 program features the promotional Cyclone GT 500. (Photo Courtesy Ford Motor Company)

The Sports Panel

Lincoln-Mercury created the Sports Panel in the fall of 1967 with some of the most famous names in sports. According to Dan Gurney, "The primary purpose of the Lincoln-Mercury Sports Panel is to be of assistance to dealers and salesmen. Nearly half of today's population is under 25 years of age. The youth market is not only a valuable source of prospects for used car sales, it also represents a tremendous potential for new car sales, now and in the future.

"These young people are interested in sports, and the Lincoln-Mercury Sports Panel provides an excellent opportunity to communicate with these potential buyers on a common ground."

The Sports Panel represented Lincoln-Mercury "at numerous community functions, charitable events, and major automobile activities."

The division also launched *Mercury Sports* magazine in the fall of 1967. "There is logic in associating the Mercury car with sports. It is a car naturally tied to the concept of an active successful life. To help us we have established a Lincoln-Mercury Sports Panel, now including Arnold Palmer and Sharron Moran, pro golfers; Bart Starr, the football player; and Al Kaline, the baseball player." Cale Yarborough was later added to the panel, which lasted through 1975.

Delivery at the Track

On March 31, 1968, Mercury won big at the Atlanta 500 with Cale Yarborough and LeeRoy Yarbrough finishing 1st and 2nd in their Cyclones. It was the perfect culmination of a month-long sales promotion organized by the Atlanta sales district that resulted in the production of specially trimmed Cyclones called Cyclone 500s.

Eighty-five dealerships (out of 138 in the region) spanning five states participated in this promotion, which was presented in front of 80,000 NASCAR fans at the Atlanta 500. The newspaper, radio, and TV media blitz kicked off after the Daytona 500 on February 28.

Said one Atlanta-based sales manager in the April 15, 1968, *Automotive News*, "It was the best promotion I've ever seen in my experience in the auto business." He claimed he even sold a Cyclone within one hour of opening the dealership on the day after the race. The customer admitted he hadn't even thought of Mercury until Cale Yarborough's victory at Daytona a month earlier, with the Atlanta 500 clinching the deal.

Marti Auto Works records show 155 Cyclones were ordered for the Atlanta 500 promotion. The Cyclone 500 was nothing more than a factory Cyclone or Cyclone GT with "500" numerals and checkered flags added to each rear fender outside the factory. All were painted Calypso Coral or Polar White and equipped with everything from a 302 to a 390.

The Cyclone 500s were lined up at the track when the gates opened up at 6 a.m., remaining in full view of the spectators for more than five hours. Customers who had purchased Cyclone 500s before the Atlanta 500 were given two free tickets to take delivery at the race, which included breakfast, Mercury race hats and jackets, photo opportunities with Mercury's drivers, and two passes around the track before the gentlemen started their engines.

Mercury's Merchandising Department manager, R. A. Ablondi, addressed Mercury dealers in an April 18, 1968, letter that highlighted the Atlanta 500 Drive-Away Program. Ablondi described delivery of 160 cars in front of 83,000 spectators, and Mercury's 1-2 victory at the race, then concluded, "There can be no greater evidence than that cited in this article about the Atlanta 500 Drive-Away Program to make the point that *performance sells cars* when properly promoted. By publicizing these victories at the local level, you can strengthen Mercury's performance image and improve sales at the same time."

Thanks to the promotion's success, it was repeated at the World 600 at Charlotte on May 26, 1968, with involvement from both the Atlanta and Washington, D.C., sales districts. Sixty 1968 Calypso Coral Cyclone GTs were ordered and rebadged as Cyclone 500s, several of them with the 428 Cobra Jet that had been introduced the previous month. Additionally, 54 1968 Polar White Cougars were rebadged as Cougar 500s. Several engines were available, from the 289 to the Cobra Jet.

CHAPTER 8

PLYMOUTH TAKES IT TO THE STREET

Chrysler created a legend with the 1955 C-300. Plymouth's first V-8 was a fine effort, but it had to compete with the "Hot One" from Chevrolet, whose small-block took off. The limited-edition 1956 Fury showcased Plymouth in a new light and created the first true Plymouth performance car. That lasted through 1958 with a 305-hp 350; for 1959, the one-year-only Sport Fury featured a 305-horse 361, but the special aspect of the original Fury was lost.

Plymouth Goes Commando

Performance received a boost in 1960 thanks to ram induction. Plymouth called it Sonoramic Commando, and it came in two flavors: a 310-hp 361 and a 330-horse 383. Either was available with a column-shifted 3-speed manual or TorqueFlite automatic. "Ram induction eliminates air-wave interference with fuel flow. When the valve is closed, the length of the ram-induction manifold pipe creates a pressure that concentrates and maintains a fuel/air buildup at the intake valve. When the valve opens, the full force of the pressure rams the cylinder full of fuel. This approximates supercharging without the complications of a supercharger."

The 1961 Plymouth was shorn of its fins and looked as if it came from outer space. Only the Sonoramic Commando 383 remained. Chevrolet had debuted its 409 and Pontiac continued to be hot (not to mention light-years more handsome), but things needed to improve, and fast!

Max-Wedge Threat

The redesigned 1962 Plymouth (the first of the B-Bodies) was maligned at the time due to reduced dimensions and funky styling, but the light weight helped Plymouth rekindle performance. Enthusiasts could opt for the dual-quad 383/343 or 413/380, but it was the Super Stock 413 that truly cemented Plymouth as a threat to the status quo.

Although different than the Sonoramic, the Max Wedge utilized similar principles: "The new engine has a one-piece aluminum 15-inch ram-tube manifold that fits between the rocker covers and serves as a tappet chamber cover. The ram tubes increase the velocity of the air/fuel mixture entering the combustion chambers, producing an effect similar to supercharging. The unit is tuned to increase output in the high-speed ranges, above 4,000 rpm," announced a February 1962 press release.

With a pair of 650-cfm Carter 4-barrels, the 413 offered 410 or 420 hp depending on compression. Transmission was either a heavy-duty T-85 floor-shifted 3-speed manual or TorqueFlite.

For 1963, Plymouth toned down the bizarre styling that had hurt sales. A new Golden Commando 383 featuring 330 hp made its appearance. It was as good as

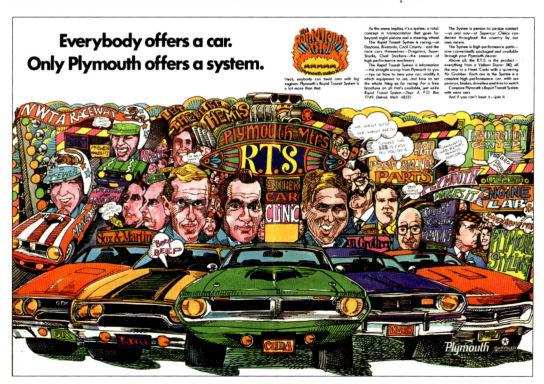

Other companies offered cars, but Plymouth offered a system. The 1970–1971 Rapid Transit System featured at least one model for each high-performance segment. (Dodge, Plymouth and the AMC design are registered trademarks of FCA US LLC)

The 1960 Plymouth's Sonoramic Commando ram induction for 361 and 383 big-blocks had an advantage thanks to Chrysler's TorqueFlite automatic. Plymouth built 1,573 Sonoramics in 1960 according to Darrell Davis. (Dodge, Plymouth and the AMC design are registered trademarks of FCA US LLC)

In 1957, Plymouth advertised, "Suddenly, it's 1960!" but by 1960, the division probably wished it were 1957. Unibody construction was new. (Tim Costello Photo)

The 1962 Sport Fury was Plymouth's sporty buckets-and-console model but suffered from polarizing styling and 7/8-scale size. The size was a mixed blessing because the Super Stock 413 wreaked havoc on the dragstrips. (Dodge, Plymouth and the AMC design are registered trademarks of FCA US LLC)

Sales picked up in 1963 thanks to Plymouth's attempt to remove 1962's styling quirks. The Super Stock 413 was upgraded to 426 ci, but the new Hurst 4-speed was available only for big-blocks up to the 383. (Andrew V. Kent Photo)

it got for street-going Plymouths except for the drag-oriented Max Wedge. A November 1962 announcement for a floor-shifted Hurst 4-speed helped give Plymouth some much-needed performance ability, but it was not up to the task of handling the Max Wedge's power.

Nevertheless, the Max Wedge grew to 426 ci, now rated at 415 and 425 hp (the latter available with aluminum components and air induction). In June, Plymouth announced the Super Stock 426-II, an update that improved airflow characteristics for a broader peak horsepower curve. Horsepower ratings remained the same.

Street Wedge Debut

By 1964, Plymouth had shed every ungainly styling item that was introduced two years prior. However, the performance market was experiencing a dynamic shift because of the introduction of the Pontiac GTO. Plymouth still had a 330-hp 383, but "383 Belvedere" didn't have the same ring or performance as "Tri-Power." Plymouth's answer was the new 365-horse Commando 426. It was streetable, in contrast to the Max Wedge, and a new 4-speed for the 426 gave it more performance appeal.

The 4-speed was also available for the Max Wedge. It began 1964 as the Super Stock 426-III, which included upgrades such as heavier and more durable connecting rods, new cylinder heads with increased intake ports, and slightly larger combustion chambers. The low-compression version kept its 415 hp rating, but the 425-horse upgrade featured compression lowered to 12.5:1 "to make the engine less critical as far as octane require-

ments are concerned without affecting performance." The latter also came standard with aluminum components.

The Hemi

The Max Wedge may have put Plymouth into the big leagues, but when the Super Commando 426 was updated with hemispherical heads in mid-1964, Chrysler rewrote racing history. The 426 Hemi changed the rules in both NASCAR and NHRA competition, with Richard Petty leading a 1-2-3 win at Daytona.

Announced on February 17, 1964, the Super Commando V-8 (aka 426 Hemi) was a distinct improvement over the Super Stock 426, as Richard Petty famously demonstrated. The 400-hp NASCAR engine featured a 4-barrel atop a two-level intake. (Dodge, Plymouth and the AMC design are registered trademarks of FCA US LLC)

The 1964 Plymouth's appearance was quite mainstream, which helped sales recover. This Belvedere featured the new 426 Street Wedge that bridged the gap between the 383 and Super Stock 426.

The Barracuda may have had to make do with a 273, but Hurst's Hemi Under Glass featured a fuel-injected 426 Hemi under the backlight. (Dodge, Plymouth and the AMC design are registered trademarks of FCA US LLC)

The new Barracuda, a distinctive Valiant-based fastback featuring a prodigious backlight, was introduced in April. Nothing performance-worthy was available initially, but it was an auspicious start for this sporty model until the Ford Mustang was unveiled 16 days later.

In 1965, Plymouth finally had a full-fledged full-size series after 1962's downsizing debacle. The new C-Body platform continued the Fury name in several guises. All featured contemporary vertical headlights and conservative, slab-sided styling that played it safe after going over the edge several years before.

But that didn't spell the end of the B-Body. It continued on, restyled and promoted as a midsize car. The series consisted of the Belvedere I, Belvedere II, and Satellite, all available with the 383/330 or 426/365. And the Hemi? Still available, although offered only as a 12.5:1-compression drag car because Plymouth was sitting out NASCAR.

Plymouth finally produced a "proper" full-size car in 1965 after 1962's downsizing debacle. The Fury name was retained and, with the 426 Street Wedge, the Sport Fury could be a very capable machine. (Dennis Kerry Photo)

With a 1965 A990 Hemi Belvedere, Shirley Shahan became the first woman to win an NHRA event. (Photo ©TEN: The Enthusiast Network. All rights reserved.)

The Super Commander A990 Belvedere I was joined midyear by an A/FX version featuring axles that were moved forward for better weight distribution. This kinda funny-looking car led to a new race car classification.

The Hemi, Part II

The B-Body was restyled for 1966, but the most newsworthy changes were under the hood. The Commando 383 was demoted to 325 hp; the Commando 426 disappeared from the option list, replaced by the all-new 425-horse Street Hemi. "This remarkable engine has smooth, dependable

The 1965 B-Body's clever new role as a midsize car featured an attractive restyle and gave Plymouth an opportunity to compete with GM's A-Bodies. But even with the 426/365, Plymouth found competing with the GTO juggernaut to be difficult. (Dodge, Plymouth and the AMC design are registered trademarks of FCA US LLC)

The B-Body was restyled for 1966, but the big news was the introduction of the Street Hemi. Because of the engine's expense (and subsequent rarity) and Belvedere/Satellite's lack of performance image, it wasn't quite enough to help Plymouth's street cred. (Tim Costello Photo)

power on the street. The 426 Hemi idles smoothly, has good low-speed response, and warms up quickly. The intake manifold features two tandem-mounted 4-barrel carburetors. The hemispherical combustion chambers make it possible to use bigger valves for better breathing and maximum efficiency." The new Street Hemi was expensive, and an owner needed to be on the ball to keep it running on all cylinders but, when it was, few cars could touch it.

And therein lay the problem: the performance segment was thriving on *image*. The GTO had it in spades, but the Belvedere? Sure, a Hemi Belvedere I two-door sedan could give a big-block Corvette a run for its money, but it lacked visual appeal, special identification, or its own nameplate that set the segment leaders apart. Considering that Pontiac sold more than 96,000 1966 GTOs, Plymouth was clearly missing an opportunity.

Plymouth Finally Fields a Contender

Plymouth finally got the message for 1967 with the introduction of the GTX. Bucket seats, simulated hood scoops, and other niceties distinguished the GTX from basic Belvederes. A new 375-hp Super Commando 440 was *standard*. Not only was that the biggest engine in the segment, but on paper its power output also was the equivalent of the competition's *optional* engines. Fifty more horses was as close as the Hemi.

The Hemi also was the basis for the Super Stock RO23 Belvedere II. All were white hardtops with a semi-modified Street Hemi (including special intake plus air induction), deleted heater and sound deadener, drag gears, and several other heavy-duty and weight-saving features.

The Hemi was also officially available for a special Belvedere II for Super Stock. However, this particular RO Hemi Belvedere was campaigned as a GTX to promote Plymouth's new image model. (Photo ©TEN: The Enthusiast Network. All rights reserved.)

Barracuda Grows Up

On the pony car front, 1967 introduced a new performance chapter for the Barracuda. Now it was more of a proper competitor to the Mustang with an expanded line-up: fastback, coupe, and convertible. All three were handsome and contemporary. The sports-minded Formula S package included upgraded suspension, tires, and standard Commando 273.

Soon after the Barracuda's introduction, the 383 became available for the Formula S. That may have sounded impressive in such a small car but,

Finally, a Plymouth with a performance image! The 1967 GTX one-upped the competition with a standard 440 Super Commando, although the Hemi was available to better maintain the advantage.

An all-new 1967 Barracuda matched Mustang's three body styles. The Formula S was the way to add speed and handling chops to the fish, but the 273 competed in a big-block world and the compromised 383 was somewhat underwhelming. (Photo ©TEN: The Enthusiast Network. All rights reserved.)

If the 1967 GTX was about time, the 1968 Road Runner was sweet revenge, a bargain-basement performance car for folks who had been priced out of the market. This Road Runner was part of a group of Plymouths special-ordered in Omaha Orange by several California dealerships. (Richard Truesdell Photo)

A study in contrasts: The redesigned 1968 GTX featured chrome trim, standard stripes, and bucket seats to give it distinction from the Road Runner. Under the ornamental hood scoops (with optional blackout) remained a 440/375 or optional Hemi. (Tim Costello Photo)

restrictive exhaust manifolds held the big-block at 280 hp. Power steering and air conditioning were not available because of the tight fit.

Plymouth Steals the GTO's Thunder

For 1968, Plymouth pulled a fast one on the industry. Once a brand late to follow the GTO's formula, Plymouth introduced a performance model that was pure marketing genius (as in Wile E.): the Road Runner.

Since the debut of the 1964 GTO, performance cars tended to be upscale with standard bucket seats and fancy trim. Even the GTX was equipped with all the usual accoutrements, including bucket seats, sill and wheel opening moldings, and nylon-blend floor carpeting.

The Road Runner was different. Based on the Belvedere two-door coupe, the Road Runner added a 335-hp 383 (with bigger cam than the 330-horse 383 available on pedestrian models), standard 4-speed, and little else, all for $2,896; in contrast, the GTX started at $3,355. It also was somewhat of a put-on thanks to Warner Brothers–approved cartoon decals and "Beep-beep!" horn. And, yes, Virginia, the Hemi was available. A companion hardtop joined midyear, helping Plymouth produce a rousing 44,599 Road Runners.

The Road Runner was part of the redesigned B-Body series that featured flowing rooflines with curves and bulges in all the right places. The GTX took over where the Road Runner left off, offering a hardtop and convertible with a higher level of appointments, lower-body racing stripes, and 440/375 or optional Hemi under the scooped hood.

Minor visual tweaks greeted the Barracuda in 1968, but under the hood, the Formula S package was revitalized with the all-new 340. Despite a 275-hp rating, the small-block quickly developed a reputation for handling much more substantial vehicles. The 383, now rated at 300 hp, thanks to new cylinder heads and intake, was optional. Power steering became available for the 383 in March.

1969: Hemi, A12 and the 'Cuda

March also was the month the Hemi Barracuda fastback was produced in conjunction with Hurst for B/Stock. Unlike the 1967 RO23 Belvedere, the Hemi Barracuda featured an honest-to-goodness Race Hemi plus cross-ram intake, Hooker headers, Plexiglas windows, fiberglass front fenders, and more.

The 1969 Road Runner returned with a mild facelift and a new convertible version. Newly branded performance and axle packages allowed buyers

After a successful 1967 redesign, the 1968 Barracuda Formula S featured a new 275-hp 340 or a 383 bumped up 20 horses from 1967. Longitudinal Sport Stripes were a new option. (Tim Costello Photo)

the beat goes on... and on...and on...

PLYMOUTH REVEALS NEW BARRACUDA BASED MONSTER

● DETROIT -- Chrysler Corporation has pulled another rabbit out of their collective hat and built an honest-to-goodness flat-out race car, one of the first since 1965. The car, based on the Barracuda-Dart series in Plymouth and Dodge, promises to be a really fantastic number. It's light -- about 3000 pounds wringing wet. And the power plant is enough to bring tears of joy to the eyes of any MoPar lover. The little monster is born with a full-race, competition 426 CID Hemi.

This is virtually the same engine that was used to power the earlier Chrysler Corp. Super Stocks. The engine is fitted with a ram-tuned intake manifold and dual Holley four-Bbl. carbs. Compression ratio is 12.5 to 1. The car comes from the factory equipped with Hooker Headers, pipes, and mufflers. Other engine components are: High-output dual point transistor ignition, high capacity oil pump, roller timing chain, and viscous fan drive.

The cars will be equipped with either Torqueflite automatic transmission of four-speed manual. All the new race cars will be equipped with Hurst shifters. Rear end ratios will be 4.88 for the manual transmission cars and 4.86 for the automatics.

The Hemi Barracuda is a lot lighter than its stock brethren and the reasons are obvious. Things like: No heater, no radio, no sound deadener or under-coating, fiberglass front fenders, fiberglass hood and hood scoop, light-guage steel doors, light weight glass windows, twin light bucket seats, and no rear seat all contribute. Oh, yes. There is one heavy item. The battery. It appears to be a truck unit and it's definitely mounted in the trunk. But of course. Squarely over the right rear wheel for traction. Price? $4400. But they might be a little tough to get. Still, you might try your dealer on order number BO29. But hurry. They're only making 50 Darts and 50 Barracudas and they'll be gone quickly.

Hurst prepared 70 BO29 1968 Hemi Barracudas for Super Stock. Professional drag racers picked them up from Hurst in gray primer with black fiberglass front fenders. (Photo Courtesy Hurst Performance)

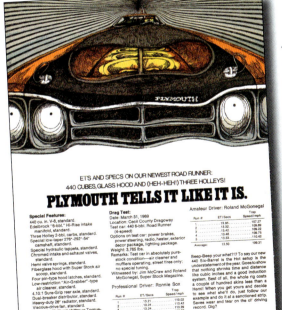

Sign of the times: In 1968, Plymouth began to use zany illustrations of its performance cars in a series of print ads, and things got even zanier in 1969, as exemplified by this A12 Road Runner. (Dodge, Plymouth and the AMC design are registered trademarks of FCA US LLC)

The 1969 Road Runner's A12 package proved that Plymouth understood what was going on in the street after all. Along with blacked-out fiberglass hood and wheels sans hubcaps, the package paired a trio of 2-barrel Holleys to the GTX's 440. (Lon Seigworth Photo)

to better tailor their Road Runners for street or strip duty. The simulated hood scoops were available with Performance Hood Paint; the hood could be made functional with the optional Coyote Duster air-induction system. Several bright colors were introduced midyear.

In March, Plymouth introduced the A12 440 6-barrel package, which included a 440 featuring 3x2 Holley carburetors and aluminum intake. Sitting atop the 390-hp engine was a unique hingeless fiberglass hood that had been designed in a wind tunnel. Testing had demonstrated that a boundary of static air on the hood surface rendered most systems useless, but the A12's scoop was several inches higher for a true ramming effect. With 4.10

The 1969 GTX was refined with new lower-body trim and other tweaks. A new air-induction system became an option for the 440 (standard with Hemi).

A new 'Cuda package for the fastback and coupe gave the Road Runner treatment to the Barracuda. The 340 and 383 were joined midyear by a 440/375. This is a pre-production Mopar 340, before Plymouth decided to change the name. (Photo ©TEN: The Enthusiast Network. All rights reserved.)

The restyled 1970 Road Runner kicked up the cartoonish-ness several notches with Dust Trails, bulge hood, and bright colors with crazy names such as Sassy Grass Green.

gears and no hubcaps, the A12 Road Runner was all business, relatively easy to maintain, and cheaper than the Hemi yet arguably faster.

The Road Runner's popularity didn't render the GTX obsolete, especially considering that the Super Commando 440 was standard. A new Air Grabber induction system was optional but included with the Hemi. Like the Road Runner, dual matte-black hood stripes were available. Gone were the lower-body racing stripes, replaced by full-length lower-body molding with black textured paint complemented by reflective red or white pinstripes.

The 1969 Barracuda featured tweaks to its grille and taillights, plus a new longitudinal stripe option. The 340/275 returned, with the 4-speed using the automatic's milder cam. Although the 340 was newly available without the Formula S package, the Formula S continued to be mandatory for the 383, producing 330 hp, thanks to a new camshaft.

In December 1968, Plymouth introduced a new performance package for the Barracuda: the 'Cuda. Available with either the 340 or 383 for the fastback or coupe, the 'Cuda was basically a Barracuda that was given the Road Runner treatment. The 'Cuda package featured a blacked-out grille, lower-body black stripes, and two black hood stripes complemented by simulated scoops placed close to the cowl.

In March 1969, Hurst Performance was subcontracted to stuff the 440/375 into the little A-Body to produce the 'Cuda 440, which included mandatory console-shifted automatic and 8.75-inch rear with 3.55 or 3.91 gears; disc brakes, power brakes and steering, and air conditioning were not available.

Plymouth's vacuum-operated Air Grabber may have been the niftiest system in the industry.

The Rapid Transit System

The year 1970 was set to be the greatest ever for high performance, and for Plymouth, that just may have been true. Flush with several new models, bright colors and stripes, and an arm's length of options, 1970 was set to break records. However, insurance rates and shifting demand began to kill the performance market.

A restyle gave the 1970 Road Runner a completely new look. The wheel arches from 1968–1969 gave way to simulated rear-fender scoops, which could be complemented by gold reflective Dust Trail stripes. A new power-bulge hood, which could be optioned with a matte-black stripe, was available with a redesigned Coyote Duster system featuring a vacuum-operated scoop. Following the trend, Plymouth also offered a spoiler for the first time. Under the hood, the 383/335 remained standard but was now backed by a 3-speed

Richard Petty made his name with Plymouth, but The King left for Ford in 1969. The 1970 Superbird brought Petty back. (Tim Costello Photo)

GTX 2-Door Hardtop

Plymouth makes it

The 1970 GTX featured new styling (with racing stripes making a return) and a 440 6-barrel as an option. The convertible was discontinued. (Dodge, Plymouth and the AMC design are registered trademarks of FCA US LLC)

manual; the optional 4-speed featured a nifty Hurst Pistol Grip shifter. The 440 6-barrel returned but sported the conventional Road Runner hood with unique cartoon-like "440+6" decals. When properly equipped, the Road Runner became a veritable cartoon on wheels.

One Road Runner model was head and shoulders the most cartoonish of all: the Superbird. As Plymouth's successor to the 1969 Dodge Charger Daytona (and the car that won back Richard Petty) the Superbird was similar, yet distinct. The 440 Super Commando (normally not available for Road Runners) was standard, with the 440 6-barrel and Hemi as options. A change in homologation rules required Plymouth to build one for each dealership, so approximately 1,935 were built.

The 1970 Barracuda was available with plenty of options; several more were added midyear, including strobe stripes in black, white, magenta, or chartreuse. (Dodge, Plymouth and the AMC design are registered trademarks of FCA US LLC)

Dan Gurney's All-American Racers team influenced the street-going AAR 'Cuda, a 'Cuda with strobe stripes, side exhausts, NACA fiberglass hood, and staggered tires front and rear. (Photo ©TEN: The Enthusiast Network. All rights reserved.)

The 1970 GTX returned for 1970, was restyled with flat-black tail panel trim and the return of racing stripes. The 440 6-barrel was added to the option list, and a redesigned Air Grabber system helped with engine breathing. The convertible was discontinued.

The Barracuda was completely revamped for 1970, shedding its Valiant origins and becoming a full-fledged member of the pony car fraternity. The new E-Body was available in three versions: Barracuda, luxurious Gran Coupe, and performance-oriented 'Cuda.

Perhaps the A-Body Barracuda was gone, but Plymouth used the inspiration to create the semi-fastback 1970 Duster. In Duster 340 guise, its price made Road Runner owners envious. (Andrew V. Kent Photo)

Plymouth never had a dedicated full-size performance car until the 1970 Sport Fury GT appeared as the executive branch of the Rapid Transit System. If the 440/350-hp wasn't enough, the Special 440 with three 2-barrel Holleys was available. (Photo ©TEN: The Enthusiast Network. All rights reserved.)

The 'Cuda started with the 383/335; next was the 'Cuda 340 (a no-cost upgrade), and then 'Cuda 440, 'Cuda 440-6, and Hemi 'Cuda. A non-functional twin-scoop "performance" hood was standard; a functional Shaker air induction system was standard with the Hemi and optional for the others. The 'Cuda included a long list of options including Elastomeric body-colored bumpers, black "hockey stick" stripes, rear-window louvers, and spoilers front and rear.

A special 'Cuda was announced in February 1970: the AAR 'Cuda, which was Plymouth's Trans-Am contender named after Dan Gurney's All-American Racers. The A53 AAR package included a 290-hp 340 6-barrel, fiberglass hood with NACA scoop, upper-beltline strobe stripes, ducktail spoiler, side exhaust trumpets, and mismatched tires, among other features.

Thanks to the demise of the A-Body Barracuda, there was room for another sporty compact. In this case, Plymouth created the Duster, a semi-fastback coupe that was available with a 340. Featuring full-length side and rear deck panel stripes, heavy-duty suspension, 3.23 gears, and Rallye road wheels, the Duster 340 was a cheap yet stylish way to get into a performance car.

The Road Runner, GTX, 'Cuda, and Duster 340 were part of a new performance team called the Rapid Transit System (RTS). This "new concept in high-performance transportation" was an integrated program that was the result of Plymouth's competition efforts trickling down to the factory and supported by dealerships and parts catalog. The RTS featured performance vehicles covering all segments including full-size cars.

Wait. Full-size? Yes, even though the days of big high-performance vehicles were long gone, Plymouth felt that the time was ripe to produce the Sport Fury GT, a *fuselage* bruiser full of 440 power with 350 hp plus

reflective strobe stripes, heavy-duty suspension and brakes, and more. Even better, the GT had the 440 6-barrel as an option, the only full-size Mopar to receive this engine. "Thus endowed, it can do things a lot of so-called Supercars can't do," said the Rapid Transit System catalog.

Plymouth Keeps the Flame Alive for 1971

Although General Motors reduced compression a year before the government-mandated emissions standards, Plymouth kept high-compression goodness for one more year. Plymouth also went all-out to produce its wildest vehicles ever.

B-Bodies were completely redesigned for 1971, and featured a unique coupe that shared little with its sedan counterpart. The Road Runner's 383, the only performance engine to experience a substantial compression cut, now produced 300 hp. Making its first appearance in a B-Body was the 340/275. The next step up was the 440 6-barrel, which dropped 5 horses to 385 because of a half-point cut in compression, but the Hemi kept on keeping on with a full 425 horses.

The standard Performance Hood was an evolution of the 1968–1969 Road Runner hood, but the Air Grabber returned in familiar form. A full host of visual aids were available for the Road Runner, such as funky strobe stripes, front and rear Elastomeric body-colored bumpers, and the Aerodynamic Spoiler Package.

The 1971 GTX came equipped with a standard 440 Super Commando, now with a 0.2-point compression drop to 370 hp. Lower-body

The 1971 GTX distinguished itself visually from the Road Runner with different striping options. Longitudinal pinstripes were standard; this transverse hood treatment was optional; the Air Grabber was also available. Only 2,942 GTXs were built.

The redesigned 1971 Road Runner was chock full of unique options inside and out, including strobe stripes, body-colored bumpers, and funky exhaust pipes. The convertible may have been gone, but a sunroof was available to fake it.

The Duster 340's sophomore year added visual pizazz such as segmented grille and new striping options. Despite emissions requirements, 12,886 Duster 340s were built. (Photo ©TEN: The Enthusiast Network. All rights reserved.)

Unbelievably, the Sport Fury GT reappeared in 1971 with 20 more horsepower. Strobe stripes and huge "GT" identification on the hood left no doubt this was a member of the Rapid Transit System. (Photo Courtesy Curtiss Lichty/Motorcar Portfolio)

The 1971 Barracuda debuted with quad headlights, but the 'Cuda's optional Billboard stripes really made it stand out. The 383 was again standard for the 'Cuda, but horsepower was reduced to 300. (Richard Truesdell Photo)

The 1971 Sport Fury GT featured new "GT" decals on the rear quarter panels and a new urethane appliqué, which was common to all Sport Furys. (Photo Courtesy Curtiss Lichty/Motorcar Portfolio)

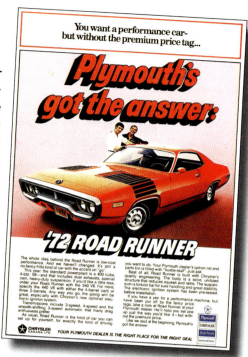

With a new grille and taillights, the 1972 Road Runner continued to look the part. However, the new low-compression lineup hurt performance, although the 440 6-barrel managed to survive several weeks before being canceled. (Dodge, Plymouth and the AMC design are registered trademarks of FCA US LLC)

longitudinal stripes, which could be complemented by optional transverse stripes that ran from the simulated hood scoops to the front fenders, were standard. Many of the best Road Runner features were also available for the GTX, but with a touch more class. Alas, this was the last year for the GTX model.

The Barracuda received a heavy facelift for 1971. Dual headlights and a segmented grille were new, while the parking lights moved to the valance. The 'Cuda stood out from other Barracudas thanks to new simulated front fender louvers, color-keyed grille (for certain colors), and wild, optional "Billboard" stripes. When built with the Aerodynamic Spoiler package, Billboard stripes, Elastomeric bumpers, and color-keyed grille, the 'Cuda looked almost magical.

The 383/300 was standard, with the 340, 440 6-barrel, and Hemi also available (the 4-barrel 440 was gone). The Shaker hood remained standard for the Hemi and optional for other engines. Sales fell to 6,228 'Cuda hardtops and 374 'Cuda ragtops.

The Duster 340 returned for 1971 with a new segmented grille and redesigned stripes. Optional visual treats included pop art–inspired performance hood paint treatment with a large "340 Wedge" emblazoned on a blacked-out hood, rear spoiler, and hood pins.

Would you believe the Sport Fury GT remained part of the Rapid Transit System? Except for a new grille and louvered taillights, the 1971 GT included revised strobe stripes plus new GT identification on the rear fenders and huge "GT" call-outs on the hood. The standard and only available engine was an upgraded 370-hp 440. Already a tough sell in 1970, only 375 were built for 1971.

Performance Takes a Nosedive

The performance market crashed in 1972. The Hemi disappeared, leaving the 440 as the top engine for the Road Runner. For E-Bodies, all big-blocks were purged from the roster, leaving the 340 as the only performance option. Horsepower was down because of lowered compression and a new net rating system; that is, if horsepower was ever mentioned in dealership literature.

The most noticeable changes for the 1972 Road Runner were a new grille and taillights. The optional strobe stripes now featured more strobes, which could be complemented by similar strobe stripes for the hood. Also new

Not only did the 1972 'Cuda lose all three of its big-blocks, its standard engine was a 318 with the 340 optional. Several new options, such as revamped stripe designs, kept the 1972 'Cuda interesting. (Photo Courtesy Mitch Frumkin)

were hood and deck lid stripes, which were only available with the Air Grabber hood. All these updates were diminished by the new low-compression engine lineup, from the standard 400/255, 340/240, and 440/280 (which gave the Road Runner "GTX" badges). The 440 6-barrel featured 10.3:1 compression (high for 1972) and was only available with TorqueFlite. It was canceled in September 1971 after a handful sneaked out of the factory.

The 1972 Barracuda reverted to dual headlights and a "new divided grille with twin deep-throat openings." Road lamp–style parking lights were mounted in the lower valance. Out back, the Barracuda featured a new look with quad circular taillights. Several new striping options were offered, including a longitudinal upper-beltline stripe and an inverse-style performance hood treatment. If you wanted your performance on the sly, the 340 was now available on the base Barracuda.

In another indignity, the 'Cuda 318 became the standard engine, although it still came with the "performance" hood, black rear panel, heavy-duty suspension, chrome trim, and upgraded tires. The grille could be color-keyed with several colors.

The 1972 Duster 340 may have weathered the storm the best, although the rear spoiler, hood pins, and performance axle options were missing from the option list. There were very few visual changes, but the value proposition remained intact, making the Duster 340 perhaps the smartest performance value of the moment.

More government mandates set up 1973 as a rough year, but how rough depended on how Plymouth embraced change. The Road Runner was restyled and included new roof and body-side stripes and a domed hood. The standard engine was downgraded to a 318, but performance enthusiasts had the 340/240, 400/260, and GTX 440/280 (now only with an automatic) to choose from. Add the Performance Axle Package, which included 3.55 gears with Sure-Grip and heavy-duty cooling, and suddenly it was *almost* 1970 all over again.

The 1973 Barracuda also was available with the Performance Axle Package, which added a power steering oil cooler. New energy-absorbing bumper guards detracted from the Barracuda's clean appearance. The performance hood treatment disappeared for the scooped hood, but the Barracuda featured a new optional longitudinal stripe design. The sporty 'Cuda continued to enjoy its role as a handling package with a horsepower nudge that was just a 340 upgrade away.

The 1973 Duster 340 continued to be a solid performance package with heavy-duty suspension, E70 bias-belted tires, and dual exhausts, among other equipment. A new grille shared a passing resemblance to the Road Runner, while redesigned side and rear deck striping (plus optional hood blackout) complemented the new look.

The year 1974 marked plenty of "lasts" for Plymouth: The last 440 Road Runner; the last E-Body. The last Hurst Pistol Grip 4-speed. If you were unsure whether the muscle car era was done and hung up wet, 1974 provided a moment of clarity. The Road Runner languished with a standard 318 with dual exhausts and bright exhaust tips, but the small-block gained horsepower with the new 245-horse 360. Alas, both the 400 and 440 lost power.

The restyled 1973 Road Runner featured a standard 318, but the 340, 400, and 440 remained available. Reshuffled trim and stripes were new for the Barracuda. The 340 remained the top engine. The Duster 340 seemed to weather the storm the best of the bunch. (Dodge, Plymouth and the AMC design are registered trademarks of FCA US LLC)

The 340 was upgraded to 360 ci for 1974, which was actually a nice improvement in an era in which there seemed to be none. It was available in all of Plymouth's performance cars, but the Duster 360 was the most popular benefactor. (Andrew V. Kent Photo)

In its final year, the 1974 Barracuda featured even larger front and rear bumper guards to keep the feds happy. As with other models, the 340 was replaced by the 360, which was an option for both Barracuda and 'Cuda. Thankfully, the Performance Axle Package was still available so that Plymouth's pony car could die with grace.

The 1974 Duster 360 featured longitudinal body side stripes that appeared identical to the 1973's, but engine identification moved from the stripe to a badge on the front fenders. Sales had been consistent for the high-performance A-Body in these lean years, but only 3,314 were built for 1974.

With no E-Bodies for 1975, what was left? A heavily restyled Road Runner that bulked up and lost even more performance pretenses. The 400 was the top engine, the last appearance of a big-block as the Road Runner moved to the compact Volaré for 1976. The Duster 360 soldiered on but was down on horsepower.

Yes, Plymouth tried, but high performance met an ignominious end.

Plymouth Supercar Clinics

According to Pontiac adman Jim Wangers, racing and performance were two different things. Taking a page from that insight, Plymouth began the Sox & Martin Supercar Clinic in 1967 in support of its racing and performance exploits. Initial kick-off was at the 1967 NHRA Winternationals, followed by 30 clinics throughout the model year. All clinics were scheduled to coincide with sanctioned drag race events, so both the Plymouth brand and the race were promoted.

PLYMOUTH EXPANDS SUPER CAR CLINIC

The 1967 Sox & Martin Supercar Clinic was so successful that Plymouth's general manager admitted "it has created a demand for the clinic that one drag team cannot possibly fill. Therefore, certain outstanding super stock drag racers who drive Plymouths will be selected to conduct supplementary clinics." (Photo Courtesy Hurst Performance)

According to the January 1969 *Drag Racing* magazine, Chrysler engineers and product planners developed the project to involve racers as "traveling showmen" in addition to their racing duties. Speaking to the public required education, so participating racers spent a week in Detroit developing their chops and learning how to represent Plymouth and its corporate values. Specialty equipment firms/sponsors were approached to financially support the promotion of their respective products.

Here's how Plymouth sold the clinics to dealerships:

- Plymouth Coming Through for You: "We do it with the Rapid Transit System and we do it with the Supercar Clinics. Two of the best ways to tap interest among the enthusiasts."
- We'll Stand on Our Record: "Plymouth has dominated drag racing with victories in just about every major event in the country. Our cars are tops . . . and the same thing can be said for our drivers. Their fame (and accomplishments) add an extra plus to the performance image you're selling. Our Rapid Transit System cars complete the picture."
- Getting it to Come Together: The clinics gave salesmen the opportunity to meet more than 1,000 performance-car prospects. Contest/drawing registrations were used to obtain personal information from enthusiasts. "And be sure everyone knows the Supercar Clinic is on its way to your showroom. That's why it's important to *promote* and *advertise* aggressively" several days before the Clinic via rock radio stations and sports and automotive news section in the newspaper."

Included in the Supercar Clinic kit were newspaper ads, radio spots, window posters, cards, handbills, and other promotional goodies.

Sox & Martin's seminars generally followed this format: overview of Plymouth's performance line, discussion of high-performance equipment and recommendations, suggestions on making Plymouths faster via tune-up tips and speed secrets, a 30-minute film, and a question and answer segment.

"Since its introduction early this year, the Sox & Martin Clinic in Plymouth dealerships has proved an overwhelming success," said Plymouth General Manager Robert Anderson in 1967. "In fact, it has been so successful that it has created a demand for the Clinic that one drag team cannot possibly fulfill. Therefore, certain outstanding super stock drag racers who drive Plymouths will be selected to conduct supplementary clinics," including Don Grotheer, Arlen Vanke, and Jack Werst.

Plymouth also distributed a publication at Clinics to help enthusiasts get the most out of their Plymouth engines, including recommendations from Clinic co-sponsors: "Nine of the best names in the high-performance business with their Chrysler Engineering tested and approved products." The sections included:

- About Sox & Martin
- Supercars: Plymouth Style
- Care and Feeding of Your Loved One: Clinic Style: A series of tips for high-performance Plymouths and the products and pieces that make them run
- Super Boots: Goodyear talks high-performance and racing tires
- Lubricate for Life: Valvoline talks oil
- An Exhaustive Subject: Hooker talks headers

- Gauges are Gauged, Too: StewartWarner talks racing instruments
- Mission: Shift: Hurst talks shifters and linkage
- Induction for Performance: Edelbrock talks intake manifolds
- A Winning Spark: Spark plug tips and ignition systems
- Your Wheel Choice: Keystone Mags talks custom wheels
- Filter Power: Fram talks oil, air, and fuel filtration

Supercar Clinic Program lasted through 1971.

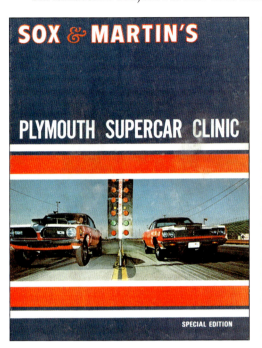

Marketing Strategy

The Rapid Transit System had all the performance bases covered, from compact, pony car, econo-muscle, its high-line big brother, and full-size muscle. To promote Plymouth's performance team and Mopar's "Hustle Stuff" parts catalog, the Division created the 1970-71 Rapid Transit Caravan as a "customized interpretation of the Plymouth Rapid Transit System."

Plymouth commissioned the country's top hot rod shops to build the Caravan, which toured dealerships, new and custom car shows, and fairs. All the custom captured the zeitgeist of "World of Wheels" car culture of the time.

Plymouth produced this magazine in 1969 for distribution at Supercar Clinics. Information on Plymouth's muscle roster, speed suggestions and tips, plus ads from the racers' sponsors was found between the covers. (Dodge, Plymouth and the AMC design are registered trademarks of FCA US LLC)

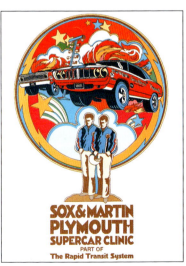

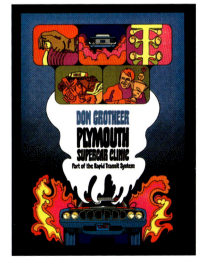

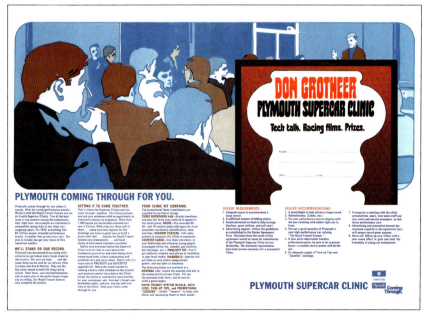

Thanks to a declining high-performance market, the Supercar Clinic program experienced its swan song in 1971. (Dodge, Plymouth and the AMC design are registered trademarks of FCA US LLC)

Following is a list of the vehicles that were a part of the Rapid Transit Caravan, along with important spec details.

1970 Duster 340

Painted in several hues of red, flat black, and pearl, the new-for-1970 A-Body was lowered 3 inches and featured a bumperless front end with quad Lucas headlights, small rectangular grille (with "DUSTER" painted above), and redesigned parking lights.

Out back was a bumperless rump with four exhaust trumpets poking from the rolled valance panel and a subtle, integrated rear spoiler above the backlight.

Other details included shaved door handles, chrome rocker panel trim, twin quick-fill gas caps, and American Dragmaster wheels.

Power came from a stock 340 with a 4-speed and 3.91 gears.

Body modifications were handled by Byron Grenfell; Butch Brinza handled the paint.

1970 Road Runner

Originally a factory Hemi hardtop, this Road Runner featured flared rear wheel wells, enlarged rear-quarter scoops, a spoiler molded into the rear

The 1970 Rapid Transit Caravan Road Runner (originally a factory Hemi hardtop) was one of the more radical Caravan cars. Note the huge Road Runner with Dust Trails coming from behind. (Dodge, Plymouth and the AMC design are registered trademarks of FCA US LLC)

quarters, and life-size version of the Dust Trail stripe. Contemporary Cibie headlights, taillight lenses with a reflective insert, shaved door handles, and Ansen mags completed the custom effect. Jerry Roman handled the pearlescent dark gold/white/flat-black paint job.

1970 'Cuda 440

Designed by Harry Bradley and painted/built by Chuck Miller's Styline Customs, the Rapid Transit Caravan 'Cuda 440 was lowered 2.5 inches. More conspicuous was a unique oval insert molded to the grille which hid Cibie headlights. Unique twin spoilers protruded from underneath the front valance. Taillight lenses were similar to production units but not recessed;

PLYMOUTH'S RAPID TRANSIT SYSTEM DUSTER 340 -- The lowness of the Duster 340 in Plymouth's Rapid Transit System Caravan is accented by the addition of a chrome molding along the rocker panel. A unique spoiler has been built into the rear of the roof line. (Photo #70-2281)

From: Chrysler-Plymouth Public Relations, P.O. Box 1658, Det., Mi.

The red 1970 Rapid Transit Caravan Duster 340 featured a bumper-less design and a unique, integrated roof spoiler. (Dodge, Plymouth and the AMC design are registered trademarks of FCA US LLC)

The 1970 Rapid Transit Caravan 'Cuda 440 was designed by Harry Bradley and built by Chuck Miller's Styline Customs. Although initially appearing similar to the renowned Sonic 'Cuda show car, the Caravan 'Cuda maintained its factory Shaker setup. (Photo ©TEN: The Enthusiast Network. All rights reserved.)

wheelie bars protruded from the rear valance (normally used by the exhaust) with a drag parachute in between. Trendsetter side pipes replaced the stock gilled rocker panels. Wheels were Cragar Super Stocks, widened in the

Byron Grenfell slightly restyled the 1970 Rapid Transit Caravan Duster 340 for 1971. Butch Brinza was responsible for the new multi-hued green paint.

The 1971 Caravan Road Runner started out as a basic 383 Road Runner. Compare it with the 1970 and see how radical and contemporary it was at the time.

Some interesting 1971 Caravan Road Runner styling features included injected-molded side-marker lights and taillights that reflected the forward motion of the vehicle.

rear, with mud deflectors at all four corners. Like its Caravan brethren, the 'Cuda 440 had its door handles replaced by solenoids.

The whole thing was painted in a pearlescent white with green and gray striping. The top received a black-out that foreshadowed the canopy-style vinyl top available on 1971 B-Bodies.

1970 'Cuda Funny Car

Don "The Snake" Prudhomme was the "hot shoe" in NHRA racing at the time, so a replica of his 'Cuda funny car was created to complement the customs. Built by Ron Scrima's Exhibition Engineering, the 'Cuda's body was a one-piece affair on a tube frame. The Hemi was authentic but wasn't set up to run under its own power.

1971 Duster 340

Lowered 3 inches and revised with a new multi-hued green paint job, the Duster also received a snout extension from its 1970 iteration, including "DUSTER" lettering in a more contemporary font. The front also featured a new custom-made "thin line bumper," rolled-under front pan, and redesigned parking lights that resembled air induction scoops. A dark green hood black-out featured huge "340" numerals. Two rectangular exhaust ports were another update.

1971 Road Runner

Perhaps the star of the 1971 Rapid Transit Caravan series, the redesigned Road Runner appeared as if it were designed as a Chrysler Corporation show car rather than by a hot rod craftsman. Only the roof, doors, interior, and engine were unchanged; the rest of the Road Runner screamed custom.

The nose was lengthened by more than 6 inches (all in sheet metal), eliminating the front valance with an open-mouth grille and distinctive custom Plexiglas headlamps nestled in both corners. A three-dimensional rendering of the head of the fabled Warner Brothers character appeared in the center of the grille and functioned as a hood release; the same rendering was used as injected-molded side-marker lights. The hood featured two planes sloping to a cowl induction system.

The trunk lid sloped from the backlight to the tail, with the sides of the lid used as support for an integrated spoiler. Taillights were custom components consisting of red, yellow, and green lights that signified the vehicle's motion. The rear valance tucked underneath and had factory slotted pipes on each side.

Flat-black custom disc wheel covers with stock trim rings mounted on Goodyear G60 x 15 tires completed the custom Runner, which was painted in candy-over-pearl orange with white. Harry Bradley was credited for the design, with body and paint handled by Chuck Miller's Styline Customs.

1971 'Cuda 440

Although the 1971 Barracuda received a heavy facelift with quad headlights and a cheese-grater grille, the 1971 Rapid Transit Caravan 'Cuda 440's styling was basically a repeat of the 1970 car with a new red/orange/white (covered in Merano pearlescent) paint scheme handled by Chuck Miller. Subtle parking lights positioned under the twin chin spoilers were new; the unique canopy roof design was discarded.

1971 'Cuda Funny Car

Don Prudhomme's replica returned for 1971, this time equipped with a functional, Keith Black-prepared supercharged and injected 1,500-hp Hemi capable of running ETs of less than 7 seconds. The 'Cuda featured respective model year updates plus a new red/orange/yellow-flamed white pearl paint job by Jack Kampney.

DON PRUDHOMME'S RAPID TRANSIT SYSTEM CARAVAN PLYMOUTH BARRACUDA FUNNY CAR
From: Chrysler-Plymouth Public Relations
P.O. Box 1658, Detroit, Mich. 48231   (71-2922)

Don Prudhomme's 'Cuda funny car returned to the 1971 Rapid Transit Caravan featuring a new grille and taillights, Keith Black Hemi, and white pearl paint with flames. (Dodge, Plymouth and the AMC design are registered trademarks of FCA US LLC)

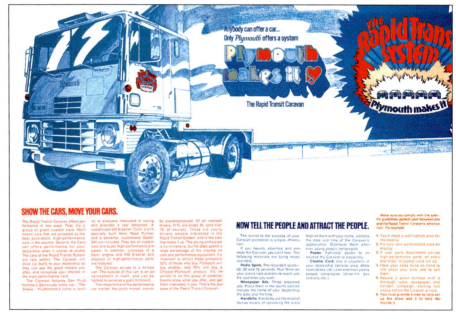

A high-performance car show for your town? That's the opportunity Plymouth offered with the 1970 Rapid Transit Caravan. Show cars and equipment arrived in a 44-foot trailer/rolling billboard. (Dodge, Plymouth and the AMC design are registered trademarks of FCA US LLC)

Also featured in the tour were "two cut-away [Hemi and 440] performance engines and a display board of performance parts."

Rapid Transit Caravan

The Rapid Transit System had all the performance bases covered, from compact, pony car, econo-muscle, its high-line big brother, and full-size muscle. To promote Plymouth's performance team and Mopar's *Hustle Stuff* parts catalog, the division created the 1970–1971 Rapid Transit Caravan as a "customized interpretation of the Plymouth Rapid Transit System."

Plymouth commissioned the country's top hot rod shops to build the Caravan, which toured dealerships, new and custom car shows, and fairs. All the customs captured the zeitgeist of "World of Wheels" car culture of the time. Also featured in the tour were "two cut-away [Hemi and 440] performance engines and a display board of performance parts."

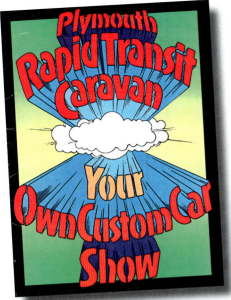

For 1971, the Rapid Transit Caravan made another tour of its "customized interpretation of the Plymouth Rapid Transit System" featuring a revised lineup that included the redesigned Road Runner plus reworked versions of the RTC Duster 340 and 'Cuda 440 models. (Dodge, Plymouth and the AMC design are registered trademarks of FCA US LLC)

In the *1970 Rapid Transit Caravan Kit*, Plymouth urged participating dealers to be actively involved. "The secret of the success of your Caravan promotion is simple: Promotion. If you heavily advertise and promote the Caravan, you can't lose." Plymouth provided the following materials for assistance. Plymouth also offered compliance guidelines for dealerships when the Caravan was in town, which included local media promotion starting two weeks before the event, and a display of the dealer's own performance cars.

Rapid Transit System Salesman's Guide

"Everybody offers a car. Only Plymouth offers a system." To assist salesmen in promoting the Rapid Transit System, Plymouth created a booklet to demonstrate to salespeople that "selling high-performance cars is easy when you have a System."

Introduction

As 10 percent of domestic new-car sales in 1969 were high-performance cars, with the number expected to be greater for 1970, Plymouth pro-

A spectator takes a look at the assortment of Hustle Stuff equipment on display at a 1970 Rapid Transit Caravan stop. (Dodge, Plymouth and the AMC design are registered trademarks of FCA US LLC)

With the new 1970 Rapid Transit System and a ramped-up marketing push, Plymouth developed this guide to show dealership sales staffs how a little knowledge made selling high performance easy and profitable. (Dodge, Plymouth and the AMC design are registered trademarks of FCA US LLC)

moted this insight: "This book is about high-performance cars. You, as a Plymouth dealer, are in the middle of the picture. The better you understand the enormous potential of the performance car market, and how to lead it down the road to your dealership, the bigger the payoff."

The average age of car buyers was going down, with half the population already under 25. Although most of this demographic wasn't financially wealthy, they were inclined to spend much of their income on cars.

It went beyond enthusiasts too: "The fact is, enthusiasts in this country influence millions of car buyers who don't know the difference between a camshaft and a crankshaft."

Making Personal Contact

"It's important to the car enthusiast to feel that Plymouth and Plymouth dealers personally acknowledge his existence. So keeping in mind that car buffs are incurable racing fans, what better way to reach them than by making it possible for them to actually get close to, and even touch, actual Plymouth race cars and talk with the drivers." The Supercar Clinics were one way, with Sox & Martin and Don Grotheer conducting clinics across the country. Plymouth claimed attendance averaged 500 with some attracting more than 1,500 enthusiasts.

The Rapid Transit Caravan was "an important supplement to the clinics," with a truck and 44-foot trailer able to put on a high-performance car show at any dealership. The Caravan's customized vehicles were "super high-performance prepared" and carried "all the latest, most popular equipment." Because Sox & Martin and Grotheer had busy schedules and clinics were often based on their racing schedules, having the Caravan parked in front of a dealership was the next best thing.

This mock showroom (featuring 1970 vehicles) demonstrated what a 1971 Chrysler/Plymouth dealership would look like with upcoming merchandising materials. (Dodge, Plymouth and the AMC design are registered trademarks of FCA US LLC)

Getting Started

Recommendations for a dealership to establish a Rapid Transit System Center included:

- Stock "the hot setups."
- "You can also stock high-performance parts."
- Hire a performance specialist and, ideally, "a mechanic who knows how to work on high-performance Plymouths."

PERFORMANCE KIT— Optional Item

With Plymouth's performance teams winning one race after another, you have every reason to capitalize on Plymouth's great performance image.

The new '71 kit consists of 2 large standing displays and 8 small pylons. These colorful, dramatic performance displays put the "Rapid Transit System" right in your showroom. And the new small pylons give you plenty of spread for getting the message through to your prospects. If you have the Performance Kit from 1970, you need only buy conversion panels (items 26 and 28) and the small pylons (item 30) to update your Performance Kit.

The 32" dimensional plastic Roadrunner is also available again this year as a separate item to give your Performance Center that finishing touch.

Item	Description	Price
24	Performance Kit (complete)	$66.90
26	• "Fury & Roadrunner" Pylon Panels (Set of 4)	7.95
28	• "Barracuda & Duster" Pylon Panels (Set of 4)	7.95
30	• Set of 8 Small Performance Pylons	7.95
29	Dimensional Plastic Roadrunner	9.95

To highlight a dealership's Performance Center, Plymouth offered a special performance kit that included two large, colorful standing displays and eight small pylons. Also available was a three-dimensional 32-inch plastic Road Runner. (Dodge, Plymouth and the AMC design are registered trademarks of FCA US LLC)

- The basic Rapid Transit System package, which included full-color car-top tents, posters, and signs.
- The Rapid Transit System Performance Kit included six-foot-high pylons featuring the "performance story" for performance models, a three-dimensional 32-inch plastic Road Runner, and a vinyl floor runner.

Understanding the Product

In addition to car features and specs to increase the salespeople's knowledge of the System, these tips were included:

- Bright colors "attract prospects. So order them on your high-performance cars."
- Big engines, especially a 440 6-barrel and Hemi in stock, help "gain credibility as a high-performance dealer."
- Axle ratios are "the second-most important attribute of a car" after the engine, "so we strongly recommend an Axle Package on virtually every high-performance Plymouth you order."
- Wheels and tires are important to consumers because the race car look is key. "Stock high-performance cars with the biggest wheels and tires available in the System."
- Transmissions should be considered when ordering stock. "In the eyes of the enthusiast, the 4-speed is where it's at."
- Air induction systems "are very popular with the buffs. Order them."
- Miscellany such as paint stripes and tachometers "are quite popular with performance buyers," but "there are some options that our research shows aren't favored by the majority of the performance enthusiasts," a lot of it dependent on age.

The introduction in the 1970 Rapid Transit System Salesman's Guide *presented three key points: know the product, understand the customer, and realize the possibilities. (Dodge, Plymouth and the AMC design are registered trademarks of FCA US LLC)*

To promote product knowledge, this section of the Rapid Transit System dealer guide covered the System's core features including models, engines and transmissions, axle ratios, colors, and more. (Dodge, Plymouth and the AMC design are registered trademarks of FCA US LLC)

Stocking the Hot Setups

"Just as there are several types of high-performance prospects, there are several types of high-performance cars." Plymouth suggested several personalities and levels of equipment for different models, such as The Spartan, The Drive-In Cruiser, The Racer for the Road Runner and the GT, The Cosmetic 'Cuda, and The All-Out 'Cuda for Plymouth's pony car.

Offering High-Performance Parts

- The incredible high-performance aftermarket: "Once the car enthusiast buys his car, the spending doesn't stop with the monthly payments."
- Chrysler high-performance parts program: "Plymouth has developed a high-performance parts program that enables you to give the enthusiast the parts he wants" with "the principal objective to make them available at *your dealership*. To make your job a little easier, Plymouth has put together several 'Rapid Transit' parts packages." All could be found in the Hustle Stuff catalog.
- Displays: With a dealership's first Hustle Stuff parts order, "a large colorful poster display [is] available for use in your showroom or service department."
- Tune-up tips: "Offering high-performance parts to the enthusiasts is one thing. There also has to be some 'how-to' information. So Plymouth is offering you a series of Tune-up Booklets," including one each for 273/318/340, 383/440, and 426 Hemi engines.

Reinforcing the Buyer

To build loyalty, salesmen were encouraged to offer extras (especially to youths) such as decals, racing jackets, and other goodies, including brochures. "Make sure you always have a supply of these catalogs at your Rapid Transit Center."

Advertising Program

Even without a proper image car until 1967, racing success buoyed Plymouth's image. Starting in 1968, Plymouth moved toward the other extreme and featured perhaps the wildest ads in the high-performance market.

Rapid Transit System

After the success of Dodge's 1968 Scat Pack, Plymouth formed its own performance team for 1970 called the Rapid Transit System. The models included Road Runner, GTX, 'Cuda (with the Hemi 'Cuda being the "Rapid Transit Authority"), Duster 340, and Sport Fury GT. Each was touted as a complete high-performance car with "suspension, brakes, drivelines, and tires to match."

The brochure stated that there were no low-performance variants in the RTS lineup because its purpose was to ensure "that our race cars and our street cars always have a lot in common.

"Anybody can offer a car. Only Plymouth offers a System." The Rapid Transit System also included Plymouth's racing efforts, Supercar Clinics,

The essence of the Rapid Transit System was that Plymouth's racing efforts trickled down to its street cars, offering assurance that the division supported enthusiasts' high-performance aspirations with the proper parts and information. (Dodge, Plymouth and the AMC design are registered trademarks of FCA US LLC)

high-performance tips, and packaged high-performance parts.

"Those of us at Plymouth who design and build high-performance cars have been inspired to go beyond just offering cars with big engines, good suspensions, great brakes and fat tires.

"We now have a System. An integrated program. It's a total concept in high-performance transportation that combines the lessons learned in competition, an information network, people who understand high-performance, trick parts and great products.

"The Rapid Transit System is years of racing experience at Daytona, Indianapolis, Riverside, Irwindale, Cecil County. It's the race cars themselves, drag racing cars, Grand National stockers, Rally, and Championship cars. And it's the input (and output) gained from all this racing.

"The Rapid Transit System is information (the straight scoop from us to you) on how to tune and modify your car, which equipment to use, and how to set the whole thing up for racing.

"The System is high-performance parts (special cams, manifolds, pistons, bearings, etc.), which are more readily available through parts centers

strategically located across the country.

"Above all, the Rapid Transit System is the product. Everything from a 'sleeper' Plymouth Duster with a 340-ci V-8, to a giant 440-ci Sport Fury GT, all the way up to a Hemi 'Cuda with a Quivering Exposed Cold Air Grabber.

"And, in between, there are Road Runners and GTXs available with 6-barrel carburetion, and vacuum-controlled induction systems. And 'Cudas with lightweight, high-winding 340 V-8s. Each one is a complete high-performance car. With suspension, brakes, driveline, and tires to match. (The system doesn't allow for a car that won't corner or stop or stand up under the strain when you stand on it.)

"And, if you come to the conclusion you can't beat it, join it."

The Rapid Transit System continued into 1971 with new prose: "First there was the car, next evolved the 'Supercar,' then came *the System*," which was the "ultimate answer to the performance enthusiast's search for a complete high-performance program.

"You could say the RTS produces complete performance, not just cars."

CHAPTER 9

DODGE CHARGES AHEAD

Dodge performance has its roots in 1953 with the introduction of the Red Ram Hemi, but real performance didn't appear until 1954 when the Dodge Royal was named to pace the Indianapolis 500. Despite offering only 150 hp, this was the shape of things to come for Dodge.

Beginning in 1956, Dodge introduced the D-500 package, available on any Dodge model. The D-500 could be purchased in several states of tune through 1959; a 345-hp 383 with dual-quads was top dog that year.

Ram Induction

In 1960, Dodge introduced D-500 Ram Induction for the 361 and 383. They were respectively rated at 310 and 330 hp, looked great under the hood, and offered the advantage of an automatic transmission, something that Chevrolet and Ford didn't offer with their top engines.

Dodge's 1960 product line was also new, divided into two segments: low-line Dart and high-line Matador and Polara. Production records compiled by Darrell Davis show 1,118 Darts and 524 Matador/Polaras were built with Ram Induction.

Dodge dealers were becoming unhappy with designer Virgil Exner, especially with his ungainly vision for the 1961 Dodge. Despite some minor model shuffling, the ram-inducted D-500 383 remained Dodge's only performance option. Thanks to stiff competition and indifferent styling, sales fell drastically: 493 Darts and 573 Polaras were equipped with Ram Induction.

Dawn of the Ramcharger

Although a funky 1962 redesign didn't help sales, the new Polara 500 injected some sportiness in the product line with standard bucket seats, a console, and the 305-hp 361. Enthusiasts could opt for a dual-quad 383/343 or 413/380, but the February 1962 announcement of the 410-horse 413 Ramcharger package was a game-changer.

The Max Wedge featured a pair of 650-cfm Carter 4-barrels atop a cross-ram manifold, solid lifters, aluminum pistons, Magnafluxed connecting rods, double-breaker ignition, and efficient 3-inch headers. Transmission choices were a floor-shifted 3-speed or TorqueFlite. Max Wedge production didn't begin until May, but Dodge's swing was a home run against the 409s, 421s, and 406s that were making waves in Super Stock.

Due to the "widespread recognition and acceptance of the performance" of the 413 Ramcharger (note spelling variation), Dodge sent out a June 1962 dealer memo that announced the division was planning a document titled *Dodge 413 Ramcharger News Flash* that would include

The Scat Pack Club of 1970 created a tribe of enthusiasts interested in getting the skinny on high-performance Dodge news and info. (Dodge, Plymouth and the AMC design are registered trademarks of FCA US LLC)

It was evident that Virgil Exner was out of touch with the performance market in 1961, but the D-500 Ram Induction 383 showed that Dodge's engineers were hard at work. (Dodge, Plymouth and the AMC design are registered trademarks of FCA US LLC)

Dodge's "downsized" 1962s were not welcomed in the market, but the 413 Ramcharger made all the difference in Super Stock. Those goofy-looking Dodges were something to be feared by the more handsome Pontiacs, Fords, and Chevys. (Richard Truesdell Photo)

The new 413 Ramcharger featured 410 or 420 horses with higher compression. Transmission choices were a 3-speed manual or TorqueFlite. (Dodge, Plymouth and the AMC design are registered trademarks of FCA US LLC)

Dodge did its best to fix its styling for 1963. The Ramcharger moved up to 426 ci and continued to make waves on dragstrips across America, including winning NHRA's Stock Eliminator title. (Dodge, Plymouth and the AMC design are registered trademarks of FCA US LLC)

Dodge cleaned up its styling for 1963 and incorporated a 3-inch wheelbase increase to counter the downsized proportions that contributed to poor sales for 1962, although the front end still had remnants of Exner's asymmetric styling. The bargain-priced Dart also moved to the new compact A-Body chassis, leaving 330, 440, Polara, and Polara 500 as Dodge's full-size models.

"helpful tuning tips, service techniques, and performance recommendations." Dodge also recommended that dealers send performance and product feedback to Dodge's Service Department to "benefit the owner, the dealer, and the factory," resulting in constant improvements "to an even higher level of perfection." By June, a higher-compression Ramcharger with 420 horses hit dealerships.

The Ramcharger was increased to 426 ci with both versions experiencing a 5-hp bump. The higher-compression 425-horse engine was available with aluminum components and hood scoop for truly competitive drivers.

In June, Dodge announced an update called Ramcharger 426-A. "The new engine is more efficient in its ability to develop maximum power over a wider engine speed range. Refinements primarily involve items that improve the airflow characteristics or increase the volumetric efficiency" such as larger carburetors, tweaked induction system and combustion chambers, and a new camshaft with longer exhaust duration and higher intake/exhaust valve lifts. Advertised horsepower remained unchanged.

Dodge also offered a 330-hp 383, which benefitted from the new availability of a Hurst-shifted 4-speed. Unfortunately, the 4-speed was not up to the task of handling the Ramcharger's power.

A New 426 for Street and Strip

Dodge continued to mainstream the B-Body's styling for 1964. The performance scene changed rapidly, thanks to the Pontiac GTO, which was focused on the street. Dodge's 383/330 was a fine alternative, but it was a middleweight that was outclassed by the Tri-Power 389. The solution was

a new 4-barrel 426 High Performance with 365 hp, "a high-performance powerplant particularly suited to everyday driving needs."

Dodge updated the Max Wedge, now known as the Ramcharger 426-B, for 1964. Advances were heavier and more durable connecting rods, new cylinder heads with increased intake ports, and slightly larger combustion chambers. The 11.0:1-compression engine was still rated at 415 hp, but the 425-horse engine featured a compression reduction to 12.5 "to make the engine less critical as far as octane requirements are concerned without affecting performance." It also featured aluminum components for racing competition.

Even better was the new 4-speed manual transmission for the 426. Dodge's advantage grew even more on February 17, 1964, when the 426 Hemi was announced. Known as the Dodge Hemi-Charger, the new engine was an evolution of the Ramcharger 426-B but featured hemispherical

For 1964, Dodge introduced the 426 High Performance to complement the Ramcharger. Dodge claimed the 365-hp engine featured the "ultimate in 'get-up' power." (Dodge, Plymouth and the AMC design are registered trademarks of FCA US LLC)

This 1965 ad touted the Hemi, which was available only as a lightweight A990 race car. It was another year until a Hemi Coronet was available for the street. (Dodge, Plymouth and the AMC design are registered trademarks of FCA US LLC)

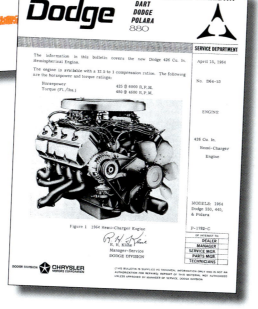

The NASCAR-spec 1964 Hemi-Charger featured a single 4-barrel 400 hp. For drag racing, the 426 used a pair of staggered 4-barrels for 425 horses. (Dodge, Plymouth and the AMC design are registered trademarks of FCA US LLC)

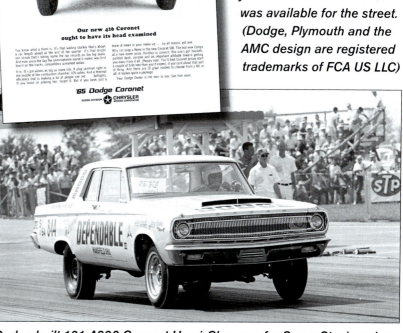

Dodge built 101 A990 Coronet Hemi-Chargers for Super Stock racing. To reduce weight, the hood, doors, front fenders, and bumpers were acid-dipped. The Hemi had new aluminum heads and magnesium intake. (Photo ©TEN: The Enthusiast Network. All rights reserved.)

By 1966, Dodge had yet to offer a performance car with proper image to compete with the GTO, but Pontiac never built a 389 Tri-Power four-door LeMans either. This is a special-order Hemi Coronet Deluxe. (Tim Costello Photo)

The 1966 Charger was simply a Coronet with a fastback roofline, special trim, and special interior. The base 318 and 361 were nothing special, but the 383 and Hemi appealed to enthusiasts.

combustion chambers and other improvements. The Hemi changed the rules in both NHRA and NASCAR competition.

The full-size C-Body car line was introduced for 1965 after several years of "downsized" cars. The sporty Polara 500 continued to satisfy the buckets/console crowd, and the new Monaco was a personal-luxury answer to Pontiac's Grand Prix. These Dodges had no true performance pretensions, although the 426/365 was available for them.

Dodge carried over the B-Body into 1965 and played a bit of sleight of hand, restyling, renaming, and promoting them as midsize cars. The Coronet name was revived, as a series in several trim levels. The 383/330 and 426/365 offered performance for the street, but they lacked the image of the ultra-successful GTO, which had been joined by similar models from GM's other brands. The Hemi still was available, but it was a race-only engine.

More Debuts for 1966

The Coronet was given another attractive restyle for 1966. The 383 was now rated at 325 hp, but the 426/365 completely disappeared. In its place was a significant upgrade: the Street Hemi. All of a sudden, the GTO's luster shimmered a bit less next to the Hemi's 425 horses. With street-friendly 10.25 compression, the Hemi was easy to live with, but its solid lifters and dual-quads weren't for everyone. It also was an expensive proposition, but the owner of a Hemi Coronet likely was *the* one to beat in Anytown, USA.

The year 1966 also marked the debut of a new Dodge specialty vehicle called the Charger. Based on the Coronet, the Charger featured a fastback roofline, a grille with concealed headlights, full-width taillights, and a cus-

tom interior. The standard engine was a 318, but performance enthusiasts could opt for the 383/325 or the 426 Hemi.

Although great for Dodge's image, only about 13,000 out of 37,344 were equipped with the performance engines, so the impact on the street was rather minimal. Dodge still needed a dedicated performance car.

Of special note was a Dart that was created for NHRA's D/Stock class: the Maximum Performance 273 Engine Dart Drag Package. Although Darts generally came with a 273/235, the D-Dart was powered by a special 275-hp version of the small-block that included 4-speed CamCraft 284-degree camshaft, Racer Brown valvesprings, Weber Speed Equipment clutch, 8¾-inch

For 1966, Dodge produced 50 D-Darts with a special 273/275 for D/Stock. "Because of the expected use, cars equipped with this package are sold 'as is,' without any warranty coverage whatsoever," read the April 1966 Dodge Product Information Bulletin. (Photo ©TEN: The Enthusiast Network. All rights reserved.)

Sure-Grip rear with 4.89 gears, and Doug's Headers with Y-pipe adapter, among other items.

It is believed that 50 white Dart GTs were converted to satisfy homologation requirements. "Because of the expected use, cars equipped with this package are sold 'AS IS,' without any warranty coverage whatsoever," according to an April Dodge Product Information Bulletin.

For the Road and the Track

For 1967, Dodge finally followed the formula that had been a success for Pontiac and others. The new Coronet R/T was nicely trimmed with buckets, louvered hood, Charger-like grille, and prominent badging. The R/T's trump card was the standard 440 Magnum with 375 hp, with the Hemi available to handle what the 440 could not.

A special Hemi Coronet 440 hardtop was created for Super Stock. All WO23 Coronets were white with black interior and included a slightly modified Street Hemi with special intake, special air cleaner for air induction, transistorized Prestolite ignition, 4.80-series gears, and other racing items.

The Charger returned for 1967, slightly changed and now offering the 440 Magnum as an option. None of the changes helped the Charger's popularity: production fell to 15,788.

The Dart was redesigned for 1967, but its top engine remained the 273/235; not muscle, but sporty nonetheless. In March, Dodge announced the 280-horse Charger 383 for the

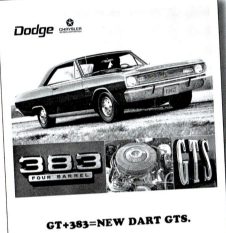

Dodge finally had a proper GTO-fighter with the 1967 Coronet R/T. Its standard 440 Magnum dwarfed the competition in size, and the optional Hemi dwarfed them in power. (Dodge, Plymouth and the AMC design are registered trademarks of FCA US LLC)

The redesigned 1967 Dart GT was sporty, but the available 273/235 wasn't quite muscle. Dodge eventually squeezed in a 383 to create the Dart GTS, the only big-block compact in the market (along with the Barracuda). (Dodge, Plymouth and the AMC design are registered trademarks of FCA US LLC)

Dick Landy received a Super Stock WO Hemi Coronet 440 and dressed it in R/T regalia to promote Dodge's new image car. (Photo ©TEN: The Enthusiast Network. All rights reserved.)

Dodge redesigned the 1968 Coronet R/T, still using a standard 440. Dick Landy campaigned this one in SS/FA. (Photo ©TEN: The Enthusiast Network. All rights reserved.)

Announcing:
CORONET "SUPER BEE"
Scat Pack performance at a new low price.

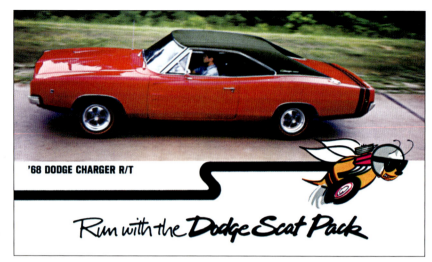

'68 DODGE CHARGER R/T

Run with the Dodge Scat Pack

When Plymouth introduced the 1968 Road Runner, Dodge had no equivalent. Several months later, Dodge created the Super Bee. (Dodge, Plymouth and the AMC design are registered trademarks of FCA US LLC)

After the 1962s turned Chrysler upside-down, the company played it safe. The 1968 Dodge Charger was Chrysler's return to form, and arguably the most exciting car in the market. The new Charger R/T featured a standard 440 Magnum; the Hemi was optional. (Dodge, Plymouth and the AMC design are registered trademarks of FCA US LLC)

Dart GT, which changed the model designation to Dart GTS. Horsepower was down from the Comet's 383s thanks to restrictive exhaust manifolds, and power steering was not available, but the GTS (and its Barracuda cousin) was the only big-block compact on the market.

The all-new 1968 Coronet featured contemporary Coke-bottle styling and trademark Delta flourishes for a fresh look. The Coronet R/T returned with a new power bulge hood that set it apart. Double body side stripes were standard, but no-cost twin bumblebee stripes on the rear was a sign that the Coronet R/T was a part of the Scat Pack, Dodge's new high-performance team that eventually included the Super Bee coupe.

As Dodge's midyear answer to the Road Runner, the Super Bee offered 90 percent of the performance of the R/T for more than $300 less. Included was a 383 Magnum with 335 hp, standard 4-speed, heavy-duty suspension and brakes, Charger instrument panel, power bulge hood, and bumblebee stripes, among other items.

Charger: The Shape of 1968

The 1968 Charger was the big newsmaker at Dodge. It stood out with its gorgeous styling and perfect proportions complemented by hidden headlights, flying buttress roofline, and subtle detailing. The top engine was a 330-hp 383, so performance fans who wanted more had to move up to the new Charger R/T.

As the leader of the Scat Pack, the Charger R/T was equipped like the Coronet R/T: standard 440 Magnum, bucket seats, heavy-duty suspension, and bumblebee stripes on the rear. When equipped with the Hemi, perhaps no vehicle from 1968 had a better combination of looks and power.

The Dart GTS became a full-fledged model for 1968, with an all-new 340 standard and the 383 optional. Mr. Norm commissioned Hurst to install approximately 48 440 Magnums to create the Dart GSS (for Grand Spaulding Sport). (Richard Truesdell Photo)

A fourth member of the Scat Pack was the Dart GTS. Previously a sub-model of the 1967 Dart GT, the 1968 GTS was given full-fledged model status and featured Dodge's new 275-hp 340 small-block, simulated hood intakes, heavy-duty suspension, 14-inch tires, full-length longitudinal stripes (bumblebee stripes were a no-cost option), and plenty of fancy trim to reflect its place as the top-of-the-line Dart. Order the 4-speed 340 and you received a more radical cam, or order the optional 383 and you'd have 300 horses on tap courtesy of new heads. Power steering finally made the 383 option list midyear.

Hurst Builds a Race Hemi

A special B/Stock Hemi Dart was produced in March 1968 in conjunction with Hurst. It featured a 12.5-compression Race Hemi, cross-ram intake, Hooker headers, and special weight-saving measures such as fiberglass front fenders and Plexiglas windows. "Since the purpose of this vehicle is only for competition, it will not be certified for driving on public roads, and a tag reflecting this fact will be affixed with the following notice: 'This vehicle was not manufactured

HEMI-DART RELEASED BY DODGE
brawny midget is scat pack superstar

• DETROIT -- Dodge Division of Chrysler Corporation has released their own answer to the Hemi Barracuda featured in our March issue. While similar, in many respects, to the 'Cuda, the Dart has a personality all its own. The outstanding features are:
• A complete fiberglass front end with stock grille and markings. This includes a massive hood scoop.
• Gutted interior with two lightweight bucket seats and no back seat.
• Rear fender openings reshaped to clear huge racing tires.
• Complete rear-end assembly from large-series Dodge to provide extra strength.
• Trunk-mounted heavy-duty battery.
• Light-gauge steel doors, lightweight window glass (with only lift straps for the door windows), no sound deadener, and no undercoating.
We have, however, saved the most outstanding feature for last. That's the power train. It starts with a 1968 version of Chrysler's famed Hemi-head engine at 426 CID and about 500 bhp. The engine (called a "Hemi" because of its ultra-efficient hemispherically shaped combustion chambers) is one of the hottest money can buy.

Standard equipment features include:
• Extra-strength cross-bolted main bearings.
• Racing pistons at 12.5:1 compression ratio.
• Dual Holley 4-Bbl. carbs on a ram-tuned intake manifold that feeds across the top of the engine.
• Hot dual-point transistor ignition.
• High-capacity racing oil pump.
• Hooker headers and dual exhausts and mufflers.
• Modified "slick-shift" four-speed manual or Torqueflite automatic transmission.
• Hurst Competition Plus four-speed or Dual/Gate automatic shifter (depending on transmission).
One of the first of these cars to be delivered was that of Dick Landy. Dick entered the car at the Hot Rod Magazine drag meet, but the rules stated that fifty of the cars had to be in existence to make the cars legal for competition. At that time, the cars were so new that this requirement could not be met, thus Landy could not compete. Enough of them have been made now, however, so watch out for these little devils through the year. They'll be making big news.

Eighty 1968 Hemi Darts were produced in conjunction with Hurst. It was all business, from the 12.5:1-compression Race Hemi to the fiberglass front end, gutted interior, and light-gauge steel doors. (Photo Courtesy Hurst Performance)

Although the Coronet R/T was Dodge's first true GTO-fighter, it was overshadowed by the gorgeous Charger R/T and bargain-priced Super Bee. However, if you wanted a midsize high-performance Dodge convertible, the Coronet R/T was it. (Richard Truesdell Photo)

for use on the public streets, roads, or highways, and does not conform to engine vehicle safety standards.'"

The 1969 Coronet received the usual styling fine-tuning to keep things fresh, and Scat Pack members received a redesigned bumblebee stripe. The Coronet R/T featured the same engine lineup but a new, optional Ramcharger air induction system was available for the 440 Magnum, standard for the Hemi. New simulated quarter panel scoops were a nice complementary addition.

The R/T distinguished itself from the Super Bee via full-width taillights. The Bee shared many of the same features but added a hardtop to the series. The 383/335 remained standard; the Hemi was the sole engine option.

Six Pack to Go

A new engine joined the Super Bee series in March. The A12 package featured three 2-barrels atop the 440 Magnum, a special fiberglass hood with raised scoop designed in a wind tunnel, no hubcaps, and a Dana rear with 4.10 gears, among other equipment. With 390 hp, the new 440 Six Pack paled in comparison to the Hemi, but a Six Pack Super Bee was less fussy and quite possibly faster out of the box. The A12 package included four new colors that were available on other Dodges: Bright Green, Bahama Yellow, Hemi Orange, and Bright Red.

After selling more than 90,000 Chargers in 1968, Dodge wisely left well enough alone. Except for a new split grille and full-width taillights, a new Special Edition package added a bit of leather-clad luxury to the Charger and Charger R/T. Low-gloss black hood stripes were a performance-inspired midyear option. The Charger R/T continued to feature the 440 Magnum standard and the Hemi optional, although no air induction system was available as with the Scat Pack Coronets.

The midyear 1969 440 Six Pack Super Bee was as fast out of the showroom as the Hemi, looked like a tough street bruiser, and came with an efficient, fiberglass air induction hood that was designed in a wind tunnel. (Rocky Rotella Photo)

The 1969 Charger 500 initiated the escalation in the "Aero Wars" in which Chrysler and Ford fought for NASCAR supremacy. To create the 500, Dodge started with a Charger R/T, then smoothed out the backlight and added a flush Coronet grille, among other tweaks. (Richard Truesdell Photo)

After Ford responded to the Charger 500 with the Torino Talladega/ Cyclone Spoiler II, Dodge developed the Charger Daytona. This was the first NASCAR stock car to reach 200 mph on the banked oval. (Tim Costello Photo)

The Greatest Charger of 'Em All

Two special Chargers appeared during the 1969 model year with the purpose of homologating their aerodynamic tweaks for NASCAR.

The Charger 500 featured a flush 1968 Coronet grille, exposed headlights, and A-pillar caps. The roofline's flying buttresses were smoothed out to reduce drag. The 500 upped the ante on circle tracks until Ford's response (Ford Torino Talladega/Mercury Cyclone Spoiler II) began to give Dodge trouble.

The Charger Daytona, successor to the Charger 500, shared the same backlight as the 500 but added an 18-inch nose, 23-inch-tall rear spoiler, and scoops mounted on the front fenders. It was the wildest thing on wheels out of Detroit and, on the NASCAR circuit, was the first car to break the 200-mph barrier.

The Dart GTS underwent a mild facelift for 1969 and, like all Scat Pack members, received a redesigned bumblebee stripe. There also were some changes under the hood: the 4-speed 340 now shared the milder cam with the automatic, and the optional 383 was bumped up to 330 hp. A 440 GTS hardtop became available midyear, but only with an automatic transmission.

The GTS also had a new Scat Pack brother: Dart Swinger 340. The Swinger 340 hardtop was akin to the GTS with a taxicab treatment à la Super Bee.

The 1970 Coronet was restyled with more prominent Coke-bottle curves and an unusual prow that exploited Dodge's delta theme. The Coronet R/T received a redesigned bulge hood with simulated scoops. The Ramcharger was not changed. The standard 440/375 was joined by the 440 Six Pack plus the Hemi. Redesigned rear quarter side scoops were now a standard R/T exclusive. Inside, standard bucket seats with integrated head restraints and Hurst's Pistol Grip 4-speed shifter were fresh additions.

The Super Bee received many of the same updates as the R/T. The base 383/335 was now backed by a standard 3-speed manual, but the 4-speed and Torqueflite remained most popular. The 440 Six Pack returned, but only as a conventional offering without the A12 package. Unique for the Super Bee was a choice of two stripes: traditional bumblebee or new "hockey stick" longitudinal stripes.

1969 Dodge Swinger 340. A bold new member of the Dodge Scat Pack.
Run with the Dodge Scat Pack

The Dart Swinger 340 joined the Scat Pack in 1969 for those who wanted the high-winding 340 without the luxurious appointments of the Dart GTS. Unlike the GTS, the Swinger 340 had no optional big-block. (Dodge, Plymouth and the AMC design are registered trademarks of FCA US LLC)

The 1970 Super Bee came standard with a new "hockey stick" stripe. The traditional bumblebee stripe was a no-cost option. A 3-speed manual became the new standard transmission. (Jim Stodolka Photo)

Like the Coronets, the 1970 Charger was in the third year of its design cycle, but the updates were not as drastic. A new loop bumper and full-width grille were the most noticeable changes.

R/Ts featured distinctive simulated side scoops on the doors. The R/T also gained a new longitudinal stripe that accentuated the Coke-bottle rear quarters, but the bumblebee continued to be a popular choice.

The flat-black performance paint treatment for the hood returned, which could be complemented by new reflective silver engine call-outs in a neat pop-art font. The 440 Magnum remained standard, but the 440 Six Pack joined the Hemi as an option.

The Dart GTS was killed for 1970, leaving the restyled Dart Swinger 340 as the sole A-Body Scat Pack member. (Dodge, Plymouth and the AMC design are registered trademarks of FCA US LLC)

The 1970 Charger featured a new loop bumper and grille and, for the R/T, simulated scoops on the doors. The bumblebee stripe was now a no-cost option, as new longitudinal stripes became standard. Engine call-outs were a new extra on top of the optional hood stripes. (Wade Ogle Photo)

The Dart GTS was put to rest for 1970, but a restyled Swinger 340 continued to represent Dodge's high-performance compact. Even though street-going A-Body Dodges never had air induction, the 1970 Swinger 340 looked the part with a non-functional Ramcharger hood that could be complemented by an optional black-out.

Dodge Finally Fields a Pony

No doubt the biggest news at Dodge for 1970 was the all-new Challenger, the division's first pony car. It was available in regular, luxury, and sporty versions: Challenger; Challenger Special Edition (SE), which added a vinyl roof with "formal" backlight, additional chrome trim, leather and woodgrain

The 1970 Challenger R/T's bumblebee stripe was paint and not a decal, so it was possible to order a Light Green Challenger with a Sublime stripe. (Tim Costello Photo)

interior trim, and an overhead consolette; Challenger R/T, which featured the 383 Magnum, performance hood, heavy-duty suspension and brakes, F70 x 14-inch tires, longitudinal stripes (bumblebee was a no-cost option), Rallye instrument cluster, and quad exhaust tips; and Challenger R/T SE.

The Challenger and SE were not performance cars, but their top engine was a 383/330. The A66 Challenger 340 Performance Package for the base

Dodge's Trans-Am package was available for the base Challenger and included exclusive use of a trio of Holleys on the 340. The Challenger T/A featured a redesigned A12 hood (now with hinges), which later became available for other performance Challengers. (Photo ©TEN: The Enthusiast Network. All rights reserved.)

The redesigned 1971 Charger absorbed the Coronet coupe and became a multi-faceted series. The Charger Super Bee came standard with the 383 but was now available with a 340 for the first time. Note the standard hood and optional hidden headlights. (Photo ©TEN: The Enthusiast Network. All rights reserved.)

Challenger included the 275-hp small-block, 15-inch Rallye wheels, and bumblebee stripe, among other equipment.

The Challenger R/T's optional engines included the 440 Magnum, 440 Six Pack, and Hemi. A new Shaker hood scoop was available for all R/T engines. The N94 fiberglass hood, which was inspired by the 1969 A12 Super Bee, was released midyear.

The same hood was standard on the Challenger T/A, which was Dodge's homologation special for the Trans-Am series. The T/A package featured a number of performance upgrades including offset tire sizes, side exhaust trumpets, unique black longitudinal stripes, and 290-hp 340 Six Pack.

Charger Tries to Follow Suit

For 1971, Coronet coupes were gone, replaced by a redesigned and expanded Charger series. The Super Bee became the Charger Super Bee, featuring new, groovy Charger styling plus 383/300, performance hood with simulated valve covers, black beltline stripe, heavy-duty suspension and brakes, and bench seat, among other items.

Optional engines began with the 340/275 then went up to the 440 Six Pack and Hemi. Notable options included the Ramcharger hood (like Plymouth's Air Grabber but with an angry bee illustration), hidden headlights, Elastomeric body-colored bumpers, sunroof, and spoilers front and rear.

The Charger R/T did the Super Bee one better with a standard 440 Magnum engine, now down 5 hp to 370. The Charger R/T differed slightly from the Super Bee thanks to simulated louvered doors, taillights, and performance hood.

Standard were bucket seats, extra-heavy-duty suspension, and G70 x 14–inch tires, among other items. Engine choices remained the 440 Six Pack and Hemi, the latter with standard Ramcharger. The R/T also shared a number of performance and visual options with the Super Bee.

The 440 Magnum continued to be standard for the upscale 1971 Charger R/T, which also included exclusive "simulated door louvers." A standard louvered hood also distinguished the R/T from the Super Bee.

Dodge replaced the Dart Swinger 340 with the new semi-fastback 1971 Demon 340, although 75 Swinger 340s were specially built for two dealerships in Saskatchewan and Alberta, Canada. (Photo ©TEN: The Enthusiast Network. All rights reserved.)

After a strong debut, the Challenger received marginal styling tweaks for 1971, such as a split grille and matching taillights. The wide grille surround (shown) and body-colored bumpers front and rear were two new optional styling treatments.

Although not part of the Scat Pack, the Charger SE was now its own model instead of a trim package. Although its luxurious trim and standard hidden headlights pointed to the personal-luxury market, an available 440/370 gave the Charger SE the opportunity to pull double duty as a performance car.

The 1971 Challenger featured a twin-scooped grille that was mimicked by split taillights. Elastomeric body-colored bumpers were a new option available in several colors. The SE models and the R/T convertible were discontinued, leaving the Challenger R/T hardtop as the only high-performance model. The 383 remained standard, although it was detuned to 300 hp.

The R/T featured unique simulated quarter panel scoops and new, wide dual stripes along the beltline, plus an R/T decal on the performance hood. Optional engines included the 340 (still available for the base Challenger), 440 Six Pack, and Hemi, with Shaker or T/A hood available for any R/T engine.

Dodge's New Small-Block Street Demon

The Demon 340, a new cousin to the Plymouth Duster, replaced the Dart Swinger 340 for 1971 (although two Canadian dealerships commissioned a small number of Swinger 340s for 1971–1972). A cartoonish logo with a cutesy disposition helped make the Demon 340 the perfect entry-level performance car. It was several hundred dollars cheaper than the Charger Super Bee.

Horns Shorn

Shuffled model lines for 1972 were a byproduct of a changing market and lowered compression. The Charger and Charger SE received new grilles and taillights, with the SE featuring a more formal greenhouse. The Rallye package, which featured a dark argent grille, power bulge hood with black performance treatment, simulated door louvers, louvered taillights, front and rear sway bars, and F70 x 14 tires, took the place of the Charger Super Bee and R/T. "This Package makes driving

The Rallye package for the 1972 Charger replaced the Charger R/T. The 318 was standard, and every performance engine now had low compression. The 440 Six Pack was initially available but cancelled soon after production began. This Rallye features optional hidden headlights.

any Charger more fun without the need for larger engines. But for those who want the big engines, Charger has them," said the dealer book, referring to the standard 318. Enthusiasts could choose from the 240-hp 340 (a Rallye exclusive), 400/255, and 440/280; the 440 Six Pack was canceled in early September.

A mild facelift carried the Charger into 1973. The Rallye lost its door louvers but featured new striping options. Despite an available 440, it was clear the Charger was moving into a more personal-luxury direction, spearheaded by the Charger SE. (Dodge, Plymouth and the AMC design are registered trademarks of FCA US LLC)

After 1972's facelift, the 1973 Challenger adopted prominent front bumper guards to withstand 5-mph crashes as dictated by law. Enthusiasts could still depend on the Challenger Rallye with 340 Magnum. (Dodge, Plymouth and the AMC design are registered trademarks of FCA US LLC)

The 1972 Challenger bore a new look thanks to an "upside-down" grille and four oval taillights. Like the Charger, the R/T was replaced by the Rallye package, which offered the 318 standard and the 340 (also available on the base Challenger) as the only upgrade. The Rallye included a black grille, front fender scoops with black strobe stripes, performance hood, Rallye instrument cluster, and F70 x 14–inch tires, among other items.

Despite lowered engine compression, the Demon 340 was little changed for 1972. A new hood with simulated hood scoops and striping were the most notable enhancements.

The 1973 Charger received a facelift with redesigned front bumpers (with the SE losing its signature hidden headlights) and rear taillights. By this time it was clear that the Charger was headed in a personal-luxury direction, but enthusiasts could still order the 340/240, 400/260, or 440/280 with the Rallye package. The package included voluptuous full-length body side tape stripes in black or gradated red.

The 1973 Challenger featured solid-rubber guards for the new government-mandated bumpers. The Rallye was dropped as a model but remained available through as a package, which offered much of the same equipment. The 340 remained an option for both the Challenger and Rallye.

The Dart 340 Sport replaced the Demon 340, and received a new grille and front bumper plus redesigned taillights. A new mid-body stripe (plus a rear deck stripe) was standard but could be substituted by an "up-and-over" stripe. A special hood with "performance treatment" and non-functional scoops was also available.

The 1974 Charger saw minimal outward changes, but the 245-hp 360 small-block under the hood replaced the 340. The Rallye Package remained chock full of handling and visual bling, including bulged hood and body-side tape stripes (standard in black, available in gradated red or gold). However, enthusiasts needed to upgrade to the 360, 400/250, or 440/275 for any semblance of performance. The Performance Axle Package included 3.55 gears, Sure-Grip differential, and Maximum Cooling Package.

The final year for the Challenger featured marginal changes, the most noticeable being even larger rubber rear bumper guards. The Rallye Package included the performance hood, front fender scoops with strobe stripes, suspension tweaks, and more, but the package was only worth its salt when equipped with the new 360 engine.

The 1974 Dart 360 Sport changed little except for the new small-block. A special black paint treatment with hood scoops was again available as an option.

After 1974, Dodge stopped trying to fake the good years and let the personal-luxury market rule the roost. Darts continued to feature the 360 as an option, and the R/T made a return on the Volaré several years later, but by then the 360 was asthmatic and had no semblance to the glory days of high performance. It wasn't until the 1980s that Dodge, with help from Carroll Shelby, offered a 14-second car from the factory.

Dealerships

Dodge made strong impressions on the dragstrip with the Ramcharger, and when the Hemi upgrade arrived in February 1964, it made history on the banked ovals. Dodge failed to develop an image-based muscle car until the Coronet R/T hit dealerships in the fall of 1966. Hemi? Yeah, that had image in spades. But how many Hemi Coronets were sold compared to Pontiac GTOs?

Luckily, Dodge had a booster on its side that helped the brand market a high-performance image before the powers-that-be at Highland Park figured out that selling racing and performance were two different things: "Mr. Norm" Kraus and Grand Spaulding Dodge.

Norm's father owned a gas station that sold used cars on the side. Business grew and he, along with his sons, expanded to the lot next door. After Norm discovered that hot V-8s with stick shifts were quick sellers, they began to focus only on high-performance cars. The dealership became so hot that Dodge approached the Krauses several times about becoming a franchised dealer. Finally, in 1962, after seeing a preview of the 1963 Dodges and the 426 Ramcharger, Norm and his brother signed on the dotted line and proceeded to build a Dodge dealership.

Mr. Norm said, "When you walked into Grand Spaulding Dodge, you knew that we were all about high performance. We started in the showroom selling new performance cars. We backed it up with the parts department, we backed it up with the service department, and we had a big selection of high-performance cars on the used car lot. Nearly everything we did was geared to promote performance. I don't know what other dealers did, but I know what we did at Grand Spaulding.

"Then I started adding! When we put in our first dyno machine and I said, 'Guys, this looks too bare. Go out and buy about four or five Sun machines.' Once they were all in place, it even impressed *me*!

"I put women in my showroom floor, and I hired 21-year-old guys in my parts department to be performance specialists. I took four stalls in the service department and allocated 40 feet for the high-performance parts department. We also built up a second floor and put on display every high-performance part we had in stock."

Grand Spaulding Dodge's 1964 Ramcharger Polara, driven by Pat Minick and tuned by Al Groll, featured aluminum components. (Photo Courtesy The Mr. Norm's Collection)

Mr. Norm claimed the new Hemi Charger was "the only production car in America guaranteed to run 11s, right off the showroom floor!" (Photo Courtesy The Mr. Norm's Collection)

Before Dodge offered a big-block 1967 Dart, Mr. Norm built his own at Grand Spaulding Dodge. (Photo Courtesy The Mr. Norm's Collection)

But Grand Spaulding Dodge wasn't just any dealership with a high-performance bent. When Mr. Norm discovered the 1967 Dart was going to have a 273 as its top engine, he took things into his own hands.

"I called up Detroit and said, 'Why can't we order a big-block in the new Dart? I'm spotting everyone a thousand pounds. We have to beat these people!'

"Detroit said it couldn't be done, so I picked up another phone. 'Denny [GSD's parts director], get up here! Get a 383 4-barrel, a 727 Torqueflite, and an 8-3/4 rear end, and get them installed in a new Dart.' Two days later he comes into my office and says it's done.

"I said, 'What's done? Oh, geez, I forgot all about that. Where's it at?' So we went to the back of the service department. It looked beautiful. What an installation! 'What did you have to do?'

"He said, 'I took a little off the K-Member, a quarter inch, so it would slide in there, and then I moved the left motor mount a little and I put a heat deflector in between the exhaust manifold and the steering box.'

"*Supah!* I took it out for a road test. Phenomenal! So I called up Bob McCurry at Dodge and said, 'I've got a 383 Dart here.'

"He says, 'Bring it to Detroit!'

"I told Denny, 'Make this car look like I'm doing a big road test. Put some gauges on it. I don't care, just mix it up and put it on there.' He did a fantastic job. Picked up a reporter from the airport and took him out the next day for a road test. Took her up to 6,000 rpm and let it drop. How's the oil pressure? How's the temperature? Great! We did it again. It was fun, fun, *fun!* Then I took it to Detroit.

"Bob comes downstairs and takes a look at the installation and says, 'Very nice.' And then he takes the car, goes down to Hamtramck and hits

it. He comes back and says, 'Magnificent, Son! I gotta call these engineers,' so he gets on the phone and says 'I want you guys to come down here,' and two engineers came down.

"'Just take a good look what the kids from Chicago did. You guys look under the hood!'

"One of them says, 'They put a heat deflector on it.'

"Bob looks at him and says, 'Why couldn't you?' That's how the car was born."

By March 1967, Dodge made the announcement that the 383 was available for the Dart.

Then, when the competition got tougher, Mr. Norm built a 440 Dart. "I said, 'The 440's gotta fit in there too! [chuckles] Gary [Dyer, GSD's head of engineering] cut off 1/4 inch of the K-member to clear the oil pan. A hole near the oil pump was drilled and tapped so a modified engine mount could be attached. The driver-side exhaust manifold was the same item used for the 383 Dart GTS. Two additional modifications were necessary because of the squeeze: a heat shield to keep the brake proportioning valve in check, and a snubber on the differential to prevent extreme U-joint angles."

Mr. Norm tried to convince Dodge to build the 440 Dart. Dodge initially couldn't accommodate the request, so the division built the first batch as 383/automatic Dart GTSs but without the engine and transmission installed.

The Darts then went to Hurst in Madison Heights to receive modifications to accommodate the 440. The battery was also relocated to the trunk. The *pièce de résistance* was the name change to Dart GSS, for Grand Spaulding Special.

Not only was Grand Spaulding Dodge the only place you could buy a 1968 440 Dart, Mr. Norm also gave it his patented Power Tune, which meant the buyer had the honor of seeing his henchmen dyno the new Dart GSS, then re-jet the carb, recurve the distributor, and return to the dyno to measure the power increase.

Mr. Norm continued, "When they came out with the 383, they had a 5-year/50,000-mile warranty on the car, so they were somewhat detuned or they simply came out that way. We picked up on that because we ran one on the dyno. Gary goes and adjusts the springs on the distributor and re-jets the primaries on the carb. And then we put it back on there: 3¼ [horsepower]! Then we thought, 'Okay, with the way these cars are detuned, we don't want our customers' cars going out that way. We're going to power tune every car we sell.' So from that point on, every 383 and 440 got a free power tune, and we started advertising it: Free Power Tune: guaranteed horsepower!

Mr. Norm wasn't your run-of-the-mill car dealer; he was the yin to the enthusiast's yang. Several years after producing the 440 Dart GSS, Mr. Norm was back with the 1971 Demon GSS with the Six Pack 340. (Photo Courtesy The Mr. Norm's Collection)

The market for high-performance cars was dismal in 1972 but, seeing an opportunity, Mr. Norm created the supercharged Demon GSS and gave the public big-block performance from a low-compression 340. (Richard Truesdell Photo)

The 1970 Scat Pack Club kit helped the dealer sales force learn about high-performance enthusiasts and how to cater to them, all in the interest of sales and profit. (Dodge, Plymouth and the AMC design are registered trademarks of FCA US LLC)

"That was the marketing, and we backed it up with real performance. If I heard of anything happening at another dealership, my salesmen knew they could beat any deal from that dealership; no questions asked. But we didn't run into that much. I was prepared for everything."

And, like Mr. Norm's 383 Dart, the 1968 Dart GSS served as inspiration to Dodge because the 440 was released as a regular factory option for the 1969 Dart GTS.

Mr. Norm returned to custom-built cars with the 1971–1973 Demon GSS, offering either Six Pack carburetion (1971) or a supercharger (1972–1973), but they were dealer-prepared vehicles not directly sanctioned by Dodge.

Dodge's racing success and performance resources were beyond reproach, but it took Mr. Norm to show the division how it was done.

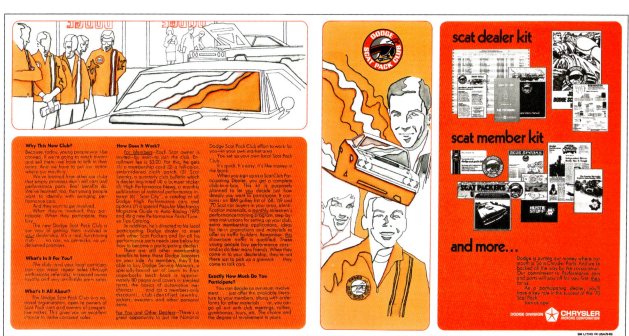

The Scat Pack Club served the obvious purpose of keeping Dodge enthusiasts in the loop, but the participation of Dodge dealers was key in maintaining the relationship. (Dodge, Plymouth and the AMC design are registered trademarks of FCA US LLC)

Marketing Strategy

The car club concept was nothing new when Dodge created the Scat Pack Club for 1970, but none had been done with the same scope. What Dodge managed to understand was that a club could be an idea all its own when it came to relationship marketing.

The Scat Pack Club kit was created for salespeople to take advantage of the performance segment. "We've been doing very well with our Scat Pack and we're going to do better. We're going to do it by making *your business* the center of interest for performance car buffs. *Our* club is built around you and your market. It's aimed, of course, at Scat Pack buyers, but its purpose is to sell cars and, certainly, parts."

Why the new club?

Because, today, young people won't be conned. If we're going to reach them (and sell them) we have to talk in their terms. And we have to put our action where our mouth is. We've learned from other car clubs that empty promises don't sell cars and performance parts. Real benefits do. We've learned, too, that young people want to identify with swinging performance cars. And they want to get involved. When they're involved, they participate.

The new Scat Pack Club is our way of getting them involved in *your* dealership. It's a real, functioning club. No con, no gimmicks, no undelivered promises.

What's in it for you?

Repeat sales (especially via referrals), increased owner loyalty, and profitable parts sales.

What's it all about?

The Dodge Scat Pack Club was a national organization open to owners of both Scat Pack vehicles and competitive makes. In other words, it was a way to maintain a relationship with customers and develop a relationship for future conquest sales.

How does it work?

For members, $3 netted a membership card, patch, the *Scat Speaks* quarterly newsletter, *Performance Parts/Tune-Up Tips* catalog, and other items.

For dealers, a "club-in-a-box" kit featuring a performance training program, club instructions, and more.

Exactly how much do you participate?

You can decide on minimum involvement. Just offer the available literature to your members, along with order forms for other materials, or you can go all out with club meetings, rallies, gymkhanas, tours, etc. The choice and the degree of involvement is yours.

How much does it cost to become a participating dealer?

$25

Is Dodge Division deeply committed to performance?

Not only Dodge, but the entire Chrysler Corporation. Today, every fifth car you and other Dodge dealers sell is a Scat Packer. With five Scat cars for 1970, we're going after an even bigger share. Commitment? We're going all the way.

How is Dodge backing your Scat Club?

- Performance-oriented service training programs
- Supercar Clinics
- Promotion via Parts Managers clubs and Dodge Service Managers Guild
- 1970 announcement materials

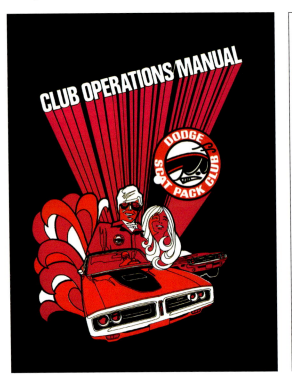

This 1971 Scat Pack Club Operations Manual featured Dodge's revamped performance car roster in a more mature style that shed its 1960s origins. (Dodge, Plymouth and the AMC design are registered trademarks of FCA US LLC)

A $25 investment was all it took to become a Scat Pack Club participating dealer. The Club offered opportunities for "repeat sales, increased owner loyalty and very profitable parts sales." (Dodge, Plymouth and the AMC design are registered trademarks of FCA US LLC)

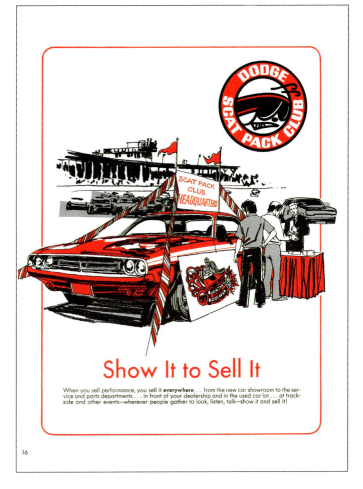

This page was both sales indoctrination and idea-generator. Selling high performance could be done at every opportunity. (Dodge, Plymouth and the AMC design are registered trademarks of FCA US LLC)

These ad templates for newspapers were created for dealerships to arouse interest in the Scat Pack Club. (Dodge, Plymouth and the AMC design are registered trademarks of FCA US LLC)

- Increased emphasis and participation in all facets of racing
- Performance-oriented national advertising

Does Chrysler Parts Division figure in the Scat program?

A performance parts merchandising package was produced to promote "Hustle Stuff" Performance Parts.

Advertising Program

Beginning in 1966, Dodge's advertising agency, BBDO, introduced a campaign whose tagline was "Join the Dodge Rebellion." Consumers were urged to "open fire on ho-hum" vehicles and go with Dodge (with Charger the "new leader of the Dodge Rebellion").

The campaign continued with "Operation 1967," with BBDO claiming in the June 19, 1967, *Automotive News* that Dodge had the "highest identification score of any car maker."

The campaign evolved into "Dodge Fever" in 1968, an irresistible, distractible force that was impossible to, um, dodge.

It evolved again in 1970, suggesting you could be "Dodge Material" based on any number of competencies that a particular model had.

Several months after the debut of the Plymouth Road Runner, the 1968 Dodge Super Bee joined the Scat Pack, eventually becoming the Pack's most popular member. (Dodge, Plymouth and the AMC design are registered trademarks of FCA US LLC)

The Scat Pack arrived in 1968 with several performance cars for several purposes, all unified by available bumblebee stripes. (Dodge, Plymouth and the AMC design are registered trademarks of FCA US LLC)

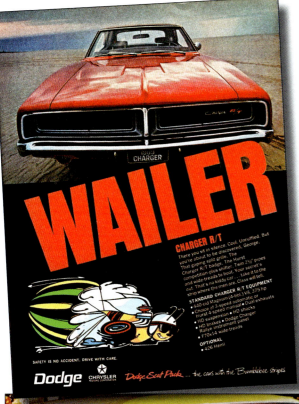

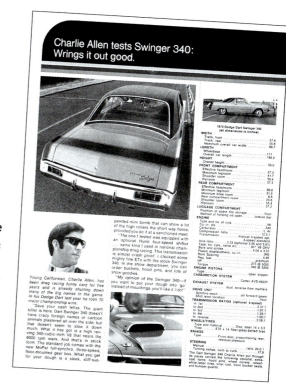

During the campaign's final year, 1971, ads proclaimed, "You can't afford *not* to be Dodge Material."

All these campaigns featured an attractive Dodge Rebellion Girl, Dodge Fever Girl, or Dodge Material Girl, all of whom endeared themselves to the public, especially veterans overseas.

High-performance Dodges were sometimes featured but, starting in 1968, they had their own targeted campaign, thanks to the Scat Pack.

Scat Pack

The high-performance market matured in 1968. Most manufacturers introduced redesigned midsize vehicles, and all offered their vision of what America's enthusiasts and youths demanded.

Dodge, however, did them one better by creating the Scat Pack, a team of performance cars for just about every purse and purpose. Featuring the Coronet R/T, Dart GTS, and Charger R/T, the

The 1971 Scat Pack picked up sophisticated 1970s style and tossed off the hyperbole that was a hallmark of past model years. (Dodge, Plymouth and the AMC design are registered trademarks of FCA US LLC)

Scat Pack could be identified by twin bumblebee stripes on each car's rump. The advertising campaign was led by a bumblebee mascot with a penchant for doing burnouts. The Scat Pack theme was so popular that when Dodge released a cousin to the Plymouth Road Runner midyear, it was called the Super Bee.

Toward the end of the model year, Scat Pack advertising hit a new level of sophistication with bold headlines, engaging photos, copy that spoke the enthusiast's language, and that wonderful bee proclaiming "Scat Pack, the cars with the Bumblebee stripes." The campaign was carried over into 1969, touting a team of cars that now included the Dart Swinger 340.

When the 1969 Scat Pack was introduced, Dodge announced a million-dollar Scat Pack Sweepstakes tie-in with the American Football League. It was part of a campaign to "turn up the fever" for Dodge. The September 2, 1968, *Automotive News* reported that more than 60 million print impressions of the contest announcement and entry forms appeared in 638 daily and weekly newspapers plus magazines such as *Life* and *Ebony*. The latter contained a 16-page insert featuring Dodge's complete lineup as well as profiles on AFL players. Joan Parker, the Dodge Fever Girl, also appeared in the promotion for both print and TV.

"The average age of a NASCAR fan is about 30," said McCurry in the June 16, 1969, *Automotive News*. "The average age of a drag fan is about 27. These people are going to be buying cars for a long time. That's another reason it's good for Dodge to be competitive, and change with the times."

He added, "You know, many of these people will find what they want in personal transportation even if no auto company gives it to them. They did it with the hot-rod shops, before Detroit saw the potential. Now they shop not for price, but for product."

Toward the end of the 1969 model year, Dodge tweaked the Scat Pack campaign once again, with models on the street and the track. This campaign continued into 1970 and included the Challenger R/T.

Dodge also created a magazine insert/brochure announcing "Scat City," a place where "competition is hot, keen, and sanctioned." The pages featured members of the 1970 Scat Pack with different celebrity racers, plus a page on Hustle Stuff Dodge Scat Packages "designed to take you from dress-up-and-show to hot-and-torrid in easy stages" such as The Showboat (a dress-up kit), The Kruncher (strip-oriented kit with ring and pinion), and The Bee-Liever (high-rise manifold and carb for better breathing).

The Scat Pack continued into 1971 with a more contemporary look and an updated performance roster. Despite trying to continue the good times, the masses were turning away from performance, and the Scat Pack died a quiet death after 1971.

Lawman Dodge

Detroit-based Al Eckstrand worked as a lawyer by day, but in his free time he raced Mopars. His first major win was at the wheel of a 1960 Plymouth Fury in SS/A at the 1960 NHRA Nationals. Through the early and mid-1960s he raced for Plymouth's Golden Commando and Dodge's Ramcharger teams, and with his own Lawman drag team.

Eckstrand changed gears in 1966, forming the American Commando Drag Team. Working with Byron Nichols, Chrysler's Vice President of Corporate Sales, Eckstrand was given a Hemi Charger (a former press pool vehicle) and took it to Europe in June to promote drag racing with a focus on Americans stationed at U.S. bases.

The *raison d'être* for visiting U.S. bases was purely pragmatic: with a performance scene developing in the States, many men were coming home to an environment that had completely changed. Put a 14-second car in the hands of a young man who has been out of the loop and bad things were bound to happen. Eckstrand presented military personnel a taste of what was being offered by American manufacturers back home and how to operate them safely.

"You know, those men had a hard time of it," he recalled. "When they got back here after serving their country, people were yelling at them and spitting on them. Most of them didn't want to be there anyway, and it was hard for anyone to make sense of it all. So in addition to the driving skills, I felt the program helped them see that there was something worthwhile, something beyond the horrible situation they were facing. That appearance of hope became more important to me as the program continued."

Eckstrand continued this effort through 1969. The following year, he formed the Lawman Performance Team and, with Ford, led a 1970 Military Performance Tour in Japan, the Philippines, and South Vietnam, plus stops in Guam, Hawaii, and Europe.

CHAPTER 10

STUDEBAKER'S LAST STAND

Studebaker is not usually the first brand that people think of when it comes to high performance, but the esteemed carriage-maker from South Bend, Indiana, produced high-performance vehicles even before the influence of the Pontiac GTO. After the "horsepower race" had begun, Studebaker borrowed Packard's 275-hp 352 and dropped it into the 1956 Golden Hawk, resulting in a 125 mph personal-luxury cruiser. For the 1957–1958 Golden Hawk, Studebaker equaled the horsepower of the 352 by bolting a McCulloch supercharger to its 289.

But Studebaker was in an unhealthy position. After being purchased by Packard in 1954 to form the Studebaker-Packard Corporation, things went downhill, exacerbated by the 1958 recession that was the final nail in the coffin for Packard. In response, Studebaker changed directions and found success with the compact Lark, which eventually outgrew its austere beginnings and benefitted from a handsome 1962 facelift courtesy of industrial designer Brooks Stevens.

That was the same year Studebaker introduced the sporty Lark Daytona, which seized on the bucket-seat trend. Studebaker had purchased Paxton Products, Inc. the year before and retained the services of the three Granatelli brothers. They quickly began working on a blown 289 for the Avanti slated to debut at the New York International Auto Show in April 1962.

Spearheaded by Studebaker Corporation president Sherwood Egbert to create a halo car to save the company, the Avanti featured a Lark chassis wrapped in fiberglass bodywork designed by a team headed by industrial designer Raymond Loewy. When the 2+2 hit the market as a 1963 model, it wowed enthusiasts the world over with its style and substance, never mind the fact that "America's only four-passenger high-performance personal car" was a fine performer.

The Avanti initially featured two Jet-Thrust 289 engines: R1 and R2. The R1 was rated at 240 hp with a Carter 625-cfm 4-barrel, but the R2 added a Paxton SN-60 supercharger (plus lowered compression) for 289 horses.

Jet-Thrust engines became available as options for the Lark and Gran Turismo Hawk for 1963. In April, two "Super" high-performance packages were introduced to create the Super Lark and Super Hawk. Both packages included Jet Thrust R1 or R2, bucket seats, heavy-duty suspension (with radius rods and rear stabilizer), heavy-duty Twin Traction differential, and front disc brakes, among other items.

Most of the equipment was available individually but, when grouped as a Super package, it gave Studebaker valuable publicity and saved customers a few dollars in the process. Studebaker also offered an exclusive Super Red paint available only for Super Studebakers. In all, 1,391 Jet-Thrust Larks and GT Hawks were produced for 1963, including 145 Super Studebakers.

During this time, Studebaker was working on an experimental Jet-Thrust engine called R3. The 289 received a 0.060-inch bore to form a

This 1963 Avanti was bought by **Sports Car Graphic's** *Bill Burke after life as an experimental car used for speed trials. Burke set new speed records with the very same car for several decades. (Photo Courtesy Studebaker National Museum)*

The struggling company designed the fiberglass 1963 Avanti in 40 days, but there was nothing expedient about its performance, especially when powered by the supercharged R2 289. (Photo Courtesy Studebaker National Museum)

The 1963 Lark also benefited from the Avanti's R2. Later in the year, Studebaker released the Super Lark package, which bundled all the desirable high-performance options. (Tom Shaw Photo)

perfectly square 299-ci engine. Other goodies included a Paxton SN-60 and exhaust manifold castings featuring gently curved runners plus a siamesed collector section for some cylinders.

The R3 was designed in South Bend but hand-built, machined, balanced, and dyno-tested at Granatelli's Paxton facility in California before being sent back to South Bend for installation. Studebaker didn't release horsepower figures, but eventually it was revealed that the R3 put out 305 hp. Andy Granatelli took an experimental R3 Avanti to Bonneville and set 29 records.

"Speed and power will be promoted by Studebaker Corp. when it offers its restyled 1964 models to the buying public. Egbert said he is convinced that a new corporate image of speed, performance, and endurance would attract the nation's young buyers into Studebaker showrooms," reported the September 23, 1963, *Automotive News*. "Egbert left no doubt that Studebaker is aiming squarely at the youth market of the country with its high-speed tests and advertising program."

Brooks Stevens gave the Lark a contemporary look that belied its compact origins. Jet-Thrust Larks and Hawks without the Super performance packages featured upgrades previously available only on Super Studebakers.

Thirteen days before its public introduction, in April 1962, the Avanti made its first record-setting run. The Avanti had been sent to the Granatelli Brothers' Paxton facility in California before achieving an SCTA-sanctioned 171.10 mph in Jean, Nevada.

Also new for 1964 was a production version of the R3 featuring several advances over the experimental 299, including an aluminum intake manifold and cylinder heads with larger ports and valves. The production R3 measured 304.5 ci and was rated at 335 hp, although it is said Andy Granatelli claimed each engine achieved 411 hp on the dyno. There also was an R4, which featured a naturally aspirated, dual-quad 304.5 with 12.0 compression rated at 280 hp.

Because of financial strife, Studebaker announced in December 1963 that all automobile production would be moved to the company's facilities in Hamilton, Ontario, Canada, effective January 1964. All Jet-Thrust engines and Super performance packages promptly disappeared, and Studebaker engines were unceremoniously replaced by a lowly Chevrolet small-block for 1965–1966. By that time, 545 1964 Jet-Thrust Larks and GT Hawks had been built, which included 241 with the Super package; of the latter, one Lark Commander with the R3 engine and another Daytona hardtop with the R4 were built.

The final Studebaker rolled off the line in March 1966 after 64 years of automobile production.

Dealerships

As Studebaker began to embrace high performance, several dealerships welcomed the newfound direction and campaigned Jet-Thrust Studebakers on the dragstrip.

Among the first to gain prominence was Ray Tanner Motors in Phoenix, who sponsored *The Whistler*, a 1963 R2 Lark Regal prepared by Floyd Mendenhall. With only two days of preparation, Mendenhall ran 14.59 at the 1963 AHRA Winternationals to clinch the A/CS class. Before the year was out, he set a class record with a 13.52 ET.

With 5 pounds of boost courtesy of a Paxton supercharger, the 9.0:1-compression R2 put out 289 hp.

Andy Granatelli asked, "Can you imagine what it is like covering a mile in 20 seconds in pitch darkness with only the car's headlights? Thanks to Avanti's aircraft instrument lighting, I had no trouble. Otherwise, it would have been impossible." (Photo Courtesy Studebaker National Museum)

speedy Studes shattered 29 records including a two-way average speed of 168.15 mph in the flying mile for American Class C Flying Start. This eclipsed the 153.67-mph record set three weeks before by Mickey Thompson in a 421 Super Duty Pontiac Catalina.

Another race sponsor was Warren and Day Studebaker in San Bernardino, California. Gordon Williams drove its R1-powered 1963 Lark sedan to victory in F/SA at the 1964 Winternationals in Pomona, later upgrading it to R2 power for C/SA.

Motor Service Company of Rapid City, South Dakota, holds the interesting distinction of selling the highest percentage of Jet-Thrust cars. Although it never sponsored a race car, the dealership was so serious about high performance that it wrote a letter to Studebaker criticizing the factory's high-performance marketing and how it prepared and tuned vehicles for magazine tests.

On February 14, 1963, Andy Granatelli returned to Bonneville with a Super Lark and Super Hawk, both equipped with R2 engine, 4-speed, and 3.31 gears. This was the run featured in a popular ad.

According to the April 1963 *Studebaker Spotlight*, both engines were certified as stock by USAC inspection teams. "Although these speeds are fantastically high for these two models, neither car was contending for

Marketing Strategy

If racing improves the breed, Studebaker took it in a different direction than the Big Three. The Big Three had enormous resources to support NHRA and NASCAR, but Studebaker didn't have that luxury. Instead, the company proved its mettle at Bonneville.

Studebaker's first Bonneville record was set by an Avanti in April 1962, 13 days before its public introduction. This Avanti (the original factory prototype) was sent to the Granatelli Brothers' Paxton facility in California before achieving an SCTA-sanctioned 171.10 mph in Jean, Utah.

The following outing on August 14, 1962, featured three Avantis with the experimental R3 299. One of the

This 1964 Lark Challenger's original owner ordered a new R3 from Paxton Products (Studebaker's high-performance division) in November and, during Christmas break, replaced the original 289. (Photo Courtesy George Krem and Robert Palma)

On August 13-14, 1963, a collaboration between Studebaker and Sears Allstate tires led to a publicity stunt where an R2-equipped Avanti left Los Angeles for New York City. In less than 50 hours (within legal speed limits), the Avanti arrived at its destination. The Studebaker then headed to San Diego, which took just over 52 hours. It didn't end there, however, as the Avanti crossed the border to Tijuana and then headed toward Vancouver, British Columbia, Canada, in a hair over 25 hours; less than 24 hours later, the Avanti returned to Mexico.

national speed records since these were primarily engineering runs," said Granatelli. "The engines in both cars, completely stock R2 supercharged powerplants, have already accounted for about 40 percent of our orders of Avanti models and have been ordered by buyers of more than 1,000 Lark and Hawk automobiles. This is truly a dual-purpose engine, equally at home in trips to the grocery or running at speed trials."

In September, upon completion of the multiple treks, the Avanti headed to Bonneville where Studebaker, Sears, and USAC timing crews were ready for the final test: top-speed straightaway runs. The only preparations were adjusted air pressure in the tires (6.70 x 15–inch), a fresh set of Champion spark plugs, and a check of the ignition dwell. Andy Granatelli ran a two-way average of 145.99 mph.

Ray Tanner Motors in Phoenix was one of the few Studebaker dealerships to race competitively. The Whistler was an R2-powered 1963 Lark. (Photo Courtesy George Krem and Robert Palma)

Hot Rod *magazine technical editor Ray Brock piloted this 1963 Avanti through the traps at 128.94 mph in the half-mile at Riverside Raceway Dragstrip. (Photo Courtesy Studebaker National Museum)*

Starting on October 14, 1963, Studebaker went loaded for bear with a dozen vehicles prepared by Paxton Products, from a lowly Commander Six to an experimental R5 Avanti named *Due Cento* ("200" in Italian, a reference to its top-speed attempt). The 8.5:1-compression R5 was based on the R3 but added twin Paxton superchargers and fuel injection for 497 dyno-certified horsepower per the September 23, 1963, *Automotive News.*

With 3.31 gears, this Studebaker/Sears Allstate Avanti traveled 8,909.7 miles with an average speed of 59.3 mph, then stopped by Bonneville for some top-end runs. (Photo Courtesy Studebaker National Museum)

Due Cento managed only 196.62 mph in poor conditions but, after 10 days, Studebakers owned 337 records in seven different classes.

By the time *Hot Rod*'s coverage of Studebaker's Bonneville runs hit the newsstands, Studebaker had already made the decision to suspend U.S. production and move it to Canada, thereby killing any opportunity to exploit the Bonneville performance. We may not have had the opportunity to properly discover Studebaker performance during the muscle car era, but we can only imagine how the company would have responded to the GTO, given the chance.

Advertising Program

When Jet-Thrust engines were introduced in 1963, Studebaker seized on the homely looks of the Lark with the headline "Q*Car" with the subhead, "How to amaze your friends by adding a few little factory-stock extras to your normal-looking Lark." The copy proceeded to educate the reader that Studebaker's parts bin had everything needed to "dust off Detroit iron and many more-expensive imports" with horsepower and handling. "It won't cost an arm and a leg, and you can drive the folks to church without causing eyebrows to rise."

- For beef: heavy-duty clutch, adjustable shocks, heavy-duty front/rear springs
- For go: supercharged R2 engine, limited-slip rear end, axle ratios up to 4.55

- For stop: power disc brakes up front, finned 11 x 2–inch drums out back
- For safety: seat belts and padded dash
- For sense: full dial instrumentation and 15-inch wheels
- For advice: write to Andy Granatelli

In the spring of 1963, Studebaker began to tout its performance exploits and announced the Super high-performance packages after Andy Granatelli took a Super Lark and Super Hawk to Bonneville. "Two new cars are born:

Avanti-inspired, Bonneville-tested! R2 Super Lark [and] R2 Super Hawk," read the headline. The results spoke for themselves: Lark hit a certified 132 mph, GT Hawk 140.

After Granatelli's October 1963 outing at Bonneville, Studebaker proclaimed, "The power is the story" and bragged how Studebaker "filled whole pages" of the United States Automobile Club's record books. Yet soon after this ad appeared, Studebaker was out of the high-performance business.

Studebaker made an assault on Bonneville with several models in several configurations, from a 6-cylinder Lark to Due Cento. (Photo Courtesy Studebaker National Museum)

Studebaker's Bonneville efforts yielded impressive results that were worth telling to the world. The Big Three had no compact that could compare to the Lark's performance. (Photo Courtesy Studebaker National Museum)

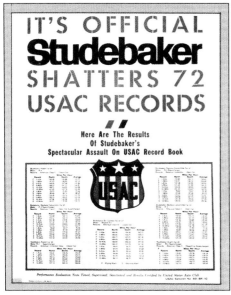

By the time coverage of the Bonneville achievements hit newsstands, Studebaker was bleeding. Ads such as this were the only way to spread the word about Studebaker performance before Jet-Thrust engines were canceled and production moved to Canada. (Photo Courtesy Studebaker National Museum)

World War II Q-boats were warships disguised as innocent-looking merchant ships. Studebaker made no bones that any Lark equipped with a Jet-Thrust engine was like a Q-boat. (Photo Courtesy Studebaker National Museum)

CHAPTER 11

AMC: RACING ON A BUDGET

Rambler was Nash's new compact series for 1950. By 1957, after the 1954 merger of Nash and Hudson to form American Motors, Rambler was its own full-fledged marque while its parents were experiencing their swan song. For a brand that was built on practicality and economy, Rambler had a vehicle in its lineup that some consider an early muscle car: Rebel.

Built only as a silver and gold four-door hardtop, the 1957 Rebel borrowed the 255-hp 327 from Nash and added mechanical lifters and a higher compression ratio. With optional fuel injection, the 288-hp Rebel proceeded to be the second-fastest vehicle at Speed Weeks at Daytona (behind a fuel-injected Corvette). For 1958, AMC applied the Rebel name to any Rambler with the 250 V-8. A high-performance Rambler didn't hit dealerships for another 10 years.

American Motors Steps Up

George Romney's departure from American Motors in 1962 allowed his successor, Roy Abernethy, to bask in the glow of being awarded the 1963 *Motor Trend* Car of the Year and Rambler's third place in sales in 1964. AMC exploited its position of eschewing performance for practicality. However,

Abernethy had bigger idea; he wanted to move away from solely providing economical transportation solutions and give Rambler buyers something to move up to. In essence, he wanted to compete head-on with the Big Three.

Abernethy made several missteps that led to several unprofitable years, so he was asked to step down early in 1967. In his place was Roy Chapin, who decided it was time to get serious about capturing the youth market and breed a more performance-oriented image via motorsports. With newfound vigor, Carl Chamakian was appointed the newly created performance activities director.

The Shape of Things to Come

The year 1967 was important for AMC, even before the changing of the guard. AMC introduced a modern 280-hp 343 with power output competitive with other engines in its size range, but when installed in the Rebel, it couldn't handle the likes of the GTO. However, when placed in the compact American, it was clear that something interesting was going on at AMC.

Ads proclaimed, "For American Motors to stuff a 343 Typhoon V-8 into an innocent-looking Rambler American is guaranteed to cause news. You can opt for a fat pile of goodies including Hi-Performance Cam kit, a 4.44 rear axle, Twin-Grip differential, special handling package, power disc brakes, electric tach, shoulder belts, and extra-wide-profile red-line nylons mounted on 5.5-inch rims."

If that wasn't a portent of things to come, AMC invested $250,000 in a project with Grant Piston Ring Company to prepare a Rambler Rebel SST funny car. With a supercharged 343 (enlarged to 438 ci) putting out 1,200 hp at 9,000 rpm, *Automotive News* reported that the Funny Car raced in X/S in 30 cities and was used as a display in dealerships to draw floor traffic.

American Motors had even more in store. In the July 10, 1967, *Automotive News* article, "Chapin Tells AMC Racing Plans," Chairman Roy D. Chapin Jr. said, "American Motors is going rallying, drag-racing and possibly even stock-car racing. And it will do everything

This 1969 Javelin SST is equipped with the Go Package, which included non-function hood scoops atop a 343 or 390, PDB, red-line Polyglas tires on 6-inch rims, and handling package. (Bob McClurg Photo)

Dick Allen Rambler in Los Angeles had a vibrant high-performance business, serving one of the largest performance markets in America. (Photo Courtesy Dennis Allen)

The 1957 Rambler Rebel may have been a four-door, but the silver and gold hardtop was one of the quickest American cars that year. (Richard Truesdell Photo)

The 1965 Rambler Marlin was AMC's first "specialty car," but Preston Honea from Bill Kraft Rambler had other ideas. He ran a 392 Hemi. (Photo ©TEN: The Enthusiast Network. All rights reserved.)

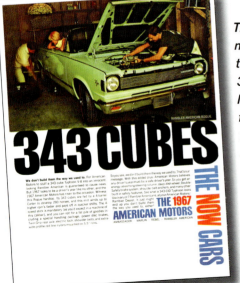

The Marlin may have looked neat, but it lacked muscle. By the time the 280-hp Typhoon 343 arrived for 1967, the Marlin had moved up to the full-size Ambassador platform. However, the 343 was available for the Rambler American (with mandatory 4-speed), creating an interesting sleeper. (Dodge, Plymouth and the AMC design are registered trademarks of FCA US LLC)

Grant Industries' 1967 Rambler Rebel SST, driven by Hayden Proffitt, featured a 343 bored to 443. The blown Rebel put out about 1,200 hp. (Photo ©TEN: The Enthusiast Network. All rights reserved.)

possible to rally and drag its dealers behind this further attempt to change the company image."

He continued, "We're interested in performance, not racing as such. It is a commercial way to prove something about our engineering. Drag racing has crowd appeal and public acceptance. Then there is the novelty of seeing a 1,200-hp Rebel capable of 200 mph."

AMC also had plans for the upcoming Javelin to be homologated for the 1968 SCCA Trans-Am series. "AMC expects to get at least 5 percent of the 1,400,000 sales in the specialty-car field," added Chapin. "We have an eager bunch of young guys in engineering who are raring to go all out in this competition area, but we are not interested in building special cars for something like Le Mans."

American Motors Builds a Better Mustang

Although 1968 was a great year for the performance segment, it was pivotal for American Motors because of the introduction of the Javelin and its two-seat brother, the AMX. The Javelin featured contemporary styling that didn't give up anything to the Mustang or Camaro despite coming from a company that was popular with a psychographic that counted frugality and utility as buying points.

Compared to the Mustang, the Javelin had a lower base price, plus it featured a roomier interior, greater visibility, a tighter turning radius, and quicker steering than its competitors. Because the Javelin was a pony car, its standard engine (either in base or SST trim levels) was rather pedestrian, but AMC did not ignore enthusiasts. The Go Package included the 280-horse 343, heavy-duty springs, beefier sway bar, and Rally stripe as a performance upgrade, among other items.

By the end of the model year, AMC's new 315-hp 390 became available. Although 3.54 gearing was as good as it got from the factory, gears up to 4.44:1 were available from the parts catalog.

AMX: Without Equal

Introduced in March 1968, the AMX was more than just a two-seat pony car with a shorter wheelbase. It was a whole new class of automobile that AMC had all to itself. AMC trimmed the Javelin's wheelbase 12 inches and gave it a standard 225-horse 290 with 4-speed transmission, reclining bucket seats, heavy-duty springs and shocks, an 8,000-rpm tach,

The Javelin was a major factor in the evolution of AMC's image. The Go Package included good stuff such as the 343/280 (eventually a 390, too), beefy components, and beltline stripes. (Dodge, Plymouth and the AMC design are registered trademarks of FCA US LLC)

Take a 290 Javelin, shorten the wheelbase, remove the rear seats, add a special hood and Bam! instant "specialty car." The AMX's two-seat configuration may have limited its audience, but it showed enthusiasts that AMC was worthy when it came to performance. (Jeremy Whitmore Photo)

and more. The optional 343 and 390 were available with the Go Package, which included dual overhead racing stripes, Twin-Grip differential, and other high-performance items.

Judging by sales of the Javelin/AMX twins, AMC proved that it could build cars that could compete with the Big Three. Things became even more interesting for 1969.

Both the Javelin and AMX returned with subtle refinements. Engines remained the same, but the Go Package for the Javelin was re-shuffled to include the 390 and non-functional hood scoops. A redesigned rally stripe was optional for the Javelin, but the AMX continued to feature an overhead racing stripe in the Go Package. Also included were Twin-Grip differential and heavy-duty cooling.

Hurst Helps Build a Super Stocker

One AMX stood out from the rest: SS/AMX. American Motors wanted to complement its racing efforts in NHRA Super Stock. A proposal was presented to AMC brass, who gave their permission to build enough to meet homologation rules. On November 4, 1968, AMC announced its collaboration with Hurst to produce the SS/AMX. AMXs were taken off the assembly line at Kenosha, Wisconsin, shipped to Hurst's facility near Detroit, and then returned to Kenosha.

"We need to obtain 50 firm orders to justify building these cars and are offering them on a first come, first served basis. This car will be sold strictly as an off-road vehicle. With the Hurst name, the opportunity to obtain a competitive Super Stocker and the need to establish our name at the dragstrips, I believe the program has all the ingredients to promote performance

"It is intended as a unique semi-finished base car from which a dealer or a buyer can tailor a competition car," said J. W. Voelpel in an AMC interdepartmental letter. The resulting 1969 SS/AMX ran 10-second ETs in NHRA racing. (Photo ©TEN: The Enthusiast Network. All rights reserved.)

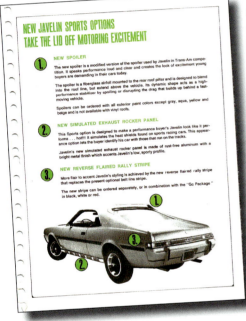

In addition to Big Bad colors, the Javelin also featured several new sports options to build the ultimate "mod" pony car: Trans-Am–inspired rear roof spoiler, simulated exhaust rockers, and rally stripes. (Dodge, Plymouth and the AMC design are registered trademarks of FCA US LLC)

AMC introduced Big Bad Blue, Big Bad Green, and Big Bad Orange mid-year for the 1969 Javelin and AMX because the youth market was "dumping the drab. It shows in their clothes, in their music, in their entertainment, and in the car they buy." (Dodge, Plymouth and the AMC design are registered trademarks of FCA US LLC)

and your dealership," said Robert W. McNealy, AMC's vice president of marketing services, in a dealership bulletin.

The price was estimated to be $5,000 (although it ended up costing over $1,000 more). A December 2, 1968, bulletin stated that only 40 orders had been received, and admitted that prototype testing was still going on to ensure low-11-second ETs at 120 mph. Hurst made modifications that included a special dual-quad manifold, competition clutch and explosion-proof bellhousing, altered wheel wells, modified cylinder heads, and other mods.

American Motors issued a press release in January 1969 announcing that production of the SS/AMX would begin in March.

AMC Digs It

Midyear 1969, American Motors introduced three day-glow colors that showed that the corporation was hip to youth culture. "They're called the Big Bad Colors: Big Bad Orange, Big Bad Green and Big Bad Blue. They

happen on the new Javelins and AMXs, from bumper to bumper, including the bumpers. And they're the boldest street machine skin covers since candy apple anythings and red lead primer."

The updated Javelin bore simulated side pipes, a new C-stripe, and special Trans Am–inspired Breedlove roof spoiler. Sounds totally mod, right? Also introduced was a 4-speed Hurst shifter, a "special short-throw version that pops through the gears as fast as your wrist can handle the situation."

Rambler Goes Out with a Bang-Shift

New at American Motors for 1969 was one of the most outlandish vehicles on the market: SC/Rambler. When AMC executives met with Hurst Performance late in 1968 to discuss their partnership that led to the creation of the SS/AMX, Hurst's Dave Landrith brought up an idea that he and adman Jim Wangers had discussed: an AMC supercar that was somewhat a reincarnation of the 1964 GTO, but with the appearance of what the public expected a 1969 performance car to look like.

As told in *Hurst Equipped: More than 50 Years of High-Performance*, Hurst envisioned installing the SS/AMX's 390 in a Rambler Rogue hardtop. AMC's Walt Czarnecki took the idea to AMC engineers, who had concerns that the torque would wreak havoc on the unibody (a lesson learned from

Yes, a Rambler that does the quarter-mile in 14.3. In conjunction with Hurst, the Rambler American went out with a bang before it was replaced by the AMC Hornet. A 315-hp 390, 4-speed, conspicuous hood scoop, and pop-art graphics were all standard. (Dodge, Plymouth and the AMC design are registered trademarks of FCA US LLC)

343 Americans). Subframe connectors had been added to all Americans starting in 1968, making the concern moot, so the engineers gave the SC/Rambler the green light.

American Motors planned to build only 500 SC/Ramblers in a boisterous red, white, and blue paint scheme, but certain circumstances changed the original plan. After AMC's 1,700 dealers got hold of the memo, they were afraid to be left out because less than a third would receive a car. Also, certain dealerships felt the SC/Rambler's paint scheme was simply too much for their conservative clientele. Lastly, there was a surplus of 390 engines due to AMX sales that did not meet expectations. By increasing production, including a toned-down paint scheme and using the 315-hp 390 already in inventory, everyone would be happy.

For $2,998, the SC/Rambler was priced directly against the Plymouth Road Runner, but the Rambler's performance was more in line with machines of higher stature because it was around 600 pounds lighter. To be factored competitively in F/Stock, AMC overrated the SC/Rambler's curb weight by 160 pounds. Special features included rolled wheel well lips, hood pins, 20:1 quick-ratio steering, rear torque links, Thrush mufflers with 2-inch pipes, Sun ST602 tach, and more. Only one option was available: an AM radio.

Hurst handled the design, marketing, and most of the modifications and components that were not standard American fare. The cars, however, were completely built in Kenosha.

Up with the Rebel Machine

The midsize Rebel never had a high-performance model, but that changed for 1970. Thanks to successful collaborations between American Motors and Hurst, they produced another performance car (although never presented or badged as a Hurst project).

Called the Rebel Machine, it was equipped with a 340-hp 390, standard 3.54 rear axle, reflective red, white, and blue striping, hood scoop with integrated tach, front and rear sway bars, 15-inch Kelsey-Hayes wheels, and heavy-duty shocks and springs to give it a raked stance. Inside were high-backed black bucket seats and floor-mounted BorgWarner Super T-10 4-speed transmission with Hurst linkage or a 3-speed automatic.

Unlike the SC/Rambler, customers were allowed to add regular Rebel options to The Machine. "But if your taste is a little less All-American, you can order The Rebel Machine in any available Rebel color. And trade your blue hood for a flat-black job," read the brochure.

The 1970 Javelin featured more aggressive styling thanks to a longer hood and revised twin-venturi grille. Taillights were segmented and no longer wrapped around, and the optional C-stripe was redesigned. In performance news, a new 285-hp 360 replaced the 343; the 390 remained the top engine option but was upgraded to 325 horses; a new "blister" hood with air induction was included when the Go Package was ordered.

A 360 Go Pack was included with the new Mark Donohue Javelin, which was American Motors' Trans-Am homologation special. Donohue designed the fat ducktail spoiler himself. Also included in the package were dual exhausts, E70 x 14 white-letter wide-profile tires on 14 x 6 wheels, handling package, and C-stripe. Enthusiasts could choose a 4-speed or automatic, and upgrade to the 390.

Another special 1970 Javelin was the Trans-Am Javelin. Built to publicize AMC's Trans-Am exploits rather than for homologation purposes, this special Javelin was produced in several batches totaling 100 units. All were Javelin SSTs with their lower trim and moldings deleted. They had a funky Matador Red/Frost White/Commodore Blue paint scheme, 390/325, 4-speed with Hurst shifter, 3.91 gears with Twin-Grip, ram air, special front and rear spoilers designed by Kaplan Engineering, heavy-duty suspension and cooling, Goodyear F70 x 14 Polyglas tires mounted on Magnum 500s, and more.

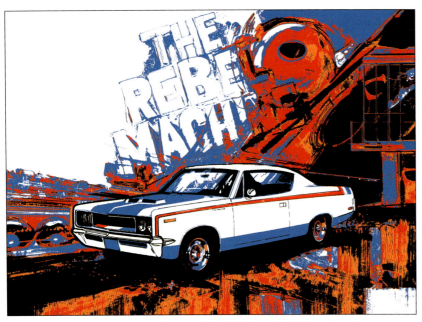

A performance Rebel was ignored by AMC until 1970 when the Hurst-inspired Rebel Machine debuted. "It is not as fast on the getaway as a 427 Corvette or a Hemi, but it is faster on the getaway than a Volkswagen, a slow freight train, and your old man's Cadillac," said the ad. (Dodge, Plymouth and the AMC design are registered trademarks of FCA US LLC)

The AMX had its own tweaks for 1970 including a simulated hood scoop (shared with the Javelin), new grille with parking lights between the headlights, and rocker panels featuring simulated side pipes. The new 360/285 was standard; the 390 remained a popular option. The Go Package featured the usual upgrades plus functional air induction. New appearance options included a beltline stripe that started at the top of the C-pillar, and the Shadow

At the 1970 Chicago Auto Show, AMC made sure the public was familiar with the Javelin's racing exploits. (Photo Courtesy Mitch Frumkin)

Mask, which consisted of flat-black paint on the hood wrapped around the edge of the C-pillar. Inside, the dashboard received the warmth of woodgrain trim, and new high-back buckets were available (even in corduroy or leather).

AMC Does a Lot with a Little

Even though 1971 was an ominous year for the performance segment, American Motors continued to move forward. The Javelin was completely redesigned, although the chassis remained the same. Immediately noticeable was a leaner front end with exaggerated wheel arches and a split-level grille. A stubbier rear accentuated the long hood/short deck that was a pony car hallmark. Above the backlight was an integrated spoiler, and under the hood was a new, optional 330-hp 401.

And the AMX? After sales that never met expectations (plus a lack of resources), the AMX gained a rear seat and became a performance package for the Javelin. The package included a standard 360 2-barrel, but the 360/285 and 401 were available. Visually, the AMX grille was a mesh screen covering the Javelin's and parking lights set between the headlights. Both front and rear spoilers were standard, the latter inspired by Mark Donohue.

The Rebel was replaced by the restyled Matador for 1971. The Rebel Machine did not return, but American

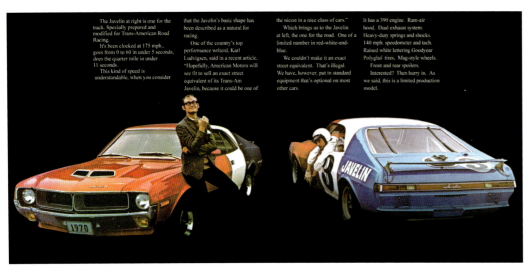

The Javelin at right is one for the track. Specially prepared and modified for Trans-American Road Racing.

It's been clocked at 175 mph.. goes from 0 to 60 in under 5 seconds, does the quarter mile in under 11 seconds.

This kind of speed is understandable, when you consider that the Javelin's basic shape has been described as a natural for racing.

One of the country's top performance writerd, Karl Ludvigsen, said in a recent article, "Hopefully, American Motors will see fit to sell an exact street equivalent of its Trans-Am Javelin, because it could be one of the nicest in a nice class of cars."

Which brings us to the Javelin at left, the one for the road. One of a limited number in red-white-and-blue.

We couldn't make it an exact street equivalent. That's illegal. We have, however, put in standard equipment that's optional on most other cars.

It has a 390 engine. Ram-air hood. Dual exhaust system. Heavy-duty springs and shocks. 140 mph. speedometer and tach. Raised white lettering Goodyear Polyglas tires. Mag-style wheels. Front and rear spoilers.

Interested? Then hurry in. As we said, this is a limited production model.

The 1970 Mark Donohue Javelin was AMC's Trans-Am homologation special, but the Trans-Am Javelin was created to highlight AMC's racing effort. All 100 were Javelin SSTs painted red, white, and blue with a unique adjustable rear spoiler, a 390 with Ram Air, the 4-speed with 3.91 gears, and other performance equipment. (Dodge, Plymouth and the AMC design are registered trademarks of FCA US LLC)

Motors offered the Machine Go Package for Matador two-door hardtops. Included in the package were either a 360/285 or 401/330, dual exhausts, 15 x 7–inch slot-style wheels mounted on E60 x 15–inch white-lettered Polyglas tires, handling package, and power disc brakes, among other equipment. No stripes or nameplates were featured on the Matador Machine. With options up to a 4-speed with 3.91 gears, a 401 Matador Machine could likely hold its own against a 400 GTO or a 402 Chevelle SS.

The Javelin wasn't the only new performance choice from American Motors for 1971. The Hornet SC/360 was a "sensible alternative to the money-squeezing, insurance-strangling muscle cars of America." The SC/360 came standard with a decidedly non-performance 360 2-barrel plus rally stripes and D70 x 14–inch Polyglas white-lettered tires on slot-style wheels. With the Go Package drivers received the 360/285 with ram air, dual exhausts, tachometer, and handling package. It was a fine effort, but AMC stopped taking orders in January 1971. Only 784 SC/360s were built.

It was a tough year for the industry in 1972, but American Motors continued to push the Javelin with reasonable success after winning the Trans-Am championship the previous year. (It won again in 1972).

Javelin AMX (7179-8)
Electric Blue/Go-Package T-Stripe

Javelin SST (7179-7)
Quick Silver/Rally Stripe/Vinyl Roof

The restyled 1971 Javelin was influenced by Mark Donohue's racing efforts, but the AMX was demoted to a Javelin performance package. The optional Go Package included the 360 4-barrel or 401, cowl induction, handling package, and a host of other performance upgrades. (Dodge, Plymouth and the AMC design are registered trademarks of FCA US LLC)

High performance may have been knocked to its knees, but racing was still relevant. AMC won the Trans-Am series in 1971, with George Follmer capturing the Driver's Championship in 1972. For the street, the hot setup remained the Javelin/AMX with the Go Package and 401. (Dodge, Plymouth and the AMC design are registered trademarks of FCA US LLC)

A new egg-crate grille lent the Javelin a new look, which was mimicked in an overlay that covered the taillights. Engines were now measured in net horsepower, so the 360 4-barrel had 220 hp while the 401 put out 255. The Go Pack remained for the AMX package but, in a sign of the times, AMX's base engine was now a 304. For all engines, Chrysler's Torqueflite (called Torque-Command by AMC) replaced the BorgWarner automatic.

The Firebird and the 1973 Javelin were the only pony cars to offer more than 400 ci. A new AMX-inspired grille and round taillights distinguished the Javelin from 1971 to 1972. The 360, 401, and Go Package continued to keep the performance flame alive. (Richard Truesdell Photo)

Speed enthusiasts found the world a grimmer place for 1973, but American Motors kept plugging away with the Javelin. New styling included an AMX-inspired grille with parking lights, and four round taillights out back. Performance engines maintained the same power levels as before, and the AMX package's Go Pack included cowl induction for both the 360 and 401.

Not much changed for 1974, besides the 401 fall to 235 hp, the elimination of cowl induction, and the eventual discontinuation of the Javelin and the AMX package. AMC was not alone in the decline of the muscle car era. The company should be given kudos for competing with the Big Three and for increasing Javelin sales during the lean times.

Dealerships

Although high-performance American Motors vehicles were practically non-existent before 1967, interesting developments took shape when the 343 became available for the Rambler American.

Randall Rambler

At the time, 17-year-old Mike Randall, the son of the owner of an AMC dealership in Mesa, Arizona, had been running an American 440 two-door sedan to the tune of high-11 ETs. He learned about racing from his dad, a hot rodder who caught the drag-racing bug several years before. Randall Rambler subsequently became one of the seminal American Motors dealerships involved in racing.

Per the June 2007 *Hemmings Muscle Machines*, the Randall family also got into road- and off-road racing, but their biggest claim to muscle car fame was the creation of the Gremlin 401-XR. Mike had pulled the 304 out of a new 1972 Gremlin and slipped in a 401, which was externally identical.

"I saw that everybody had those little Novas with the Yenko big-blocks. I said, 'Heck, a 401 fits right in that Gremlin,' so I found a 401 and put it in. It upset Dad, but I told him I could sell it."

Out of the box, the Gremlin was a 12-second car with a low-compression engine, all for the price of a 401 Javelin AMX. Magazine coverage followed, as did 360 Pacer transplants several years later.

Bev Smith Rambler

Another AMC dealership inspired by racing was Bev Smith Rambler of West

Although Rambler introduced the thin-wall 290 in 1966, performance really didn't make its mark at AMC until 1967 when the 343 Typhoon became available for the American. Available only with a 4-speed, the 343 was embraced by a handful of enterprising dealerships such as Bev Smith Rambler in Florida. (Photo Courtesy Nick Smith)

Bev Smith Rambler ordered this 1967 American 440 two-door hardtop with the 280-hp 343 and special-order Ford Poppy Red. (Photo Courtesy Nick Smith)

Palm Beach, Florida. Bev Smith started out in 1946 with a Ford dealership, but in the mid-1960s, he had a facility that was begging to be filled with new cars. Feeling that there was an opportunity to penetrate the area with AMCs, Smith made a bid to add an AMC franchise to the Bev Smith family.

Things got under way for the 1967 model year; perfect timing, as AMC was ramping up its performance image with the 343 American. Bev's son Nick felt that the new Rambler could be a winning combination as it fell within a favorable class in the NHRA.

Nick special-ordered an American 440 hardtop in Ford Poppy Red with the 280-horse engine and went to work. It didn't require a steep learning curve because both the suspension geometry and engine shared similarities with Ford's. The vermilion American garnered a lot of attention and won everywhere it went, even arousing the consternation of a certain Don Garlits, who was not happy that a Rambler had a bigger crowd than his race car next to it.

Nick raced the Rambler in C/Stock through 1969, making enough of an impact to bring new customers to the American Motors brand despite a lack of factory racing support. Bev Smith ended his association with AMC in

1970, however, because the corporation didn't have deep enough pockets for a solid financial foundation. Despite solid ideas and competitive products, AMC's financial instability caused it to lose a strong dealership in the South.

Marketing Strategy

It wasn't newsworthy to talk about the Big Three being involved in racing of any kind (even with the AMA ban), but little AMC? *That* was a different story. American Motors knew that if it were going to seduce the youth market (and those young at heart), racing needed to be part of the program. In addition to a slew of concept cars that were a portent of things to come, and a new advertising agency to help change the public's perception of the brand, AMC knew that it had to go all in if it were going to compete.

With new blood via the youthful Chairman Roy Chapin, and President William Luneburg replacing Roy Abernethy as President, AMC was on the hunt for someone to develop a racing program for the new management team.

New Team at the Top

Victor Raviolo, 20-year Ford veteran, came on as group vice president in charge of research engineering, styling, and product planning. He soon promoted Carl Chakmakian to performance activities director. According to Larry Mitchell's *AMC Muscle Cars*, this new management team was responsible for changing AMC's paradigm and bringing new ideas to its vehicle portfolio. They worked with several manufacturers from the automotive aftermarket to produce speed equipment for AMC V-8s; these items were gathered under the Group 19 banner starting in 1967.

Another person responsible for racing support was Chris Schoenleb, who was hired as director of merchandising. Formerly an executive on the Betty Crocker account for a Chicago ad agency, Schoenleb mentioned in the August 4, 1969, *Automotive News* that he "wouldn't have known a race driver [several years ago] if he had fallen over him. Now he's become a race fan who wants to win so bad 'I can taste it.'" He helped bring AMC dealers and customers in line with its youthful new direction, which included inviting high-volume dealers and members of the Dealer Advisory Council to Lake Geneva, Wisconsin, for a crash course in the high-performance market.

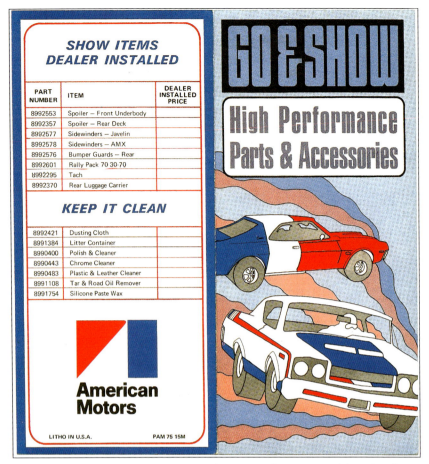

GO ITEMS—DEALER INSTALLED

PART NUMBER	ITEM	DEALER INSTALLED PRICE
4486719	Camshaft Kit. . . 66-69 (290) (343) (390)	
4486169	Camshaft. . . 70 (304) (360) (390)	
4485728	Forged Crankshaft. . . 66-69 (290) (343)	
3208750	Heat Blocker Manifold Gasket. . . 66-69 (290) (343) (390)	
3210297	Heat Blocker Manifold Gasket. . . 70 (304) (360) (390)	
3191737	Cast Iron Intake Manifold. . . 66-69 (290) (343)	
3197035	Cast Iron Intake Manifold. . . 70 (304)	
4485725	Forged Connecting Rod. . . 66-69 (290) (343)	
4485731	Edelbrock High Riser Aluminum Manifold and Single Holley Carburetor. . . 66-69 (290) (343) (390)	
4488410	Edelbrock High Riser Aluminum Manifold and Single Holley Carburetor. . . 70 (304) (360) (390)	
4486587	Rear Axle Gear Set (9:45-5. 00:1). . . 68-70 (290)(304) (343) (360) (390)	
3208551	Rear Axle Gear Set (9:40-4. 44:1). . . 67 (290) (343)	
3209854	Rear Axle Gear Set (9:40-4. 44:1). . . 68-70 (290) (304) (343) (360) (390)	
3208546	Rear Axle Gear Set (10:41-4. 10:1). . . 68-70 (290) (304) (343) (360) (390)	
4485750	Rear Axle Gear Set (11:43-3. 91:1). . . 68-70 (290) (304) (343) (360) (390)	
4485749	Rear Axle Gear Set (11:41-3. 73:1). . . 68-70 (290) (304) (343) (360) (390)	
4487900	Mallory Rev-Pol Ignition System (Less Tachometer Drive). . . 66-70 (290) (304) (343) (360) (390)	
4487901	Mallory Rev-Pol Ignition System (With Tachometer Drive). . . 66-70 (290) (304) (343) (360) (390)	
4485753	Torque Link Kit. . . 67-69 01 (V8)	
4486228	Cross Ram Dual Carburetor Aluminum Manifold. . . 67-69 (290) (343) (390)	
4488411	Cross Ram Dual Carburetor Aluminum Manifold. . . 70 (304) (360) (390)	
4485582	Torque Link Kit. . . 68-70 70	
4487989	Heavy Duty Competition Rocker Arm Kit. . . 66-70 (290) (304) (343)(360) (390)	
4486997	Detroit Locker Positive Locking Differential. . . 66-70 (290) (304) (343) (360) (390)	
4485727	Header (Left)	
4485726	Header (Right)	
4485741	Oil Pan (8½ Qt.)	
8992649	Air Traction Spring — Javelin, AMX	
8991917	Locking Gas Cap	
4485738	Wheel, Road (15 x 8")	

FOR MORE INFORMATION—SEE YOUR AMERICAN MOTORS DEALER

AMC's high-performance parts and accessories were sold under the Group 19 banner. Named after the 19th section of AMC's master parts catalog, Group 19 parts offered parts for show and go. (Dodge, Plymouth and the AMC design are registered trademarks of FCA US LLC)

AMC's performance management team worked with several aftermarket manufacturers to create parts that enthusiasts wanted. These Group 19 items were even invoiced with an AMC part number. (Dodge, Plymouth and the AMC design are registered trademarks of FCA US LLC)

Schoenleb's efforts paid off in AMC's initial foray into competition. With only seven weeks to prepare, a Craig Breedlove-prepped and -driven AMX broke the 24-hour endurance record at Bonneville by 39 mph, and shattered 105 other records. Several days later, Schoenleb brought an edited film of the record run to show at the AMX's debut at the Chicago Auto Show on February 24, 1968.

Schoenleb was instrumental in bringing AMC into the world of drag racing, Trans-Am racing, and NASCAR GT racing. He organized a special pre-race Javelin promotional parade assisted by regional dealerships.

Despite no 1969 Trans-Am victories, Schoenleb remained positive: "If we can compete so closely with the big guys, it shows the public our cars are as good as anyone's and therefore AMC is putting out a product that's not a second choice. When we do win, incidentally, it's still the David-Goliath thing and America responds to that."

It's All About the Dealers

With American Motors' new venture into racing, it required a team effort beyond its corporate offices in northwestern Detroit and the racing teams it hired. According to the July 22, 1968, *Automotive News*, "American Motors has turned to its dealers to bring a new dimension to factory participation in auto racing. It's a massive 'bring-a-dealer' campaign, a program to encourage AMC dealers, their personnel, families and friends to become acquainted with AMC's racing efforts."

Starting with March's race at Sebring, AMC set up a "tent city" as a place for dealers to "gather, exchange ideas and impressions of racing and also visit with and question AMC personnel involved in the Trans-Am series." The reaction was so positive that AMC sales personnel used similar promotions at subsequent Trans-Am events.

Another dealer immersion in racing was an AMC-sponsored day-long event at Eastex Dragway in Porter, Texas, in the summer of 1968. Per the

A regional marketing blitz in conjunction with AMC's Chicago dealer association promoted the brand by supplying the pace car for the July 7, 1968, Trans-Am race at Meadowdale International Raceway. Approximately 100 nearly identical Javelins were parked in the infield for all to see. (Ron and Dan Spannraft Photo)

August 19, 1968, *Automotive News*, 15 Houston-area AMC dealers attended with the intention to familiarize themselves "with the finer details of the drag-racing sport. The 80 participants also met professional drag racers, who explained the basic mechanics and demonstrated the various techniques and systems of drag racing."

Once participants oriented themselves with talking points of AMC's high-performance arsenal, they competed on the strip with ten Javelins and AMXs equipped with a myriad of engines, transmissions, and performance equipment. During the six-hour segment, 227 passes were made without any mechanical complication.

Dealerships were a key point in American Motors' performance strategy because they were able to carry the weight when AMC could not. Without the participation from dealers that embraced performance, AMC's efforts would not have been so successful.

Trans-Am Pace Car

The Indianapolis 500 is renowned for its factory-produced pace car replicas produced for public consumption, but smaller tracks usually don't receive factory involvement. In the case of Meadowdale International Raceway in Dundee, Illinois, the American Motors Dealer Association of Chicago supplied a Frost White/black stripe Javelin to pace the 1968 Trans-Am race.

Tens of replica Javelin pace cars were supplied to race officials and members of the press a week prior to the race. Dealerships were encouraged to use pace car decals in showrooms to promote the tie-in. Additionally, they served as headquarters to sell

---

redliner

AMERICAN MOTORS DEALER PERFORMANCE REPORT
VOL. 1 NO. 3. MAY 1969

Ray-Wel Motors AMX Runner-Up at Springnationals

The Ray-Wel Motors SS/E AMX from Kokomo, Indiana was class runner-up at the recent N.H.R.A. Springnationals in Dallas, Texas. Although the Ray-Wel car turned a quicker elapsed time than the winning Camaro, a momentary loss of traction at the starting line cost the race.

Driven by John Beachy, the AMX had low elapsed time of the class with an 11.17 second run in the semi-final round. Beachy defeated the Sox & Martin Plymouth in that race to make it to the finals.

The fine showing at Dallas was to be expected. The car has terrorized the Division Three Super Stock circuits with a win at Muncie, Indiana, runner-up at Indianapolis Raceway Park and a match race win against SS/BA Hemi-Dodge. Consistent low eleven-second elapsed times have been the rule in all these meets for the hard-running AMX.

The car is prepared by driver John Beachy, his brother Ez, and Larry Vitatoe, son of Ray-Wel's owner, Welby Vitatoe. In addition to running selected events in the Midwest for the rest of the season, the team is looking forward to the Big one—the Nationals in their own backyard at Indianapolis in August. Judging from the results at Dallas, there just might be an SS/E AMX in the winner's circle at Indy—and it just might be from Kokomo.

James Garner Joins AM Performance Field

American Motors Corporation has retained actor James Garner's American International Racing, Inc. as a representative in certain areas of high performance.

Under terms of the agreement outlined by R. W. McNealy, AM vice-president of marketing services, American International Racing, Inc. will concentrate its efforts in two phases of motor sports.

These are:
1. The Sports Car Club of America's Formula A road racing series for single seat, open-wheel vehicles. It is officially designed as the Continental Championship, a 13-race series from coast to coast.
2. Off-road endurance racing. For the Formula A series, American Motors' 305 cubic inch V8 engines, parts and other components will be utilized in AIR chassis designated as the Garner T/S 5.

In the off-road racing, AM's newly introduced SC/Rambler two-door sedan is being adapted and modified. This car will be powered by AM's 390 CID V8 engine.

"We are pleased to announce this new association with American International Racing," McNealy said. "We now

feel we have some of the finest talent and racing knowledge available to represent American Motors in these two fast-growing segments of motor sports.

"AIR made a strong showing with their Lolas this year in the Daytona Continental and were winners in the rugged Baja California 1,000-mile race. Those performances give you a good measure of their capabilities."

McNealy emphasized that the new agreement does not mean AM is changing direction in its participation in high

performance activities. The company will continue to support factory racing teams in both the SCCA Trans-American Sedan Championship and the NASCAR Grand Touring Division series, as well as selected drag race programs around the country.

"This new association with AIR is a logical extension to our existing high performance programs," he said.

"The experience we have gained in just a little over one season in Trans-Am continued on page 4

Wayne Nissen, sales and racing representative for Chuck Milner's Port Rambler in Shreveport, La., is pictured with Milner's SS/E AMX. Wayne drives the car at drag meets throughout the southeast and is aiming toward a National's win.

Nationals Entries Limited

The N.H.R.A. Nationals, the largest drag racing event of the year, is scheduled for August 27-September 1 at Indianapolis Raceway Park in Indianapolis, Indiana. Since entries for this meet are limited to 1,500, it is advisable to get your entry blank in early if you hope to participate.

Nationals entry blanks may be obtained by writing to the National Hot Rod Association, 3418 W. First St., Los Angeles, California 90004.

As We Go to Press . . .

The SS/E AMX campaigned out of Peterson Motor Co. in Kearney, Neb., won Super Stock Eliminator at the N.H.R.A. Divisional Points Meet at Brainerd, Minn. The car, driven by Lou Downing, turned an 11.20 e.t. on the final run against a hemi-Barracuda. Watch this car at the Nationals in August.

Jim Moore in an SC/Rambler won the Eliminator I bracket recently at York (Pa.) U.S. 30 Dragway. He waded through a field of 28 entrants in the bracket to take the win.

Jim Paschal in a Javelin won the 100 mile NASCAR GT race at Columbia, South Carolina. Paschal finished more than two laps ahead of the second-place Camaro. This is Javelin's third win of the season in the G.T. circuit.

American Motors' **Redliner** *newsletter gave enthusiasts the latest news on AMC's factory- and dealer-sponsored successes. In typical AMC fashion, even the little guy was not ignored. (Dodge, Plymouth and the AMC design are registered trademarks of FCA US LLC)*

CUSTOMIZING PACKAGES

American Motors recognized the magic of custom vehicles to attract new clientele. In the May 1968 Sales Ideas of the Month bulletin, "A custom idea for extra exposure, extra floor traffic, extra sales!" spotlighted Tri-City Rambler in Bakersfield and its promotional tie-in with local customizer Bob Reisner.

Reisner added Rebel SST side scoops to a Javelin and repainted it in pearl; he also customized the interior. Several hop-up items (Iskendarian camshaft, Doug's headers, Offenhauser intake, valvecovers, and Flame-Thrower ignition) were added to the 343, resulting in an impressive 14.25 at 103.68 mph. Tri-City claimed "the local teen group went wild about Javelin" and Javelin sales increased, all from a $700 investment.

XP Javelin Package

The Javelin and AMX brought many new customers to American Motors dealerships who ordinarily wouldn't have considered an AMC product before. Now that AMC produced a pony car, what could be done to offer enthusiasts even more distinction in this very competitive segment?

In 1969, DLR Engineering worked out a deal with AMC to offer a "mid-year prestige package to all Javelin buyers." The XP dress-up kit was available through AMC as a dealer-installed package to give the Javelin "that low, sleek race car look that is in keeping with the modern day automotive design." It included:

- Fiberglass hood: "With functional air intakes when unlocked, or when left covered continues to add a low and wide hood scoop treatment."
- Fiberglass spoiler: Nicely integrated full-width spoiler with end caps to complement the Javelin's lines, it was claimed to be functional at "increased speeds" and "adds to the appeal of the Javelin."
- Racing-type wheels: "Five wheels add luster and beauty to the overall appearance of the XP package."
- Wood steering wheel: A racing-inspired wheel that couldn't be beat for its "comfortable, smooth feel of the road" while making "driving a pleasure with the sure grip for handling."
- XP emblems: These helped set the XP kit apart "from all other sports type automobiles."

California-based DLR Engineering gave the Javelin more distinction with the XP package, which was sold directly through AMC as a dealer-installed kit. The XP's core features were a fiberglass hood and spoiler, mag wheels, and a wooden steering wheel. (Photo ©TEN: The Enthusiast Network. All rights reserved.)

Badger Javelin

To celebrate 15 years of American Motors in Milwaukee, 200 dealers and associates from the region (including several from Michigan's Upper Peninsula) attended an event hosted by AMC President William Luneburg. After breakfast, the milestone was marked by a drive-away featuring a fleet of 80 "Badger" 1969 Javelins. All were Frost White Javelins equipped with several mid-year options, including red reverse C-stripes and Breedlove backlight spoiler, plus matching red interior and black hood scoops. It is believed that all were equipped with either 343 or 390 engines.

Sidewinders

The popularity of options to doll-up your car took off in 1969. American Motors offered several midyear 1969 factory items to make a car stand out, such as "simulated

The 1969 Badger Javelin was part of a regional sales promotion commemorating 15 years of American Motors in Milwaukee. This regular-production fleet, sold only in Wisconsin and Michigan's Upper Peninsula, featured Frost White exterior with red interior, Go Package, red C-stripe, and roof spoiler. (David DeHaan Photo)

exhaust rocker panels" for the Javelin, but the real thing was sanctioned by AMC for dealer installation. "Sidewinders do it all. They instantly improve any car's appearance and give it a rich, distinctive sound," read the flyer. Up to a 20-hp gain and a weight reduction of up to 50 pounds was claimed for the chambered pipes. "They tell their own selling message everywhere they go."

Sidepipes were not a regular production item for Javelins or AMXs, but AMC's sparse resources were an opportunity to get creative and work with aftermarket manufacturers to provide custom-designed equipment it simply could not make itself.

Sidewinders were grouped under Group 19 performance equipment series complete with their own AMC part number, adding legitimacy to a product that was tailor-made for AMC vehicles.

where exciting ideas come to life

AMERICAN MOTORS

Sidewinders do it all. They instantly improve any car's appearance and give it a rich, distinctive sound. Dead weight is reduced and horsepower is increased. Sidewinders are a high quality, high ticket item that's loaded with features.

Sidewinders

Custom engineered for Javelin & AMX

AMC's merchandising manager offered dealerships a special price on dealer-installed Sidewinders in 1969 to help increase profit opportunities. "Mount a Sidewinder kit on a demo or showroom car. Remember, displays sell goods. Goods displayed sell." (Dodge, Plymouth and the AMC design are registered trademarks of FCA US LLC)

advance tickets for the event. Employees were motivated to attend with their families.

Those driving the promotional Javelins (including dealers) were given a special section in the infield for parking directly across from the grandstands, and they were urged to wear red, white, and blue racing jackets. An American Motors Hospitality Suite provided food and beverages (which included 100 cases of beer).

In anticipation of the event, a Javelin marketing blitz was initiated for Chicagoland television viewers. About 25,000 Meadowdale spectators (1,200 of them were regional AMC dealers, salespeople, and their families) were exposed to an infield flush with approximately 100 white Javelins, not to mention Peter Revson giving AMC a 2nd-place victory.

A special section in the infield was provided for parking across from the grandstands. An American Motors Hospitality Suite provided food and beverages (which included 100 cases of beer).

Although smaller tracks usually don't receive factory involvement, the Meadowdale International Raceway in Dundee, Illinois, received a Frost White/black stripe Javelin to pace the 1968 Trans-Am race, supplied by the American Motors Dealer Association of Chicago.

In anticipation of the race, a Javelin marketing blitz was initiated for Chicagoland television viewers. About 25,000 Meadowdale spectators (including 1,200 regional AMC dealers and their families) were exposed to an infield flush with white Javelins, not to mention Peter Revson giving AMC a 2nd-place victory.

The Day at the Races was a June 1969 gathering at Orange County International Raceway. AMC's Bob Stephenson claimed it was a test of the effectiveness of AMC's turnaround "to grab the eye of the performance-oriented younger generation" by allowing owners to test their driving skills and the performance characteristics of their vehicles. (Dodge, Plymouth and the AMC design are registered trademarks of FCA US LLC)

Newsletters

Two years after investing in the high-performance segment, American Motors started publishing *Redliner*, "American Motors Dealer Performance Report." The charter March 1969 issue touted AMC's four entries in the Citrus 250 at Daytona, featured a summary previewing Javelin's racing exploits for the rest of the year, and profiled several successful independent AMC racers. The issue also announced that Shirley "Drag On Lady" Shahan had committed to campaigning an SS/AMX.

Other issues featured the AMX pace car for the Pikes Peak International Hill Climb, Javelin/AMX Sport Car Club events around the United States, the announcement of a contingency cash award program for NHRA and AHRA events, and James Garner's participation in AM Performance in SCCA Formula A and off-road endurance racing.

Another newsletter to keep AMC aficionados in the loop was *Rallye American*. Billing itself as the "Official Publication of the National Javelin-AMX Sports Car Club," this monthly then bi-monthly promoted and covered events such as Auto-X, poker runs, treasure hunts, and rallies from 1970 to 1973. Perhaps the most interesting event was Challenge Day, an organized drag race against Brand X car clubs. Of course, being a member of the club meant discounts on aftermarket parts from brands such as B&M and Ansen.

Day at the Races

During 1968, American Motors stopped being part of the counterculture and officially joined the racing world with the introduction of the Javelin and AMX. AMC now spoke the language of enthusiasts and kids alike and, remarkably, didn't appear out of place. True to the grass-roots nature of AMC's racing efforts, Los Angeles zone manager R. M. Stephenson spearheaded the Day at the Races event at Orange County International Raceway on June 8, 1969.

The zone office and Los Angeles–area dealers invited owners to test their car's performance and driving skills at the dragstrip. Everything from 6-cylinder Americans to 4-speed 390 Big Bad Green Javelins were in attendance. In front of approximately 1,800 attendees, 265 competitors in 16 classes made more than 1,500 timed runs.

All 300 or so cars (among an estimated 1,800 attendees) that participated in Day at the Races received this plaque. (Jeff Overman Photo)

Mr. and Mrs. Breedlove went for a nice, long, Sunday drive in an AMX.

They drove right into Monday and 3,380 miles later they broke 77 speed records.

On Thursday and Saturday they came back and broke 13 more records.

And on the following Tuesday, they broke 16 more. All in all the Breedloves set a total of 106 records in the 1968 AMX.

90 Class C records were broken (with a modification of the standard AMX 290 CID engine bored out to 304 CID).

That's every record in the book from 25 kilometers to 5,000 kilometers. From 1 hour to 24 hours. From standing starts and flying starts.

Here's just one to be specific: in Class C the

AMX's average speed for 24 hours was 140.790 m.p.h. The old mark was 102.310.

The AMX also broke 16 records in Class B (with a modification of the optional 390 CID engine bored out to 397 CID).

For 1,000 kilometers standing start the AMX averaged 156.548 m.p.h. The old record was 148.702.

For 75 miles flying start it averaged 174.295 m.p.h. The old record was 172.160.

Every record set by the specially prepared and modified AMX's was sanctioned by USCA and FIA.

And this is just the beginning.

American Motors
Ambassador · Rebel · Rambler American · Javelin · And the new AMX

The best way for American Motors to build credibility among the high-performance set was to go racing. Craig Breedlove was recruited and broke record after record at Bonneville. (Dodge, Plymouth and the AMC design are registered trademarks of FCA US LLC)

In 1967, while American Motors was revamping its image, the manufacturer changed its advertising agency of record to Wells, Rich, Greene, a Madison Avenue upstart. The agency cemented its place in American popular culture with campaigns such as Alka-Seltzer's "Plop plop, fizz fizz" and "I [Heart] NY".

The agency was also responsible for smart campaigns for AMC. In fact, according to the May 20, 1968, *Automotive News*, a University of Michigan poll of businessmen suggested that the "appointment of Wells, Rich, Greene as its advertising agency was rated the best single business decision of 1967." Special credit was given to the agency's "swinging, brash comparison advertising with changing AMC's 'loser-economy-car-Aunt-Martha' image to that of a 'comeback-minded manufacturer with dash and pizzazz.'"

AMC's cheeky series of ads comparing its cars to Brand X, and other individual musings, were among the strongest automotive campaigns during the era. For 1971, as the focus on changing consumers' attitudes evolved, a new campaign was ushered in with the tagline, "If you had to compete with General Motors, Ford, and Chrysler, what would you do?"

For all that American Motors needed to do to run with the big boys, despite the lack of funds, the manufacturer handled it with aplomb. The power of advertising demonstrated it at least as well as AMC's products.

A Rambler that does the quarter mile in 14.3.

American Motors and Hurst have collaborated on the custom-built SC/Rambler.

It's a limited production car; only 500 units are planned at this time.

Enough to qualify the SC/Rambler for stock classes in drag racing.

The price is $2,998. Which is very little money when you see what it buys.

1. 390 cubic inch AMX V-8 Engine.
2. 4-speed all-synchromesh close-ratio transmission.
3. Special Hurst 4-speed shift linkage with T-handle.
4. A Sun tach mounted on the steering column.
5. Dual Exhaust system with special-tone mufflers and chrome extensions.
6. Functional Hood Scoop for cold-air induction.
7. Twin-Grip differential.
8. 10½" diameter clutch.
9. 3.54:1 axle ratio.
10. Power disc brakes (front).
11. Rear axle torque links.
12. Handling package (heavy-duty front sway bar plus heavy-duty springs and shocks).
13. Heavy-duty cooling system (heavy-duty radiator,

power-flex fan and fan shroud).
14. A 20:1 manual steering ratio.
15. Special application of new Red, White and Blue exterior colors.
16. Two hood Tie-Downs with locking safety pins and cables.
17. Custom Tear-Drop racing mirrors (one each side).
18. Custom Grille.
19. Custom SC/Rambler-Hurst emblem on front fenders/rear panel.
20. Mag styled wheels, 14" x 6", painted specially to complement exterior color scheme.
21. Five E 70 x 14 Goodyear Polyglas™ Wide-Tread tires.
22. Sports steering wheel.
23. Custom-upholstered head restraints in Red, White and Blue vinyl.
24. All-vinyl charcoal seat upholstery with full carpeting.
25. Individually adjustable reclining seats.

There's more, but you get the idea. With this car you could make life miserable for any GTO, Roadrunner, Cobra Jet or Mach 1.

**American Motors/Hurst
SC/Rambler**

1. Manufacturer's suggested retail price includes all items listed and federal taxes. State and local taxes, if any, and destination charges excluded.

Advertising agency Wells, Rich, Greene deserves as much credit for helping turn around AMC's reputation as the AMX and SC/Rambler thanks to cheeky advertising that reflected the absurdity of competing against the Big Three. (Dodge, Plymouth and the AMC design are registered trademarks of FCA US LLC)

Donohue puts his mark on the Javelin.

Starting now you can buy a Javelin with a spoiler designed by Mark Donohue.

You couldn't before this, but an exciting development has changed everything.

Mark Donohue and Roger Penske, the most successful driver-manager team in road racing, recently signed a three year contract with American Motors.

Together they've won two straight Trans-Am championships. They'll go for a third with the Javelin.

One of the modifications in their Trans-Am Javelin is a spoiler designed by Donohue.

This means that according to Trans-Am rules, the spoiler has to be homologated.

In other words we must incorporate the spoiler into 2,500 Javelins

that the public can buy.

And that's just what we've done. But the Donohue designed spoiler isn't the only extra these Javelin SST's will have.

Dual exhausts, power front discs, E70 x 14 white lettered wide profile tires, 14 x 6 wheels, handling package, and a Ram-Air induction system with an AMX hood are also part of the deal.

And you can choose between a 360 or a 390 CID engine. Console shift automatic or 4-speed with a Hurst shifter.

We expect that a lot of the competition are going to see the rear end of Mark Donohue's Javelin this season.

**American Motors
Javelin**

Mark Donohue signed with American Motors for 1970 and immediately made his mark with a rear spoiler he designed for his Javelin race car. AMC produced the Mark Donohue Javelin to homologate the spoiler. (Dodge, Plymouth and the AMC design are registered trademarks of FCA US LLC)

INDEX

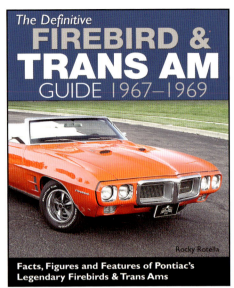
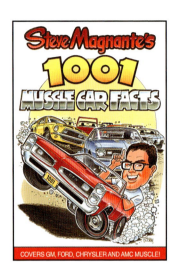
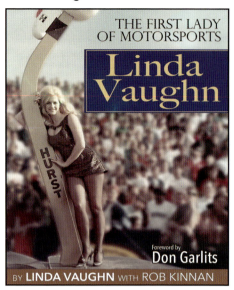
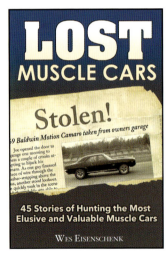

Mercury has the word for a new performance scene.

It's streep*. From street 'n strip. A new word, for a new breed of performers. Bred from the bold, brash bombers of Cale, LeeRoy, Gurney and "Dyno" Don. They move. They groove. They corner and haul it. They're StreepCars. Maxi-performance machines for Mini-E.T.'s, crisp cornering, startling speed. StreepCars make every scene. The big oval. 1320 Smoke Outs. Roadcourses. StreepCars do it all. Give 'em the good eye. See what's happening. Why streep is . . . some car . . . some scene.

*Streep is pronounced . . . in the staging lanes, by slipping your tranny in low, stomping the loud pedal, and laying down the long black stuff to clean your tires.

scene stealer—Marauder X-100

This beauty comes with most everything standard on its big 121-inch wheelbase: 360 hp/429 cid engine, 4-V carb, Select-Shift, dual exhausts, WSW H70x15 belted traction tires, styled aluminum wheels, fender skirts, two tone paint, 3-spoke rim-blow steering wheel, leather w/vinyl bench seat or all vinyl bucket seats with console or twin comfort lounge seats, clock & unique ornamentation. Suggested options: competition handling pkg, P/B (front disc/rear drum), 2.80 or 3.35 power transfer axle, remote L/H mirror "solid state" cruise control, & tilt steering wheel.

streep sweeper—Cyclone C.J.

Sweep the strip clean with a Cyclone CJ va-room bristling with CJ 335 hp/ 428 cid "Ram Air" (Includes: engine dress-up, 4-V carb w/flapper door air cleaner, hood scoop, striping, bench seats, black-out grille, dual exhausts, extra cooling, comp hand pkg, BSW F70x14 belted traction tires w/"raised" white lettering on 6" rims, 4-speed close ratio box & 3.50 conv axle). Optional: Select-Shift transmission, hood lock pins, Traction-Lok axle (3.50, 3.91, 4.30), P/B (front disc/rear drum), tach & styled steel wheels. Also may want sports appearance options: bucket seats, L/H remote racing mirror, turbine wheel covers & 3-spoke rim-blow steering wheel.

the prowler—Cougar C.J. 428

Before "looking," stuff this Cougar with CJ 335 hp/428 cid "Ram Air" (Includes: engine dress-up, 4-V carb w/flapper door air cleaner, hood scoop, striping, dual exhausts, extra cooling, comp

sure footed cat
Cougar 351-4V

scene stealer
Marauder X-100

streep sweeper
Cyclone C.J.

GROOVE

the prowler
Cougar C.J. 428